THE AFRICAN I
IN THE INDIAN OCEAN

With best wishes

Maly. N...

With my Compliments.

Shih de Silva Jayasuriya

THE AFRICAN DIASPORA
IN THE
INDIAN OCEAN

edited by
SHIHAN DE SILVA JAYASURIYA
and
RICHARD PANKHURST

Africa World Press, Inc.

P.O. Box 1892  P.O. Box 48

Trenton, NJ 08607 — Asmara, ERITREA

Africa World Press, Inc.

P.O. Box 1892
Trenton, NJ 08607

P.O. Box 48
Asmara, ERITREA

Copyright © 2003 Shihan De S Jayasuriya & Richard Pankhurst
First Printing 2003

Book design: Jonathan Gullery
Cover design: Ashraful Haque

Library of Congress Cataloging-in-Publication Data

The African diaspora in the Indian Ocean / edited by Shihan de Silva Jayasuriya & Richard Pankhurst.
    p. cm
Includes bibliographical references and index.
 ISBN 0-86543-979-6 (hard cover) -- ISBN 0-86543-980-X (pbk.)
 1. Africans--Indian Ocean Region--History. 2. African diaspora. I. Jayasuriya, Shihan de S. II. Pankhurst, Richard.
 DS339.3.A34 A34 2001
 909'.0496--dc21
                        2001005511

CONTENTS

ON THE AFRICAN DIASPORA IN THE INDIAN OCEAN REGION

Shihan de Silva Jayasuriya

& Richard Pankhurst

The Indian Ocean region is a region of social and cultural diversity inhabited by peoples with numerous languages and religions. The region straddles three continents: Africa, Asia and Australia. The men, women and children from Africa who were transplanted to the region came into contact with socio-cultures much older than those encountered by African slaves who were taken to the Atlantic Ocean region.

This book is concerned with Ethiopians and other inhabitants of Africa, south of the Sahara, who were dispersed (whether forcibly or by free will) to non-African lands in the Indian Ocean region. We are therefore not concerned solely with the slave trade.

This trade, in which Africans and non-Africans participated, was but one of several mechanisms by which innumerable men, women and children from Africa were dispersed, over centuries, throughout much of the Indian Ocean region. The African diaspora has very old roots in the Indian Ocean region, therefore, which are not entirely the consequence of the slave trade. Africans came to India as policemen, traders, bureaucrats, clerics, bodyguards, concubines, servants, soldiers and sailors from the 13th century onwards[1].

In Asia, and in particular India, people of Ethiopian, and other African descent were generally referred to by three alternative names: Habshi, Sidi and Kaffir. These words which were all derived from Arabic have different histories and connotations.

The term Habshi was a corruption of Habash, the Arabic for Abyssinia.

This latter name is believed to be derived from Habashat, the name of a Semitic people, who lived in northern Tegray in present-day Ethiopia, and part of Eritrea, and are thought by many to have migrated from Yaman in ancient times. The term Habshi seems to have at first been used for Abyssinians (or Ethiopians) alone, but was later more widely employed for all Africans. Most of those taken to India came, however, from the continent's eastern flank, and would probably have included a predominant number of Abyssinians, or Ethiopians, as the origin of the word Habshi, in fact, suggests. Ethiopians, or Abyssinians enjoyed a unique position in the Indian and Asian slave context. They had been known to the Islamic world since the time of the Prophet Muhammad, whose first muezzin in Mecca had been the son of an Abyssinian slave-girl. They were, moreover, generally liked on account of their 'Oriental' physiognomy, and were considered to make brave soldiers, loyal servants, and beautiful wives and concubines. Their homeland, with its temperate and agreeable climate, was also known as the "Third India".

The term Sidi was derived from the Arabic Saiyid, or 'master', but was used in India as a designation for African slaves, particularly those on the sub-continent's western coast. The word was, however, also often used, together with a personal name, e.g. Sidi Yaqut, as a kind of title.

The term Kaffir, sometimes also spelt in English Caffer or Coffree, was a rendering of the Arabic Kaffir, or Infidel. The word was often used fairly indiscriminately by the Arabs, and later by the Portuguese, for a Pagan, or Black, but had different connotations at different times and places. It thus sometimes served to designate slaves irrespective of their race or colour; at other times to refer to anyone not of the Muslim faith.

Slavery was widespread in the ancient world, from the Mediterranean to China. Within the Indian Ocean region,

Africa and South East Asia were the major sources of slave supply, but slaves from the latter area remained within the area itself. By the 4th century, the entire African region from Ethiopia to Madagascar had become a major source of slaves for markets from Europe to China[2]. Until the 8th century, the traffic in slaves appears to have been both small and intermittent, but it later flourished at the peak of the Arab empire, between the 9th and 11th centuries. In due course a regular network of slave routes developed across the Indian Ocean, from Madagascar to the Moluccas, with Africa and the Indonesian Archipelago as the main suppliers. East Africa, Madagascar, the Sudan and Ethiopia supplied slaves, via the Red and Arabian Seas, to many countries in the East, including Egypt, Arabia, Mesopotamia, Persia, and India. The slave trade subsequently decreased, as a result of the decline of the Arab Empire, but it received a fillip in the early 16th century on account of fighting in Ethiopia and the Horn of Africa, where many slaves were captured and taken to India, and in particular to Gujarat, in the north-west of the sub-continent . The trade increased again in the mid-17th century, initially in response to a growing demand for slaves by the Ottoman and Mughal empires. In the 18th century, Kilwa and Pate dominated this trade, and exported slaves from the East African coast and Madagascar to the Gulf, the Makran coast (in modern-day Pakistan) and Gujarat, where they were distributed among the north Indian elite, and in European settlements as far afield as Bengal (in North-East India). In India, African slaves were considered luxury and prestige commodities. An owner's social status in India, as indeed in Ethiopia, was measured by the number of his slaves, who constituted an important part of his retinue and an ostentatious way of displaying wealth and power[3]. African slaves undertook tasks which Indians could not perform on account of caste restrictions, or tasks which they would simply not perform, or which the British deemed unsuitable. In the princely states, which were free of British rule, African slaves served as domestics, concubines, eunuchs, water carriers, barbers, personal guards, stable-boys etc. The British East India Company records the arduous work performed by slaves, mainly

Malagasy, as soldiers, sailors, dockers and agricultural labourers.

European involvement in the slave trade was intermittent, with occasional Portuguese vessels carrying slaves from the Mozambique coast to South Asia, Brazil and Portugal. In the late 17th and early 18th centuries, European slave activity in the Western Indian Ocean was dominated by freebooters, mostly French, who pioneered the regular movement of slaves out of the Indian Ocean area to other parts of the world. The activities of such slavers centered on Madagascar.

Indians were significant and persistent participants in the East African slave trade, although they were of less consequence than either the French or the Arabs. In 1853, Major Hammerton, the British consul and government agent at Muscat, reported to the British government in Bombay that a lively slave trade existed between Zanzibar and the Indian states of Cutch and Kathiawar. The British were likewise involved in the African slave trade to Bombay, as early as the 18th century. African slaves were inducted into the British navy, but when British cruiser commanders reported that it was impossible to make "Madagascar slaves" useful on board ship, the Council of the United Company of Merchants of England agreed to transfer them as labourers in the marine yard. Slaves from Africa were also bought from slaving vessels, and were trained as calkers for the East India Company, which advertised contract slaves for anyone desiring such labour. In the Portuguese seaborne empire, which developed in the 16th century, slavery was the solution to the manpower shortage. De Oliveira Marques[4] points out that the large number of slaves involved was unique to Portugal although slavery as a social phenomenon was not. Magalhaes[5] states that black slaves were preferred to Moorish ones as they were both more open to conversion to Catholicism, and more compliant. He adds that in the Portuguese Asian settlements, a black slave presence was vital, mainly for military defence. Although slaves from Africa were traumatized by the violence of their capture and removal to completely different cultures, they had little problem in integrating into Asian societies. Moors, if

Christianised, were by contrast considered dangerous and potentially treacherous. The main concern of the Portuguese was the control of the sea route to India. It was for this reason that, they built a major coastal fortress at Mombasa (Fort Jesus in 1593-96), and smaller fortresses at Zanzibar. By the 17th century, Portuguese supremacy in the Indian Ocean was challenged by the Omani Arabs, Dutch, British and French. By the mid-18th century, the Portuguese had withdrawn from the East African Coast north of the Ruvuma river, and the Arabs were left in sole control. The Arabs and Portuguese were thereafter able to farm their respective portions of the East African coast for slaves[6]. The Anglo-Zanzibar Treaty of 1873 prohibited the export of slaves from the mainland, and urged the immediate closure of slave markets. By about 1880, the slave trade from the East African dominions of the Sultan of Zanzibar almost ceased. Slavery was abolished on Zanzibar and Pemba in 1897. Although the authorities in British East Africa, later Kenya, were not interested in slave trading[7], slavery continued on the Kenyan coast until 1907, and on that of German East Africa, later Tanganyika, until 1919.

In the 16th century, the Portuguese developed political and economic control over the west coast of India, especially the Konkan coast, where many African slaves were imported. Most of these slaves were from Mozambique, but the Portuguese also seized African slaves when they defeated the Muscat Arabs at the Indian port of Diu in 1670. The Portuguese employed slaves in businesses, farms, domestic work, and other menial jobs. Some slaves, on the other hand, were trained as teachers and priests in religious schools, especially in Goa, which became the headquarters for Portugal's Asian and East African colonies. This would seem to demonstrate the pragmatic approach taken by the Portuguese empire, which was built and sustained on limited resources. The Portuguese shortage of personnel obliged them to delegate some of their tasks to newly converted ex-slaves who were deemed indeed to be more loyal than Portuguese colonials. Slavery was one of the main pillars of the Lusitanian empire. In the 16th century, however, the Portuguese were mainly active along the west coast of

Africa which supplied the markets in the Atlantic Ocean region. Slaves from the eastern and southern coasts of Africa, for reasons of geography, were taken mainly to the Indian Ocean region, where they were required mainly as domestic servants and bodyguards. The number of slaves taken to the East was, however, much smaller than those taken to the West[8].

The Portuguese first sighted Madagascar in 1500, and officially discovered it in 1506, under a squadron led by Dom Francisco de Almeida. They called it Ilha de San Lourenco, or 'Island of Saint Lawrence'. They made two attempts to establish a factory at Matitana, in 1514 and 1521, but abandoned both on account of local hostility, and the absence of any important trading commodity[9]. The Portuguese, French and British wanted to establish a permanent presence on the island, and succeeded to varying degrees. Slaves were exported from Madagascar until its conquest by the French in 1896.

The Dutch entered the slave trade in the early 17th century. In 1602, the VOC (Verenigde Oost Indische Compagnie) was given a monopoly of Dutch trade and navigation east of the Cape of Good Hope and west of the Straits of Magellan for an initial period of twenty-one years. The Heeren XVII (governing body or court of 17 directors), was empowered to conclude treaties of peace and alliance, to wage defensive wars, and to build fortresses in the region. In the Cape, the Dutch were faced with an agricultural labour shortage which was solved by importing and employing slaves. As the Heeren XVII forbade the enslavement of Hottentots and Bushmen, the authorities in Cape Town obtained their slaves from further afield, namely from Mozambique, Madagascar, the Bay of Bengal and Indonesia. At the beginning of the 18th century, there were only 800 adult slaves in Cape Town, but this number increased within fifty years to 4,000, and by 1780 had reached almost 10,000[10].

In 1807, the British Parliament passed an Act to abolish the slave trade, and the institution of slavery was abolished in 1834. Britain also led attempts to regulate, if not abolish, the Arab slave trade in the Indian Ocean region. Sizable numbers of slaves nevertheless continued to be exported from Africa to Asia. Exports from the Red Sea and Gulf of Aden ports of Massawa, Beilul, Tajura and Zayla were for instance still running in the first half of the 19th century at almost 10,000 per annum. Further south, one of the principal slave markets was on the island of Zanzibar. The principal markets in the Gulf of Oman were probably Sur and Muscat. No statistics were kept, but it was estimated that in the eighteen sixties and seventies 13,000 slaves reached the Gulf annually from East African ports, and that at least 4,000 or 5,000 of them went to Sur.

When the slave trade by Europeans was abolished, the British joined other European powers in abolishing the wholesale slave trade in the Indian Ocean. The retail trade, however, continued for much longer[11].

The struggle between the French and the British for supremacy in the Indian Ocean which began in 1793 led to the British capture of Mauritius in 1810, and the surrender of Réunion and Seychelles. In 1815, however, Réunion was returned to France. Although the British had already passed an Act to abolish slavery, the French wanted slave labour for the plantations. This led to the Anglo-Merina treaty in 1820 which offered the Merina King a subsidy of 20,000 dollars per annum in return for banning the export slave trade. Ironically, the treaties intended to abolish slavery only acted as catalysts to boost slaving activity. The French found new suppliers, and slavery continued until it was finally abolished, in 1848, by the French government. Then, the French sought contract labourers from the Comoros, Mozambique and Madagascar.

Even when Africans were transported as slaves from Africa, their fate changed on reaching their destination. In Réunion for instance they were transformed from French slaves to French citizens. In Mauritius, Seychelles, Rodrigues and the Chagos, they formed a new culture, neither African nor Asian - a second Caribbean. Slaves from Portuguese Goa were transformed into soldiers in Sri Lanka. Africans were trained to be clergymen in Goa, (which was known as the 'Rome of the Orient'), and sent as churchmen to the *Estado da India* (the Portuguese 'State of India' which extended from Mozambique to China and was linked by a common administration with its headquarters in India).

This book comprises eight papers from scholars who have been researching the African diaspora in different geographical locations in the Indian Ocean region, and whose expertise includes history, linguistics, anthropology, sociology, politics, and international relations. The work covers a topic that has thus far been overlooked, and which remains largely an uncharted water. The study shows that the African diaspora was not a consequence of the slave trade alone. Africans were trading in Sri Lanka as early as the 5th century and they were warriors in the 13th century. They were also engaged in agate mining in Gujarat.

Edward Alpers considers the applicability of the term 'diaspora' to the movement of Africans to the Indian Ocean region, and establishes a framework in which to place the global scattering of Africans. He thus compares the African diaspora in the Indian Ocean region with that in the Atlantic Ocean region. His paper weaves into the next paper on the Mozambican Diaspora and sets the scene for the papers that follow.

Eduardo Medeiros surveys the Mozambican diaspora in the Indian Ocean Islands (Madagascar, Seychelles, Rodrigues, Mauritius and Réunion), and the cultural identities they developed. He demonstrates that the 'Creole' culture in these islands is the result of the fusion and innovation of European and African cultures, which have also incorporated elements from Asian (Indian and Chinese) cultures.

Malyn Newitt's paper on African migration (both free and forced) to Madagascar, which has taken place for two millennia, discusses the African contribution to Malagasy culture today. While most African slaves integrated into Malagasy society, the Makoi remained distinct throughout the colonial period.

Helen Hintjens deals with the fate of the African diaspora in the island of Réunion which had two origins: East African (via Mozambique and Zanzibar), and Madagascar. The Afro-Asiatic origin of the Malagasy, however, complicates the notion of the African diaspora in the Indian Ocean region. In the 19th century, indentured labourers were brought from India to replace former African slave labour. This, in fact, constitutes an Asian diaspora in the Indian Ocean region. Slavery was abolished twice in Réunion (in 1792 and again in 1848). Her paper also touches on the contribution of the African diaspora to Réunion, in terms of economy and society, politics and culture.

Jean Houbert's paper deals with the colonisation-decolonisation of the Indian Ocean Islands of Mauritius, Réunion, Rodrigues, Seychelles and Chagos in the context of the struggle between the European powers for hegemony over the Indian Ocean and trade monopoly in Asia. These islands, whose political regimes are largely a construction of European colonialism, are unique in that they form a 'Little New World' in the Indian Ocean.

Although geographically nearer to Africa than Asia, the islanders are culturally more akin to the Carribeans. These settler colonies were peopled by 'unwilling settlers' who lost their culture and were 'creolised'. Decolonisation in the Indian Ocean region did not, however, signify the abandonment of sea power. Whereas the Soviet Union could influence the Asian Rim overland, the West could intervene only by sea. The redeployment of Western power in the Indian Ocean entailed the dismemberment of two small British colonies (Mauritius and Seychelles), in order to locate an American military base at Diego Garcia in the Chagos archipelago. This was facilitated by the collaboration of the creole islands which were in the process of decolonisation.

Richard Pankhurst's study deals with the Ethiopian, and more generally African, diaspora in India, from early medieval times to the end of the 18th century. His paper traces the transition whereby Habshis and their descendants rose from slavery to important military positions, and eventually established ruling dynasties in the Deccan (in south west India) and elsewhere. He argues that the slave trade to India began as early as the early 13th century, but increased greatly in the early 16th century as a result of extensive fighting on the Horn of Africa.

Helene Basu discusses the historical aspects of the East African slave Trade and its involvement with Gujarat and

Gujarati merchants. She contextualises historically the information on prominent Habshi military leaders of Medieval
India. She also examines the diaspora from the global and
political elite context and delineates local constructions of
Sidi identity in Gujarat that are embedded in a hitherto little
studied cult of African saints.

The final paper, by Shihan de Silva Jayasuriya, presents
a historical survey of the African diaspora in Sri Lanka, and
examines the largest community of Ceylon Kaffirs living on
the island. The discovery, or rediscovery, of the origins of
the Ceylon Kaffirs raises complex issues. Although a distinction was made between Abyssinians and East Africans in
the 17th century, today all people of African descent in Sri
Lanka are given the ethnic label, Kaffir. The word, however,
has no racial connotation. The Kaffirs, over the centuries,
have integrated into multi-ethnic Sri Lanka, and it is timely
to examine the fast disappearing African culture now limited
to music and dance which signal the African presence on
the island.

A survey of the diaspora further east of Sri Lanka has not
been undertaken in this book, and remains for a later
work. However, the papers here published demonstrate that
the fates of the Africans who went east was radically different from that of those who went west. Despite the rigid-
ity of the Indian caste system and its constraint on social
mobility, many Habshis in Muslim India were employed as
soldiers, and rose to supreme power in several parts of the
region. This was no doubt due to the fact that India had an
adequate supply of labour, and therefore did not require
slaves for manpower. By contrast African slaves in the
Atlantic Ocean region, where labour was scarce, were
employed as manual workers in plantation and other pro-
ductive work.

The Portuguese, who were the pioneer European
colonisers of the Orient, were exposed to Islamic customs
and ideals when they were part of Moorish Iberia. This may
have caused them to follow the Muslim Indian custom of
employing slave and other immigrants from Africa as soldiers and other military personnel. This practice was later
revived by the British, as is evident from the case of Sri

Lanka, where the Kaffirs proved themselves perhaps some of the best soldiers in the Indian Ocean region.

The papers in this volume demonstrate that the African diaspora in the Indian Ocean region was not fully a consequence of the coming of 'unwilling migrants'. Some immigrants from Africa were motivated by trade, others came to settle or to seek work. The multi-disciplinary approach taken in this book is thus an attempt to view the African diaspora in the context of the African civilization, and not merely as a consequence of the slave trade.

Notes

1. Irwin, G W (1977). Africans Abroad: A Documentary History of the Black Diaspora in Asia, Latin America and the Caribbean During the Age of Slavery. Columbia University Press, New York, p.138.
2. McPherson, K (1993). The Indian Ocean: A History of People and the Sea. OUP. p.82.
3. Knight, F W, Talib, Y & Curtin, P D (1989). The African diapsora. In: General History of Africa VI. Ed J F Ade Ajayi. p. 755.
4. De Oliveira Marques, A H (1987). Portugal Quinhentista (Ensaios). Lisboa: Quetzal. p.179
5. Magalhaes, J R (1997). Africans, Indians and Slavery in Portugal. Paper presented at a Conference 'The Strangers Within' from 30 June to 2 July 1994. Department of Portuguese Studies, King's College London. p.143-146.
6. Beachey, R W (1976). The Slave Trade of Eastern Africa. Rex Collings, London. pp.9-10.
7. Alpers, E A (1967). The East African Slave Trade. Historial Association of Tanzania Paper No. 3. Nairobi: EAPH. pp.12-20.
8. Boxer, C R (1961). Four Centuries of Expansion, 1415-1825: A Succinct Survey. Witwatersrand University Press, Johannesburg. p.34.
9. Newitt, M (1983). The Comoro Islands in Indian Ocean Trade before the 19th century. Cahiers d'Etudes africaines, 89-90, XXIII-1-2, pp.139-165. p.146.
10. Boxer, C R (1965). The Dutch Seaborne Empire 1600-1800. Hutchinson, London.
11. Villiers, A (1952). The Indian Ocean. Museum Press Ltd, London. p.196

THE AFRICAN DIASPORA IN THE INDIAN OCEAN: A COMPARATIVE PERSPECTIVE

Edward A. Alpers

Studies of the African diaspora focus disproportionately on the Atlantic world and ignore that of the Indian Ocean. I have previously discussed the historiography of the latter, which I do not wish to reiterate here.[1] Suffice it to say that although this important subject has not been entirely overlooked by scholars, it remains largely uncharted territory.[2] In this paper, I seek to probe the applicability of the term "diaspora" to the African diaspora in the Indian Ocean as a first step towards establishing a comparative framework in which to situate the larger global scattering of Africans. Philip Curtin observed two decades ago that, "The African diaspora may have been unique, but aspects of it clearly belong to other aggregates of human experience that should be studied comparatively. This has barely begun, probably because fields of historical research are too narrowly compartmentalised."[3] I believe we must first take Curtin's challenge a step backwards by looking comparatively at the African diaspora. What do we imply by using this word, a term that is pregnant with meaning, both specific and general, for peoples all over the world? Do the descendants of Africans in the Indian Ocean world consider themselves to be African in any sense at all? Do they have collective memories of Africa as their homeland? Do they harbor irredentist aspirations? At first glance, our responses would seem to be negative; but a complete answer is more complicated, both less than an African American or "Black Atlantic" projection of the meaning of "diaspora" onto the African presence in the region and more than an Asian or Islamic assimilation of African peoples that negates race and culture.

Defining diaspora

"Diaspora" is a fraught term, highly politicized and largely untheorized. As James Clifford questioned, "what is at stake, politically and intellectually, in contemporary invocations of diaspora"?[4] A rapid search of the university on-line catalog under the "Find Subject" command reveals that virtually all studies address either the Jewish or the African diaspora exclusively; but a parallel search under the heading "Find Title" excavates some dozen-and-a-half different ethnicities, nationalities, races, and religions that lay claim to this distinction. This suggests that defining diaspora and who is included as a diasporic community is somewhat problematic.

Robin Cohen has recently sought to address this complex, indeed confusing, situation in a well-argued volume on *Global Diasporas* that inaugurates a new series of studies under the same title.[5] While Cohen does not succeed in theorizing "diaspora," which he considers to be impossible,[6] his typology of diasporas provides a useful beginning for anyone interested in this topic that promises to become a standard reference. Cohen argues for the existence of different categories of diaspora and specific common features that must be present if we are to be able to compare diasporas. He begins by exploring and then seeking to transcend the dominant Jewish tradition of diaspora. Building on a revised version of Safran's model, Cohen suggests that there are nine "common features of a diaspora":

1. Dispersal from an original homeland, often traumatically, to two or more foreign regions;
2. alternatively, the expansion from a homeland in search of work, in pursuit of trade or to further colonial ambitions;
3. a collective memory and myth about the homeland, including its location, history, and achievements;

4. an idealization of the putative ancestral home and a collective commitment to its maintenance, restoration, safety and prosperity, even to its creation;

5. the development of a return movement that gains collective approbation;

6. a strong ethnic group consciousness sustained over a long time and based on a sense of distinctiveness, a common history and the belief in a common fate;

7. a troubled relationship with host societies, suggesting a lack of acceptance at the least or the possibility that another calamity might befall the group;

8. a sense of empathy and solidarity with co-ethnic members in other countries of settlement; and

9. the possibility of a distinctive creative, enriching life in host countries with a tolerance for pluralism.[7]

In successive chapters of his concisely argued book, he then presents his examples of the different categories of diaspora that conform to these common features:

- victim diasporas: Africans and Armenians
- labor and imperial diasporas: Indians and British
- trade diasporas: Chinese and Lebanese
- diasporas and their homelands: Sikhs and Zionists
- cultural diasporas: the Caribbean (postmodernism; Gilroy's "Black Atlantic")
- globalization and diasporas

This is where it gets tricky for the African diaspora in the Indian Ocean. The African disapora is one of Cohen's quintessential examples of a diaspora, but it is based entirely upon the Atlantic experience of forced migration, which is basically a phenomenon spanning the 16th-19th centuries, and return to Africa, real or imagined, which is largely a 19th and 20th century phenomenon. The Indian Ocean setting complicates this situation by having experienced both a much longer history of forced migration (see for example, the Zanj slave revolts in 8th and 9th century lower Iraq) and a considerably later mass slave trade (18th and 19th centuries, even into the early 20th century), as well as a more modest tradition of free labor migration that muddies the waters. In addition, there is very little on record that points to a well developed sense of "collective memory" about Africa or a "sense of distinctiveness" among Africans in the Indian Ocean world. Cohen especially emphasizes that "The myth of a common origin acts to 'root' a diasporic consciousness and give it legitimacy," and concludes: "It is true that some homelands are more imagined than others, but it is rare that a diaspora does not seek to maintain or to restore a homeland to its former glory." Similarly, he emphasizes the importance of a "return movement," yet almost nothing like this exists in the Indian Ocean world, where even Garveyism appears never to have penetrated.[8] I could continue with such examples, but the point is clear: if one accepts Cohen's definition of a diaspora, then it will be stretching the point to include the African presence in the Indian Ocean within this rubric.

Because of the restrictive nature of Cohen's "common features," therefore, I prefer the more organic approach advocated by Clifford, who proposes that "it is not possible to define 'diaspora' sharply, either by recourse to essential features or to privative oppositions. But it is possible to perceive a loosely coherent, adaptive constellation of responses to dwelling-in-displacement."[9] Clifford observes that "Diaspora cultures ... mediate, in a lived tension, the experiences of separation and entanglement, of living here and remembering/desiring another place."[10] This seems a much more flexible and usable notion than Cohen's emphasis on a more formalized "collective memory" and it certainly works more effectively in the Indian Ocean context, as we shall soon see. Clifford contends that

> Diaspora consciousness is . . . constituted both negatively and positively. It is constituted negatively by experiences of discrimination and exclusion....

Diaspora consciousness is produced positively through identification with world-historical cultural/political forces, such as "Africa" or "China." The process may not be as much about being African or Chinese as about being American or British or wherever one has settled, differently. . . . diasporic consciousness "makes the best of a bad situation." Experiences of loss, marginality, and exile (differentially cushioned by class) are often reinforced by systematic exploitation and blocked advancement.[11]

In a sensitive exegesis of Paul Gilroy's conceptualization of the Black Atlantic, Clifford adds that "diasporic cultures work to maintain community, selectively preserving and recovering traditions, 'customizing' and 'versioning' them in novel, hybrid, and often antagonistic situations."[12] Continuing his discourse on Gilroy, he further qualifies his thinking by arguing that "Diaspora cultures are, to varying degrees, produced by regimes of political domination and economic inequality. But these violent processes of displacement do not strip people of their ability to sustain distinctive political communities and cultures of resistance."[13] He concludes his debate with Gilroy by stating pointedly that "There is no reason his privileging of the black Atlantic . . . should necessarily silence other diasporic perspectives" and that "If diaspora is to be something about which one could write a history . . . it must be something more than the name for a site of multiple displacements and reconstitutions of identity." It must, like Gilroy's Black Atlantic, be "a historically produced social formation."[14]

From the Black Atlantic, Clifford next considers the Jewish connection, where - like Cohen - he engages Safran. But where Cohen adjusts and expands upon Safran's diaspora characteristics, Clifford worries "about the extent to which diaspora, defined as dispersal, presupposed a center." Indeed, he argues vigorously that

The centering of diasporas around an axis of origin and return overrides the specific local interactions (identifications and ruptures, both constructive and defensive) necessary for the main-

tenance of diasporic social forms. The empowering paradox of
diaspora is that dwelling *here* assumes a solidarity and connection *there*. But *there* is not necessarily a single place or an
exclusive nation.
How is the connection (elsewhere) that makes a difference
(here) remembered and rearticulated?[15]

Clifford finds an answer in the anti-Zionist perspective on
the Jewish diaspora of Daniel and Jonathan Boyarin, who
contend: "'Diasporic cultural identity teaches us that cultures
are not preserved by being protected from 'mixing' but
probably can only continue to exist as a product of such
mixing. Cultures, as well as identities, are constantly being
remade.... diasporic identity is a disaggregated identity'"[16]. As
a basis for understanding the African diaspora -whether in
the world of the Indian, Atlantic, or Mediterranean Ocean -
I find Clifford's a much more suggestive and potentially
rewarding comparative framework than that of Cohen.[17] My
reasons will become clear below.

Some models for comparison

There are a variety of scholarly models upon which one
can begin to build a systematic comparison of the African
diaspora in the two hemispheres. For example, a sufficiently well developed literature exists on slave revolts,
marronage, and other forms of resistance in both the New
World and that of the Indian Ocean, that one can certainly
outline the basis for such a history that permits us to encom-
pass the different time dimensions of the diaspora in these
two oceanic systems. On the Atlantic side, there are key
works in English by Craton, Heumann, James, Price, Reis,
and Thornton, among others, not to mention the voluminous
literature in French and Portuguese.[18] On the Indian Ocean
side the literature is characteristically thinner. While we do
have a major study on the great slave revolts in 9th century
lower Iraq,[19] we do not have anything more than a few references to two slave revolts at Zanzibar in the first half of the
19th century.[20] The situation is somewhat more promising for

studies of slave revolt and flight that produced "maroon/*marron*" societies in the Indian Ocean world, where we have the excellent work of Cassanelli for the Gosha communities formed by runaway Bantu-speaking slaves in southern Somalia;[21] Morton's interesting study of slave flight on the Kenya coast;[22] Glassman's exemplary discussion of *watoro* (runaways), rebellion and community formation in Makorora on the Swahili coast by slaves who shared East Central African origins with many of the Gosha Bantu;[23] Asgarally's overview of slave revolts in the Mascarenes, a detailed study by Barassin of a major slave revolt at Réunion in the 18th century, and important discussions of revolt and marronage for Mauritius by Allen, Teelock, and Barker, as well as a shorter note by Peerthum.[24]

On another front, John Thornton's provocative thesis makes a particularly strong case for the importance of cultural manifestations - specifically language, social structure, aesthetics, and religion - in the African diaspora which I have found to represent an especially fruitful avenue for research in the northwestern Indian Ocean.[25] By rigorously combing the historical record for evidence of these cultural phenomena, Thornton establishes an interdisciplinary methodology that represents a powerful analytical tool for students of the Indian Ocean diaspora. At the same time, however, Thornton's emphasis on port-to-port connections across the Atlantic regarding cultural transference raises a number of challenging questions about ethnogenesis in the Atlantic world that have been recently taken up by other scholars.[26] Another suggestive model along these lines comes from cultural geography and concerns the transfer of African knowledge systems, which Carney has convincingly demonstrated for rice cultivation in South Carolina.[27] But in order to make use of these models for comparison, we must first determine what questions need to be asked and how we might begin to answer them in the historical context of the Indian Ocean.

The Indian Ocean setting

Perhaps the first questions to ask are quantitative: what

are the dimensions of the forced migration of Africans in the Indian Ocean world and is a meaningful census even possible? Though many have proposed wildly differing numbers for the slave trades of eastern Africa, only Ralph Austen has attempted a systematic survey for the Red Sea zone, while he, Patrick Manning, and Abdul Sheriff differ considerably in their calculations for the mature slave trade of the Swahili coast.[28] Similarly, the quantitative dimensions of the trades of the Mozambique coast and Madagascar are still under construction.[29] At the receiving end, only for the Mascarenes is it possible to more than guess intelligently at the numbers of enslaved Africans who were incorporated into Indian Ocean societies over time and even for the mature trade of the later 18th and 19th centuries.[30] One thing seems certain, however: the dimensions of the Indian Ocean trade do not rival those of the Atlantic trade, but the lateness and intensity of the 19th century trade may well have done so.

Regarding the matter of sources of the slave trade, however, it is no less important to understand what are the regional export zones for the Indian Ocean than for the Atlantic commerce. Similarly, this knowledge must be put together with an understanding of the areas where African labor was absorbed in the Indian Ocean. [31] In our case, the main zones are Northeast Africa, which drew captives from Ethiopia, Somalia, and the Sudan (including as far away as the Western Sudan), and for which export markets certainly included the Red Sea littoral, but also extended to the Hadramaut, Persian Gulf, South Asia, and even down to Zanzibar; East Africa, sources for which included the hinterland of the Swahili coast and extended to the west of Lake Tanganyika, and which mainly supplied the markets of Zanzibar, southern Somalia, the Hadramaut, Persian Gulf, South Asia, and the Seychelles; East Central Africa, drawing upon northern Mozambique, Malawi, Zambia and Zimbabwe, and feeding the same markets as East Africa plus those of the Comoros, western Madagascar, the Mascarenes and Seychelles; South Central Africa, reaching into the deep coastal hinterlands of southern Mozambique and onto the Zimbabwean plateau, and supplying labor to the Cape, western India, and the Mascarenes; and Madagascar, which was an early source for slaves at the Cape and a principal provisioner for the Mascarenes. What emerges from this exercise in mapping are two noteworthy characteristics. First, as in the Atlantic world, in the Indian Ocean there was some degree of overlap between areas of supply and receiving areas, as well as important communities of bondsmen on the principal offshore islands that are considered part of the general African region. Second, the African diaspora in the Indian Ocean included the seaborne exportation of slaves from two major sub-regions in continental eastern Africa to other sub-regions in continental eastern Africa. If this phenomenon was not entirely different from the 16th century Atlantic context, it was certainly more significant in that of the Indian Ocean. For example, in the 20th century there have been distinguishable communities of both Zigua from mainland Tanzania and Yao from Mozambique in southern Somalia. Accordingly, for purposes of comparison, there will be a solid basis for considering both meaningful similarities and striking contrasts with respect to the process and consequences of forced migration.

Understanding labor demands in the Indian Ocean serves as a further basis for comparison of these two diasporas and helps to explain why the initial spike in the dimensions of the slave trade that is reflected by the slave revolts in 8th-9th century southern Iraq was the exception, rather than the rule. Under normal circumstances there seems to have been a steady, though undramatic demand for personal slaves, sailors, and soldiers throughout the Middle East and South Asia that was at least partially met by the forced migration of Africans before the 16th century. The intervention of the Portuguese clearly created a new source of demand in the 16th and 17th centuries, though the nature of the Portuguese demand in no way departed from existing patterns of Indian Ocean usage.[32] While the demand at the Cape in the 17th and 18th centuries was motivated primarily by the need for agricultural labor, this was limited to farm holdings and was not driven by a plantation economy.[33] What drove up the demand for labor in the 18th and 19th centuries was certainly the development of plantation economies (first indigo and then sugar in the

Mascarenes, coconuts and cloves at Zanzibar and Pemba, grain on the Kenya coast, dates in the Persian Gulf), but also the demands of urban and port development around the Arabian peninsula, pearl diving in the Red Sea and Persian Gulf, grain cultivation by slave villages in Madagascar and riverine Somalia, and even political consolidation and expansion in the Hadramaut. Accordingly, while comparisons with the western hemisphere are familiar, they are by no means precise.

We next need to confront the issue of periodization and layering, by which I mean the fact that in the cases of the Tihamah of both Saudi Arabia and the Yemen, as well as for Madagascar, there are African sub-strata that antedate by centuries the more modern African populations that reflect the slave trade of the 19th century. In the case of Madagascar, Campbell has made significant progress towards untangling these different population layers;[34] but for the Tihamah such issues have not, to my knowledge, even been broached and are greatly complicated by the fact that there has been a continual process of population exchange across the Red Sea among people who are members of the same Afrasian language family. This may also be true to some extent for South Asia, though the situation is not yet clear in that case. Here again the Indian Ocean context poses some challenges not obtaining in the Atlantic world.

Thus far I have implied that forced migration was the only means by which Africans were scattered abroad in the Indian Ocean. To be sure the slave trade was clearly the main mode of diaspora for Africans in the Indian Ocean, but it was not the only means. For example, the Aksumite conquest of South Arabia in the 3rd century C.E. and close commercial relations for the following centuries before the rise of Islam in the 7th century C.E. produced an ancient African population element that might be considered as colonization, as is also the case for the earlier era of African settlement on Madagascar. The long history of African maritime labor and trade around the Indian Ocean littoral also undoubtedly left its mark on overseas coastal communities, from earliest times right through to the present century. For example, an early instance of commercial settlement would appear to be the case of Bava Gor (or Ghor), the most widely revered African Muslim saint (*pir*) of Gujarat, who is remembered as an Abyssinian trader who pioneered the lucrative agate industry as long ago as the 14th or 16th century.[35] For more recent periods, the current research of Janet Ewald explores this maritime theme for the western Indian Ocean in the 19th century, while Noel Gueunier suggests that at least some of the Makua around Maintirano claim to have come to Madagascar in the 19th century as traders, no doubt in slaves.[36] Although free migration, whether for trade, settlement, or labor was clearly a subsidiary phenomenon in the total picture of the Indian Ocean diaspora, it signals a relative difference from that of the Atlantic that bears further research.

What were the human consequences of this different, yet similar, diaspora? At one level they were not so different from those of Africans in the Atlantic world. The big distinction was that, with the exception of the Cape and the Mascarenes, the worlds into which Africans were introduced were neither European nor Christian. In most cases this world was Islamic, but culturally and linguistically the variations between the Swahili coast (including the Muslim communities of northwest Madagascar, the Comoros, and the Benadir coast of southern Somalia, for all of whom Swahili was a lingua franca rather than a mother tongue), the riverine areas of southern Somalia, the Hijaz, Yemen, Hadramaut, Oman and the Persian Gulf coast up to Basra, coastal southwest Persia, Sind, and Gujarat were very considerable. In the case of western India and the Deccan, however, the religious context was Hindu, Muslim, and at Goa Christian, with the cultural and linguistic variation equally diverse; in Madagascar the context was entirely Malagasy; at the Cape, although the cultural context was European, the religious context was both Christian and Muslim, with significant "Malay" cultural influences; only in the Mascarenes and the Seychelles was the cultural, linguistic, and religious context "Atlantic," even to the added dimensions of major infusions of Indian indentured labor and limited Chinese immigration in the 19th century. Thus, in addition to grappling with familiar problems of reconstructing diaspora cul-

ture history, in the Indian Ocean context we must also confront host societies whose cultures differ significantly from
each other and from those of the Atlantic world.

Nevertheless, if we focus our attention on cultural manifestations, we can see important innovations and retentions
in music, song and dance, spirit possession and healing,
medical pluralism, and popular religion, all of which are
linked and can be compared with the situation in the
Americas and Caribbean islands. In some cases we can also
identify linguistic influences and retentions which open up
similar opportunities both for regional research and for
hemispheric comparison. Related to this aspect of the diaspora, but essentially distinct, are issues of culture and identity. In the Atlantic world there is little question as to who
are the Africans or their descendants; the Euroamerican construction of race leaves little room for questioning and is
manifest to scholars who study these questions. At the
level of both popular consciousness and that of the intelligentsia, in the Atlantic diaspora, these matters are relatively
clear. This is not so in the Indian Ocean where, by and
large, the cultural contexts are more obfuscating and have
tended to mystify scholars who have bothered to look, especially in the Islamic world. Both the construction of African
(and Malagasy) identities and the silencing of their memory
are only beginning to be studied in the Indian Ocean context. Moreover, the absence or delayed formation of an educated class among the diaspora that parallels that of the
Atlantic world (for all its variation) has meant that with few,
and very recent exceptions, there has been no literate
yearning for Africa that compares with that in the Atlantic.

I will explore some of these cultural issues in the next
section of the paper, but before doing so I want to add one
more interesting complication to the picture. Precisely
because it was not a European world, the colonial rulers of
Africa sent African troops all over the Indian Ocean to
fight in their wars or to help retain their territories. While the
posting of African troops cannot be considered diasporic,
any more than oscillating labor migration can be subsumed
under this rubric, their presence in areas where there were
African communities is something that I have never heard of

for the Atlantic with the exception of the stationing of the West Indian Regiment in Sierra Leone in the 19th century. [37] The question that this raises is what cultural influences, if any, were exercised on Africans in the Indian Ocean diaspora by Mozambican troops in Portuguese India, where they were stationed throughout the colonial period? By regiments of the King's African Rifles (KAR) posted to Mauritius from 1943 to about 1956 and where the barracks of the Special Mobile Force at Vacoas is still remembered as the "Camp des Zulu"? And by African regiments of Allied troops stationed in Madagascar during the Second World War?[38] One example comes from a story collected in 1981 from the Makoa grandson of a slave who probably came from Mozambique in about 1860, but certainly before Makoa emancipation in 1877. According to Pierre Sômany Talata, an old Makoa man named Morasy from the village of Menabao who was "born on the Morima [from *mrima*, Swahili for coast] on the other side of the sea [i.e. the Mozambique Channel]," encountered African soldiers stationed on the island who bore the same facial scarifications as did he, and he was able to ascertain from them in the emakhuwa language that they came from his natal village. At their separation, according to the storyteller, they said:

> "We would take you back to our country, they said to him, but we are, as you see, in service, and we can't lead you there. But what we can do is to relate, when we return to our village, we can relate that we have seen you with our own eyes."[39]

Even if this message in a bottle stretches the boundaries of credibility, it serves as a vivid reminder of the power of popular memory and connection to Africa, as well as the mnemonic role that these African troops may have played in the Indian Ocean diaspora.

Culture and identity in the Indian Ocean diaspora

If we survey the Indian Ocean world we find that

Africans generally do not identify themselves as African in any diasporic sense or do not feel that the social space exists for them to do so comfortably in their societies. Of course, such a broad generalization will vary according to the place and time, but as the transition from first generation slave to creole (in the broadest meaning of the word) is made, African identity seems to lose much of its salience as people seek to integrate themselves into their host society. The absence of an intellectual elite to articulate irredentist sentiments and to place them in public discourse is a major factor in silencing the kind of African identity, whether it be defined culturally or racially, with which we are familiar in the Atlantic world. Nevertheless, whatever the cultural context of the host society, there is plenty of evidence to suggest that at the level of lived experience, people were well aware of such differences that derived from their being of African descent.

For example, although all sources indicate that today, African populations in Oman primarily identify themselves as members of the tribe into which their forbears were incorporated as slaves, there is clear evidence that racial hierarchies that denigrate blackness operate in precisely those areas where Africans are most noticeable in the population.[40] At the same time, African musical traditions have been retained in forms that are clearly traceable to specific regions of Northeast and East Africa to this very day.[41] And if the languages that Africans brought with them to Oman were surrendered to Arabic in the process of social integration, then at least at Muscat, Swahili has been consistently reinforced by the maintenance of commercial relations throughout the 20th century and given a distinct boost by the aftermath of the Zanzibar Revolution of 1964 and more recent political changes that have intensified connections between Zanzibar and Oman. Indeed, throughout the coastal regions of the Arabian peninsula and across the Strait of Hormuz in coastal southern Iran, consciousness of Africa is maintained by the widespread popularity of *zar* and *tanburah* possession cults that derive from Ethiopia and the Sudan and incorporate African spirits, African musical instruments and rhythms, African dance forms, and African songs (the meaning of which are usually unintelligible to modern adherents of these cults), all in the context of popular Islam. To take only one specific example, in coastal southern Iran, which maintained close maritime connections with both India and Africa, *zar* possession has become an integral part of the local Persian culture, afflicting the poor and dispossessed in particular, although all the adepts in the cult are of African descent. In larger towns there were separate black quarters, while on the coast, this was not the case; nevertheless, Africans apparently acknowledged that they were different in character from Persians. Not surprisingly, the most powerful and dangerous spirits in this popular belief system came from Africa. As is the case throughout the Arabian peninsula, in addition to *zar*, the name of another category of spirits, *Noban* (from Nuba), has clear African roots, as do individual *zar* spirits, such as *Pepe* (from Swahili *pepo*, the generic term for any possessing spirit), *Maturi* (from Swahili *matari*, a specific spirit), *Dingmaro* (still another Swahili spirit, *Dungomaro*), *Chinyase* (from Chinyasa, the language of the Nyasa peoples of southern Malawi, who constituted a major source for the slave trade of East Central Africa), and *Tagruri* (a generic name for slaves from the Western Sudan - Takrur - in Arabia).[42] Thus, in what for many will be an unexpected corner of the world in which to find an African outpost, awareness of being both a part of coastal Persian Islamic culture, and in command of something distinctly African as a part of that culture, has survived to the present day, although since the Iranian Revolution there are some indications that a certain level of commercialization of regional folk culture is occurring. While this may not represent a diasporic consciousness in the usual sense of that expression, it surely bears witness to a level of popular consciousness of a community's African heritage.

A different example of popular consciousness comes from India, again in an Islamic religious context, where certain Afro-Gujarati communities are designated as Scheduled Tribes, placing them outside the caste system, and display both ethnonyms and clan names that can be clearly traced to Africa. In addition, there are the various Habshi and Sidi

communities whose dances and religious practices unambiguously connect their ancestors to Africa, though not
through spirit possession cults.[43] No more powerful example of how song persists as social memory can be found
than in the poignant encounter by a team of historians and
anthropologists from the University of Iowa who visited
members of the small African community remaining in
Hyderabad, whose fathers and grandfathers had formed an
African Bodyguard to the former Nizam of Hyderabad.
According to team co-leader Allen Roberts,

> Our first contacts with these latter were somewhat awkward
> though cordial, and literally held in the street, with a large audi-
> ence of non-Afro-Indians surrounding our little party and the
> several Afro-Indian people who had been contacted in advance
> and who agreed to meet with us. At first, because of rank dis-
> crimination against them as "Africans," there was general
> denial that anything "African" is known or remembered by con-
> temporary Chaush [as they are called locally], and that such
> information was lost more than a generation ago.
>
> We had read that Chaush still perform at certain kinds of
> public events, being hired to play music and dance in what are
> described as "African" ways, at weddings and such. When I
> asked about this, my questions were again met with initial
> denial, but then a white-haired gentleman probably in his 50s
> or so, stepped forward and said that he did indeed remember
> a song and accompanying dance that he had learned from his
> grandfather. He informed us that he did not know what the
> words mean, but that he would be happy to sing the song and
> perform the dance for us. Again, this was still out in the street,
> amidst a growing audience of young men, in particular, who
> thought the whole affair was quite novel and amusing. The man
> sang his song and did a little dance, which [we] recorded with
> our digital camcorder. Barbara Thompson [an anthropology
> graduate student studying spirit possession in Tanzania and a
> member of the team] - much to our surprise, and that of our
> Indian hosts - then sang the refrain to the same song. She was
> immediately swept up by the gentleman and several other

excited men, who applauded and asked that their picture be taken with Barbara. As she then explained (filling in details later on), she was astounded to hear the song, and her eyes welled with tears, for it was sung in Shambaa [a Bantu language spoken in northeastern Tanzania], and is a song still commonly used in the first moments of possession rituals, performed to effect healing.

Roberts explains that this song "remains esoteric" and is not the sort of song anyone could have heard on the radio, even in Tanzania. "In other words, it appears very unlikely that the man could know the song in any other way than the means he himself explained: he learned it from his grandfather, who, he told us, had come from Tanzania early this century . . . when he was recruited as a soldier into the army of the Nizam." [44] Systematic research on the various Afro-Indian communities, I am confident, is likely to reveal still further examples of such popular survivals embedded in the consciousness of the people.[45]

Although there are similarities with respect to African culture and identity on the Indian Ocean islands, there are many differences, as well. In Madagascar, Makoa have tended to live apart from their Malagasy neighbors in separate villages even after their emancipation in 1877. This situation holds both for the principal areas of their concentration around Nosy Be and Tambohorano among the Sakalava and in more isolated groupings in Imerina. Living in distinct villages seems to have facilitated the preservation of the emakhuwa language at least into the 1920s, when it appears that most Makoa decided to stop teaching it to their children as part of their desire for social acceptance into Malagasy society. Nevertheless, this process has neither been easy nor is it complete. Even where they have sought full integration, their status as the descendants of slaves creates social barriers that are difficult to overcome. For example, in a community not far from the national capital, where in the 19th century their men served as stone masons for the building of the principal royal palaces, where they constitute only about a quarter of the population, and where one of their number was elected regional mayor, they are "more or less forced" to

continue to marry endogamously. This restriction consequently maintains "certain African traits visible to the naked
eye" that inhibit complete social integration. In addition, the
Malagasy name by which the Makoa or Masombika are
also known, *Zazamanga*, reinforces this separateness, since
"*zaza*" means child and *manga* means blue, "a Malagasy
way of indicating a black person."[46] The problem is, not surprisingly, more burdensome where Makoa continue to speak
both Malagasy and emakhuwa.[47] In both of these cases it is
evident that the functioning of the highly stratified Merina
social system continues to work to the disadvantage of
Africans in Madagascar. Similarly, even in the Sakalava
region, the existence of joking relationships between Makoa
and their Malagasy neighbors signals the existence of social
distance.[48] Thus African cultural retentions vary, but as
recently as within the last two decades, researchers have succeeded in collecting both word lists and folk tales in
emakhuwa from older members of this population.[49] Finally,
a different kind of African consciousness continues to exist at
the island of Nosy Be where a poetic genre in Swahili is
known as Manganja, a name unambiguously derived from
one of the major ethnic groups of southern Malawi that com-
prised a major source of the African slave population of
Madagascar.[50]

The situation is altogether different, yet surprisingly
similar, on the smaller Indian Ocean islands, though significant differences exist with respect to the Africanness of individual island societies, ranging from the Seychelles to
Rodrigues (which is a part of the nation-state of Mauritius)
to Réunion to Mauritius, where the immigration of indentured Indian labor has yielded a majority Hindu society
today. All of these island cultures share important common
features, such as related but distinct French Creole or Kreol
languages,[51] and *sega*, a dance of slave origin and musical
form with Afro-Malagasy roots. Linguistically, despite the significant numbers of East Africans who were introduced to
the islands as slaves or so-called "free emigrants" during the
18th and 19th centuries, there are remarkably few substrate
East African influences in these Kreols and certainly no independent survivals of East African languages, such as exist

among some Makoa at Madagascar.[52] That said, when Freycinet visited Mauritius in 1818, he recognized "Mozambique Creole" among the several dialectical variations within this emerging language, as did Baissac, the renowned student of Mauritian Kreol, several decades later. Similarly, Baker has identified a significant number of riddles of varying African origin from Baissac's collection.[53] In Réunion Kreol, however, references to Africans tend to be pejorative, as these proverbs in French translation indicate:

> *Au bout de cent ans dans le pays, le "cafre" mange toujours*
> *les patates douces avec la peau.*
> *Parole de Noir, pet de chien.*
> *Un Noir, un chien, deux cousins germains.*
> *Un Noir n'a point de milieu.*
> *Le "cafre" a sept peaux.*[54]

By way of contrast, influences from Malagasy are both greater in number and not pejorative.[55]

This situation was not, however, always the case. During the 19th century there is plenty of evidence that Africans and Malagasy on the Mascarenes were well aware of their roots. In the 1840s, the remarkable French ethnographer Eugène de Froberville, interviewed "more than three hundred natives of these countries [of East Africa], among whom about fifty had recently left their country" in search of information on their customs and traditions. He collected some sixty masks and figurines, "fifty portraits designed with the characteristic tattoos that these races like to trace on their faces and bodies," and thirty-one "vocabularies of their languages." Among those peoples for whom he recorded this information were Makua and so-called Niambana or Jambane (from the south central port of Inhambane) from Mozambique, and Ngindo from southern mainland Tanzania.[56] A decade later, a British missionary noted that the freed slaves "retained the superstitions and practiced the idolatrous rites peculiar to their native land" including "respect for their ancestors." They also cast lots to foretell the future and generally carried a talisman "known by the name of *grisgris*." Referring

specifically to Malagasy at Mauritius, he observed quite
accurately:

> Attachment to their native land was not a mere sentiment; it was
> incorporated with, and formed part of, their religious belief.
> They believed that when the soul quitted the body it returned not
> to God, but to the place of their birth, there to exist under some
> other form . . . . The desire that their bodies should be interred
> in their native land was perhaps as influential as the love of lib-
> erty in inducing many of them to put to sea [which he notes in
> a discussion of marronage], and thus expose themselves to a
> lingering death. This desire, probaby connected in some way
> with their religious belief, is still prevalent among the inhabitants
> of Madagascar.[57]

Over the course of the past century-and-a-half these
beliefs have been effectively suffocated on Mauritius by conversion to Catholicism and the role of the Church in denying meaningful cultural synthesis within its boundaries,
although Moutou asserts that "in the Creole milieu, certain
practices originally from Madagascar, indeed from Africa, are
still present in such funeral ceremonies."[58]

Whatever the role of organized religion on the
Mascarenes, popular religion appears to be one area where
Afro-Malagasy influences, comingled especially with those
deriving from India, survive. The relative coherence of
Malagasy culture compared with the more fragmented origins of Africans on the Mascarenes, and the high development of magical practices among the Malagasy, give them
real prominence in this area of social discourse. Réunion,
where there are also strong inputs that can be traced to rural
France, enjoys a rich and well studied popular religious culture that draws significantly upon Afro-Malagasy beliefs
and expertise.[59] Some of this has deep roots, but certain specific beliefs are more recently derived, such as the cult
devoted to Sitarane, the nickname for a Mozambican worker
named Simicoundza Simicourba who arrived in Réunion in
1889 and who together with several accomplices terrorized
the island in the first decade of the 20th century and was

hanged for allegedly committing robbery, murder, desecration of the dead, and sorcery.[60] Although few have bothered to look seriously into similar practices in Mauritius, a recent popular, indeed sensationalist, study suggests that such beliefs are alive and well there, too, and that Malagasy figure significantly both as major spirits and as adepts.[61] Anthropologist Linda Sussman's study of medical pluralism on Mauritius suggests that the widespread tradition of specialized secular healers "may represent a blend of European, and perhaps Malagasy and African, herbalism and Christian practices such as the laying on of hands," which also exists on Réunion. They treat a variety of illnesses, especially "*tambave*, an illness syndrome widely recognized on the Mascarenes and Madagascar," that is treated by "markings." She notes also that convulsions are often referred to as "*crises malgasses.*"[62] Further indication that such syncretism may well have been the case in the recent past in other settings comes from a conversation with two Hindu Mauritian colleagues who attributed to Afro-Malagasy influence the very unorthodox practice of placing offerings of cigarettes at Hindu shrines around the island.[63] Finally, it is worth noting both the significance of prominent African place names on Mauritius, such as Camp des Yolofs in Port-Louis, Gris-Gris, and Maconde (after the northern Mozambican Maconde), both on the south coast of the island, as well as the alleged erasure of such names replaced by those of Hindu leaders.[64]

Without question, the most well known example of African cultural influence in these islands is sega, also known today as *maloya* on Réunion. Rooted in the experience of slavery, sega combined African and Malagasy music and dance forms and instrumentation, although today instrumentation has been considerably modernized. Indeed, Mauritians usually assume that sega is the only remaining example of Afro-Malagasy culture on the island and in some respects its survival and popularization serve as a sharp reminder to Mauritian Creoles of Afro-Malagasy descent of their second class status in society.[65] The history of sega remains to be written in full, but until it was "rediscovered" and championed for being African by Creole intellectual Jacques Cantin, who subsequently wrote sega song lyrics, it remained despised for its slave origins and did not enjoy general popularity. General acceptance can be traced to the recording career of the late Alphonse Ravaton, popularly known as Ti-Frère, whose image has become a national symbol for sega.[66] Mauritian sega has now entered the larger orbit of world beat, while the latest variation in its evolution is known as seggae for its incorporation of rhythms from Caribbean reggae and its message of African liberation. Certainly, Mauritian Creoles today face greater problems than the commoditization of sega. These economic and social dilemmas have given rise to what is usually described as "le malaise créole" and has officially been recognized by completion in 1997 of an official report on what is locally called "exclusion."[67] On the occasion of the 150th anniversary of the abolition of slavery in 1835, a movement evolved among certain members of Créole society to advocate for identification as Afro-Mauritians, which in the Mauritian context constitutes a political statement. Sega loomed large in this invocation of Africa, as did calls for recognition of Kreol as an official language.[68] As Mauritius seeks to identify itself more with the African continent, where it is currently forging new economic relationships, it will be interesting to see how popular cultural awareness of Afro-Malagasy roots is either revived or coopted.[69]

Before concluding, I examine briefly a quite different example of irredentism among Africans scattered abroad in the Indian Ocean. The Bantu people of Gosha in riverine southern Somalia are among the chief victims of the civil war in that country. Since their forced migration to Somalia in the 19th century, these peoples have maintained an awareness of their non-Somali origins and identity through a variety of social and cultural institutions, dance being one of the most important.[70] In the wake of the chaos created by the civil war, several thousand individuals from the Zigua communities of southern Somalia have been resettled in their ancestral homelands in Handeni District of eastern mainland Tanzania, where they have drawn upon their matrilineal clan identity (despite the fact that they are now Muslim) to establish kinship with indigenous Zigua.[71] More recently, a similar claim has been made by various southern Somalia Bantu peoples claiming Mozambican origins. Numbering about 10,000 souls, in 1998, these refugees were located in camps at Dabaad in Kenya. According to a Mozambican fact-finding mission headed by the director of that country's Refugee Support Nucleus, they found that some of these people "did indeed share some cultural and linguistic affinities with certain Mozambican ethnic groups." One old man could speak Yao and "claimed his grandparents had come from Inchinga - which is today's Lichinga, capital of the Mozambican province of Niassa," while another was able to speak Makua, "the most widespread language of northern Mozambique." Moreover, "some of their dances seemed reminiscent of Mozambican ones," including the *chioda* and *tufu* dances of the north and *zore*, "a dance from Inhambane."[72] The fact that Mozambique is not willing to acknowledge these refugees as Mozambicans does not alter the fact that they are now claiming a Mozambican diaspora identity as preferable to that of Somali refugees. As Clifford notes, "The currency of diaspora discourses extends to a wide range of populations and historical predicaments."[73]

Some general comparisons

I began this paper by questioning whether we could apply the term "diaspora" in any meaningful sense to the displacement of Africans in the Indian Ocean world. By embracing the flexible definition of diaspora advocated by Clifford, I think we can indeed utilize this concept for the Indian Ocean and thus employ the notion of diaspora in order to compare the African presence in the Atlantic with that in the Indian Ocean world. By now the similarities and differences between these two worlds with respect to the African diasporas in each hemisphere should be reasonably clear. The following summarizes the issues.

The Atlantic world was the outcome of its being a Euroamerican ocean created by European expansion; Africans were major players in shaping this world, while indigenous cultures were marginalized, though not without their own influences. Oceanic transportation was on the high seas and intercontinental, while race was predicated on Euroamerican constructs of master-slave/white-black relations. The timing of the mature slave trade was somewhat different, beginning earlier and ending earlier than that of the Indian Ocean world, thus allowing for a greater passage of time among Africans in the New World. Christianity and access to western education for a limited number of Africans raised consciousness of Africa and generated an irredentism among African intellectuals in the western hemisphere that produced back to Africa movements and Pan-Africanism. In contrast, the Indian Ocean was an Asian sea of much greater cultural antiquity than that of the Atlantic; European intrusion eventually drew it into the evolving world capitalist system, but only affected its indigenous cultures at the margins until very late in the day. Oceanic transportation was historically restricted to coastal sailing, which explains how it was that the smaller Indian Ocean islands (except for the Maldives, which were not populated by Africans) remained unpopulated until European sailing vessels arrived on the scene. This also helps explain the intracontinental seaborne forced migration of Africans in the Indian Ocean, which was a distinguishing feature of this current of African slavery from other continental examples, again with the exception of the early Atlantic trade. The principal religious dimensions of this Indian Ocean world were Islamic, though not exclusively and race relations were determined by indigenous ideological systems, except for the Mascarenes, Seychelles, and the Cape, and finally there was the colonial overlay that seized the rest of this world in the 19th and 20th centuries. The abolition of slavery in the Indian Ocean began at about the same time as it did in the Atlantic world, but it was not completed until well into the 20th century in the Hadramaut. The lack of Western educational opportunities among diaspora Africans and different historical circumstances inhibited the formation of any diasporic consciousness in the Indian Ocean. Finally, the impact of indentured Indian labor migration into areas previously dominated by African slave labor has obvious parallels in the Caribbean, while the stationing of colonial African troops in the Indian Ocean basin does not. While I do not deceive myself that I have exhausted the parameters of such a comparison, I believe that my analysis provides a reasonable basis for further comparison and critical commentary.

Notes and References

1. Edward A. Alpers, "The African Diaspora in the Northwestern Indian Ocean: reconsideration of an old problem, new directions for research," *Comparative Studies of South Asia, Africa & the Middle East*, 17/2 (1997), pp. 62-81. An earlier version of this paper was presented at the conference on Black Diasporas in the Western Hemisphere, Humanities Research Centre, Australian National University, 7-9 April 1998. I am grateful to Mischalgrace Diasanta for research assistance.

2. The pioneers in recognizing the Indian Ocean dimensions of the African diaspora are Joseph E. Harris, *The African Presence in Asia: Consequences of the East African Slave Trade* (Evanston, 1971) and George Shepperson, "The African Abroad or the African diaspora," in T.O. Ranger (ed.), *Emerging Themes of African History* (Nairobi, 1968), pp. 152-176.

3. Philip Curtin, "The African Diaspora," in Michael Craton (ed.), *Roots and Branches: Current Directions in Slave Studies* (Toronto, 1979), pp. 1-17, takes the Indian Ocean and Islamic dimensions of the diaspora quite seriously, and is here quoted at p. 7.

4. James Clifford, *Routes: Travel and Translations in the Late Twentieth Century* (Cambridge, Mass. and London, 1997), p. 244.

5. Robin Cohen, *Global Diasporas: An Introduction* (Seattle, 1997).

6. Ibid., p. xii.

7. Ibid., p. 26, Table 1.1; cf. W. Safran, "Diasporas in modern societies: myths of homeland and return," *Diaspora*, 1/1 (1991), pp. 83-99.

8. Cohen, *Global Diasporas*, pp. 184-185. In making his point about roots, Cohen specifically cites the contribution of Elliot P. Skinner, "The Dialectic Between Diasporas and Homelands," in Joseph E. Harris (ed.), *Global Dimensions of the African Diaspora*, 2nd ed. (Washington, D.C., 1993), pp. 11-40. For confirmation of the absence of references to Garveyism in the Indian Ocean I thank my colleague Robert A. Hill, General Editor of the Marcus Garvey and Universal Negro Improvement Association Papers.

9. Clifford, *Routes*, p. 254. Although Cohen discusses Clifford's work on diasporas, which first appeared in 1994, he limits his discussion of it to specific elements that clearly do not affect his conclusions.

10. Ibid., p. 255.

11. Ibid., pp. 256-257.

12. Ibid., p. 263.

13. Ibid., p. 265.

14. Ibid., p. 267. For less sympathetic critiques of Gilroy's work, see the contributions by Simon Gikandi, Joan Dayan, and Natasha Barnes in Gikandi (Guest Editor), "The 'Black Atlantic'," *Research in African Literatures*, 27/4 (1996).

15. Clifford, *Routes*, p. 269.

16. Daniel and Jonathan Boyarin, "Diaspora: Generational Ground of Jewish Identity," *Critical Inquiry*, 19/4 (1993), p. 721, as cited by Clifford, *Routes*, pp. 270-271.

17. For the Mediterranean dimension, see the important work of John Hunwick, "African Slaves in the Mediterranean World: A Neglected Aspect of the African Diaspora," in Harris (ed.), *Global Dimensions*,

pp. 289-323; "Black Slave Religious Practices in the Mediterranean World," Paper presented to the SSHRC/UNESCO Summer Institute "Identifying Enslaved Africans: The 'Nigerian' Hinterland and the African Diaspora," York University, Canada, 1997; and "The Same but different: Approaches to Slavery and the African Diaspora in the lands of Islam," Paper presented to the Northwestern University Workshop on Slavery and the African Diaspora in the Lands of Islam, 30 April-2 May 1999. My thanks to Professor Hunwick for sharing these unpublished papers with me.

18. Michael Craton, "The passion to exist: slave rebellions in the British West Indies," *Journal of Caribbean History*, 13 (1980), pp. 1-20; Gad Heumann (ed.), *Out of the House of Bondage: Runaways, Resistance and Marronage in Africa and the New World* (London, 1986); C.L.R. James, *The Black Jacobins: Toussaint L'Ouverture and the San Domingo Revolution*, 2nd ed. (New York, 1963); Richard Price (ed.), *Maroon Societies* (Baltimore, 1979); João José Reis, *Slave Rebellion in Brazil: the Muslim Uprising of 1835 in Bahia* (Baltimore, 1993); John Thornton, *Africa and Africans in the Making of the Atlantic World, 1400-1800, 2nd ed.* (Cambridge, 1998), Ch. 10.

19. Alexandre Popovic, *La révolte des esclaves en Iraq au IIIe/IXe siècle* (Paris, 1976).

20. See C.S. Nicholls, *The Swahili Coast: Politics, Diplomacy and Trade on the East African Littoral 1798-1856* (London, 1971), p. 256; Frederick Cooper, *Plantation Slavery on the East Coast of Africa* (New Haven & London, 1977), pp. 202-203.

21. Lee V. Cassanelli, "Social Construction on the Somali Frontier: Bantu Former Slave Communities in the Nineteenth Century," in Igor Kopytoff (ed.), *The African Frontier: The Reproduction of Traditional African Societies* (Bloomington and Indianapolis, 1987), pp. 216-238.

22. Fred Morton, *Children of Ham: freed slaves and fugitive slaves on the Kenya coast, 1873 to 1907* (Boulder, Colo., 1990).

23. Jonathon Glassman, *Feasts and Riot: Revelry, Rebellion, and Popular Consciousness on the Swahili Coast, 1856-1888* (Portsmouth, N.H., 1995), pp. 106-114.

24. Issa Asgarally, "Les Révoltes d'Esclaves dans les Mascareignes ou 'l'Histoire du Silence'," in U. Bissondoyal and S.B.C. Servansing (eds.), *Slavery in South West Indian Ocean* (Moka, Mauritius, 1989), pp. 176-189; Jean Barassin, "La révolte des esclaves à l'Ile Bourbon (Réunion) au XVIIIe siècle," in *Mouvements de Populations dans l'océan Indien* (Paris, 1979), pp. 357-391; Richard N. Allen, "Marronage and the Maintenance of Public Order in Mauritius, 1721-1835," *Slavery & Abolition*, 4 (1983), pp. 214-231; Anthony J. Barker, *Slavery and Antislavery in Mauritius, 1810-33: The Conflict between Economic Expansion and Humanitarian Reform under British Rule* (London and New York, 1996), Ch. 8; Vijaya Teelock, *A Select Guide to Sources on Slavery in Mauritius* and *Slaves Speak Out: The Testimony of Slaves in the Era of Sugar* (Bell Village, Mauritius, 1995), Part Two; S. Peerthum, "Resistance against Slavery," in Bissondoyal and Servansing (eds.), *Slavery in South West Indian Ocean*, pp. 124-130.

25. Thornton, *Africa and Africans*, Chs. 8-9; cf. Gwendolyn Midlo Hall, *Africans in Colonial Louisiana: The Development of Afro-Creole Culture in the Eighteenth Century* (Baton Rouge and London, 1992); Alpers, "Northwestern Indian Ocean."

26. See Douglas B. Chambers, "'He is an African But Speaks Plain': Historical Creolization in Eighteenth-Century Virginia," in Alusine Jalloh and Stephen E. Maizlish (eds.), *The African Diaspora* (College Station, Texas, 1996), pp. 100-133, and "'My own nation': Igbo Exiles in the Diaspora," *Slavery & Abolition*, 18/1 (1997), pp. 72-97; Peter Caron, "'Of a nation which the others do not Understand': Bambara Slaves and African Ethnicity in Colonial Louisiana, 1718-60," *Slavery & Abolition*, 18/1 (1997), pp. 98-121; Philip D. Morgan, "The Cultural Implications of the Atlantic Slave Trade: African Regional Origins, American Destinations and New World Developments," *Slavery & Abolition*, 18/1 (1997), pp. 122-145; Michael A. Gomez, *Exchanging Our Country Marks: The transformation of African Identities in the Colonial and Antebellum South* (Chapel Hill and London, 1998).

27. Judith Carney, "From Hands to Tutors: African Expertise in the South Carolina Rice Economy," *Agricultural History*, 67/3 (1993), pp. 1-30; "Landscapes of Technology Transfer: Rice Cultivation and African Continuities," *Technology and Culture*, 37/1 (1996), pp. 80-110, and "Rice Milling, Gender and Slave Labour in Colonial South Carolina," *Past and Present*, 153 (1996), pp. 108-134.

28. For the general problem of quantitative reconstruction, see Ralph A. Austen, "Slave Trade: The Sahara Desert and Red Sea Region," p. 103, and Alpers, "Slave Trade: Eastern Africa," pp. 96-97, both in John Middleton (ed.), *Encyclopedia of Africa South of the Sahara* (New York, 1997), 4. For the mature trade, see Austen, "The 19th Century Islamic Slave Trade from East Africa (Swahili and Red Sea Coasts): A Tentative Census," in Gervase Clarence-Smith (ed.), *The Economics of the Indian Ocean Slave Trade in the Nineteenth Century* (London, 1989), pp. 21-44; Patrick Manning, *Slavery and African Life: Occidental, Oriental, and African Slave Trades* (Cambridge, 1990), pp. 52-53; Abdul Sheriff, *Slaves, Spices, and Ivory in Zanzibar: Integration of an East African Commercial Empire into the World Economy, 1770-1873* (London, 1987), pp. 33-60.

29. Alpers, *Ivory and Slaves in East Central Africa* (London and Berkeley, 1975); José Capela and Eduardo Medeiros, *O tráfico de escravos de Moçambique para as ilhas do Índico 1720-1902* (Maputo, 1987); Gwyn Campbell, "Madagascar and Mozambique in the Slave Trade of the Western Indian Ocean 1800-1861," in Clarence-Smith (ed.), *Economics*, pp. 166-193, "Madagascar and the Slave Trade, 1810-1895," *Journal of African History*, 22 (1981), pp. 203-227, and "The East African Slave Trade, 1861-1895: The 'Southern' Complex," *International Journal of African Historical Studies*. 22 (1989), pp. 1-26; Pier M. Larson, "A Census of Slaves Exported from Central Madagascar to the Mascarenes between 1769 and 1820," in Ignace Rakoto (ed.), *L'Esclavage à Madagscar: Aspects historiques et résurgences contemporaines* (Antananarivo, 1997), pp. 131-145.

30. See, e.g., R.R. Kuczynski, *Demographic Survey of the British Colonial*

Empire, 2 (Oxford, 1949), Part 4; J.M. Filliot, *La traite des esclaves vers les Mascareignes au XVIIIe siècle* (Tananarive, 1970); Huguette Ly-Tio-Fane Pineo, "Les esclaves 'de plantation' de l'Ile Maurice à la veille de l'abolition, d'après le recensement de 1823," in *Histoires d'outre-mer: Mélanges en l'honneur de Jean-Louis Miege* (Aix-en-Provence, 1992), II, pp. 635-655; Barker, *Slavery and Antislavery*, Ch. 5; Richard Allen, *Slaves, Freedmen, and Indentured Laborers in Colonial Mauritius* (Cambridge, 1999).

31. Although slaves from eastern Africa, including Madagascar, entered the labor market of the Atlantic world, I do not consider them here.

32. See Alpers, "Northwestern Indian Ocean" and sources cited therein at n. 24-26.

33. See Nigel Worden, *Slavery in Dutch South Africa* (Cambridge, 1985); Robert Shell, *Children of Bondage: a social history of the slave society at the Cape of Good Hope, 1652-1838* (New Haven, 1994).

34. See Campbell, "The Origins and Demography of Slaves in Nineteenth Century Madagascar: A chapter in the history of the African ancestry of the Malagasy," in *Fanadevozana ou esclavage: Colloque internatioanl sur l'esclavage à Madagascar* (Antananarivo, 1996), pp. 5-37.

35. See sources in Alpers, "Northwestern Indian Ocean," n. 102, and also Helene Basu, *Habshi-Sklaven, Sidi-Fakire: Muslimische Heiligenverehrung im westlichen Indien* (Berlin, 1995).

36. Noël Gueunier, "Documents sur la langue makhuwa à Madagascar et aux Comores (fin XIXe-début XXe siècles)," in *Fanadevozana ou esclavage*, p. 315

37. Roger Norman Buckley, *Slaves in Red Coats: The British West India Regiments, 1795-1815* (New Haven and London, 1979), pp. 95-96.

38. See Miguel de Noronha de Paiva Couceiro, *Diu e Eu* (Lisboa, 1969), p. 137; Eduard Maunick, Tristan Bréville, and Yves Martial, *Maurice, Le Temps d'une Île* (Paris, 1993), p. 29, for a photograph of the KAR on parade during VE Day celebrations at Curepipe in 1948; personal communiction from Tristan Bréville, Port-Louis, 2 August 1997; H. Moyse-Bartlett, *The King's African Rifles: A Study in the Military History of East and Central Africa, 1890-1945* (Aldershot, 1956), pp. 680, 702-703 (Appendix F); E.F. Whitehead, "A Short History of Uganda Military Units formed during World War II," *The Uganda Journal*, 14/1 (1950), pp. 1-14. In a conversation with Ramon Cundasamy, Acting Town Clerk, and Tristan Bréville, Port-Louis. 18 June 1999, both men recalled listening to the weekly request show of the KAR on Radio Mauritius, which featured African music, including songs in Swahili.

39. Maurice Schrive and Noël J. Gueunier, "'Histoire du Peuple': Souvenirs sur l'esclavage des Makoa du nord de Madagascar," *Études Océan Indien*, 15 (1992), pp. 177-197, quoted at 195, my translation.

40. Frederick Barth, *Sohar: Culture and Society in an Omani Town* (Baltimore/London, 1983), pp. 42-49, 98-99.

41. For details, see Alpers, "Northwestern Indian Ocean."

42. Gholam-Hossein Sa'edi, *Ahl I Hawa* (Tehran, 1966). I am indebted to Touraj Daryaee for translating this important anthropological study for me from Persian. See also, Taghi Modaressi, "The Zar Cult in

South Iran," in Raymond Prince (ed.), *Trance and Possession States* (Montreal, 1966), pp. 149-155; Kaveh Safa, "Reading Saedi's *Ahl-E Hava*: Pattern and Significance in Spirit Possession Beliefs on the Southern Coasts of Iran," *Culture, Medicine and Psychiatry*, 12 (1988), pp. 85-111; for details on these phenomena in Arabia, see Alpers, "Northwestern Indian Ocean."

43. Ibid.

44. I am indebted to Allen F. Roberts for sharing this fascinating encounter with me, first in the comfort of his home and then as an email To: alpers@history.ucla.edu From: Allen Roberts allen-roberts@uiowa.edu Subject: Shambaa song in India Date: Fri, 13 Mar 1998. The term "Chaush" is the term by which this Afro-Indian community refers to itself and is derived from a military title that approximates "sergeant." The University of Iowa project was sponsored by a "Crossing Borders: Revitalizing Area Studies" grant awarded to the University of Iowa by the Ford Foundation. For illustration of this encounter, see also the video produced by Mary Nooter Roberts, "Memory across the Indian Ocean," 1998.

45. Here I should draw attention to current research by Helene Basu among Siddis in Pakistan, by Amy Catlin-Jairazbhoy on the music of Siddis in Gujarat and North Karnataka, and by Charles Camara in these latter communities.

46. Michel Razafiarivony, "Les *Zazamanga* d'Antanetibe Ambato: de la servitude à la lutte continue pour la reconnaissance réelle," in *Fanadevozana ou esclavage*, pp. 548-559, my translation; see also, Henri Lavondès, *Bekoropoka: Quelques aspects de la vie familiale et sociale d'un village malgache* (Paris & The Hague, 1967), pp. 137-138.

47. Malanjaona Rakotomalala and Célestin Razafimbelo, "Le problème d'intégration sociale chez les Makoa de l'Antsihanaka," *Omaly sy Anio*, 21-22 (1985), pp. 93-113.

48. Narivelo Rajaonarimanana, "Les parents à plaisanterie des Makoa," *Études Océan Indien*, 8 (1987), pp. 119-123. See also, Lavondès, *Bekoropoka*, pp. 42, 92, 116; Lesley A. Sharp, *The Possessed and the Dispossessed: Spirits, Identity, and Power in a Madagascar Town* (Berkeley, 1993), pp. 59, 68, 77.

49. Gueunier, "Documents;" Schrive and Gueunier, "'Histoire du Peuple';" Gueunier, with J.M. Katupha for emakhuwa text, *Contes de la côte ouest de Madagascar* (Antananarivo and Paris, n.d.), pp. 78-96; Razafiarivony, "Les *Zazamanga* d'Antanetibe Ambato, p. 559.

50. Gueunier, "Les poèmes de Maulidi Manganja: Poèmes swahili recueillis à Nosy Be," *Bulletin des Études africaines de l'Inalco*, 3/6 (1983), pp. 7-76; for slave origins, see Campbell, "Origins and Demography."

51. A major debate rages among Creole linguists concerning whether Réunion Kreol is the source of all the others or whether it and Mauritian Kreol are different languages. Cf. Robert Chaudenson, *Le lexique du parler Créole de la Réunion* (Paris, 1974), 2 vols., and Philip Baker and Chris Corne, *Isle de France Creole: Affinities and Origins* (n.p. USA, 1982). My Mauritian Creole friends claim that while Mauritian and Seychelles Kreol are mutually intelligible, they cannot understand Réunion Kreol.

52. For the lack of significant African linguistic influence in Réunion Kreol, see Chaudenson, *Le lexique*, II, pp. 1093, 1106-1109; but cf. Baker and Corne, *Isle de France Creole*, pp. 100-101, n.3, and *passim* for evidence of significant West African language influence as a consequence of the presence of "Senegalese" slaves imported by the Compagnie des Indes when Mauritian Kreol was forming during the middle decades of the 18th century.

53. Louis de Freycinet, *Voyage autour du Monde . . . Executé sur les corvettes de S.M.* l'Oranie et la Physicienne, *pendant les années 1817, 1818, 1819 et 1820* (Paris, 1828), Vol. 1, Part 2, p. 407; Charles Baissac, *Étude sur le patois Créole Mauricien* (Nancy, 1880), pp. 104-108; Philip Baker, "On the Origins of the Mauritian Creole Riddles in Baissac 1880," *Journal of Mauritian Studies*, 2/2 (1988), pp. 40-85.

54. Chaudenson, *Le lexique*, I, p. 323; see also p. 108. Since the French is itself a translation from Réunion Kreol I consider it best not to translate these proverbs into English.

55. Ibid., II, pp. 1082-1086.

56. Eugène de Froberville, "Notes sur les Moeurs, coutumes et traditions des Amakoua, sur le commerce et la traite des esclaves dans l'Afrique orientale," *Bulletin de la Société de Géographie*, 3.me Série, 8 (1847), pp. 311-329, quoted at 311-312, my translation; also his "Notes sur les Va-Ngindo," and "Tribus de nègres bégayeurs au nord de la cafrerie," *Bulletin de la Société de Géographie*, 4.me Série, 3 (1852), pp. 425-443, 517-519. For evidence of the existence of Makua speakers at Mauritius in the 1850s, see Vincent W. Ryan, *Mauritius and Madagascar: Journal of an Eight Years' Residence in the Diocese of Mauritius, and of a Visit to Madagascar* (London, 1864), pp. 165-167. For more on African survivals and the construction of an African identity at Mauritius, see Alpers, "Becoming 'Mozambique': Diaspora and Identity in Mauritius," in Vijayalakshmi Teelock and Edward A. Alpers (eds.), *History, Memory and Identity* (Port Louis, 2001), pp. 117-155.

57. Patrick Beaton, *Creoles and Coolies; or, Five Years in Mauritius*, 2nd ed. (Port Washington/London, 1971; 1st ed. 1859), pp. 78, 79-80. The importance of burial in one's ancestral land to Malagasy is well documented, but nowhere so succinctly as by Sharp, *Possessed and Dispossessed*, pp. 59 and 297, n. 4.

58. Benjamin Moutou, *Les Chrétiens de l'île Maurice* (Port-Louis, 1996), p. 372. For a major critique of the role of the Roman Catholic Church in suppressing Afro-Malagasy culture in the process of proselytization, see Didier Colson, "Approches de la Pratique Missionnaire Catholique à l'ile Maurice entre 1840 et 1895: Une église locale edificatrice et/ou edifiante?" D. Theol., Institut Catholique de Toulouse, 1980, pp. 187-206, 479-495, 614-619; I am grateful to Jocelyn Chan Low for bringing this important study to my attention.

59. See Prosper Eve, *La religion populaire à la Réunion* (Réunion, 1985), 2 vols.; Chaudenson (ed.), *Encyclopédie de la Réunion*, 6 (Saint-Denis, 1980), pp. 79-103; Chaudenson, with Ch. Barat and M. Carayol, *Magie et sorcellerie à la Réunion* (Saint-Denis, 1983); Gérard Mouls, *Études sur la sorcellerie à la Réunion (Désir et Réaltié)* (Saint-Denis, 1982); *La Revue Grand Océan* (Réunion), 4,

"Les Âmes Errantes: Sorcellerie et Magie dans les Mascareignes" (n.d., but mid-1990s).

60. All of the sources mentioned in the previous footnote discuss Sitarane, but see especially Jean-François Sam-Long, "Sitarane ou le jeu des maléfices," in ibid., pp. 78-86.

61. Pierre-Edmond Pulvenis de Seligny, *Vraies et extraordinaires aventures de . . . chez les sorciers de l'Île Maurice: "Traiteurs" et "Longanistes" au travail et des Scènes terrifiantes d'exorcisme* (Port-Louis, 1996), pp. 42, 44, 55, 57, 77, 79, 83, 101-102, 139, 143, 147. See also Brinda Chetty, "Un chauffer de taxi sauvé par 'un esprit malgache'," in the popular weekly newspaper, *Le Défi Plus*, 26 June-2 July 1999.

62. Linda Kaye Sussman, "Medical pluralism on Mauritius: a study of medical beliefs and practices in a polyethnic society," Ph.D. dissertation, Washington University-St. Louis, 1983, pp. 152-154, 160.

63. For a photograph of offerings of cigarettes at the tomb of Sitarane at Saint-Pierre Cemetery on Réunion, see Chaudenson, *Magie et sorcellerie*, p. 55.

64. This last complaint was expressed to me by several young Creole Rastafarians at the small village of Chamarel, in Rivière-Noire, which is reputedly the most African part of the island. I found these young men playing African drums on the verandah of a house that was decorated with a large mural featuring Hayla-Sellase inside the head of a schematic Lion of Judah, and featuring a variety of cultural expressions that included specific language referring to Africa and Ethiopia. A second mural cries out "Respecter nou culture, nou droit ça! Droit fondamentale tou mauricien. [Respect our culture, our rights here! The fundamental rights of all Mauritians.]" Field notes, 27 July 1997, and photographs taken at Chamarel. For examples of African place names in the Hadramaut, see Alpers, "Northwestern Indian Ocean."

65. No better example of this sort of officially sanctioned popular incorporation of sega exists than its performance at every tourist hotel on Mauritius and its representation as African on tourist items like post cards and tea towels

66. The best study of Mauritian sega is Claudine Ricaud, "Séga-Laë: aspects of traditional music in Mauritius," B.A. thesis, University of Sydney, 1986. I am also grateful to her for the information on Jacques Cantin: personal communication, Quatre Bornes, Mauritius, 2 August 1997. Also see Iswarduth Nundlall, *Music in Mauritius* (Vacoas, Mauritius, 1984; reproduction of a M.Mus. thesis for Bhatkhande University of Music, Lucknow, 1957), pp. 37-67. Current research by Daniella Police of the University of Mauritius promises to expand our knowledge of sega. See her "Mauritian Sega: The Trace of the Slave's Emancipatory Voice," *The UTS Quarterly*, 6/2 (2000), pp. 57-69. For sega and maloya in Réunion, see Chaudenson (ed.), *Encyclopédie de la Réunion*, 5 (Saint-Denis, 1981), pp. 77-83, 91-95, 101-103; for Rodrigues, see Christian Barat, Michel Carayol, and Robert Chaudenson, *Rodrigues: La Cendrillon des Mascareignes* (Réunion, 1985), pp. 103-109. Two short studies of Ti-Frère are Marcel Poinen and Jean-Clément Cangy, Ti Frer (n.p., 1990) and Colette le Chartier, *Ti-Frère: Poète du quotidien* (Port-Louis, 1993).

67. See Norbert Benoit, "Les séquelles de l'esclavage - le malaise créole," in *Fanadevozana ou esclavage*, pp. 572-592; Asgarally (ed.), *Étude pluridisciplinaire sur l'exclsion à Maurice-Rapport Final 1997* (Réduit, Mauritius, 1997). For two important interpretations of the recent violence associated with Creole disaffection in Mauritius, see William F. S. Miles, "The Creole Malaise in Mauritius," *African Affairs*, 98 (1999), pp. 211-228; Jocelyn Chan Low, "Roots, Rastas and Riots," paper presented to the Conference "Post-Emancipation Mauritius 1839-1911," Mahatma Gandhi Institute, Moka, Mauritius, 23-26 June 1999.

68. See Gaëtan Benoît, *The Afro-Mauritians: An Essay* (Moka, 1985); Marcel Didier, *Pages Africaines de l'Île Maurice* (Bell Village, Mauritius, 1987). For a critical reading of this movement, see Thomas Hylland Eriksen, "Creole Culture and Social Change," *Journal of Mauritian Studies*, 1/2 (1986), pp. 59-72.

69. Official support for cultural recognition of African connections probably dates to Mauritius serving as host to the July 1976 Organization of African Unity Heads of State meeting. (Among the participants at that gathering was then President of Uganda Idi Dada Amin, who had once served with the KAR on Mauritius. I owe this detail to Tristan Bréville.) For example, see the volume produced by the Ministry of Education and Cultural Affairs for the Second World Black and African Festival of Arts and Culture at Lagos, Nigeria: *Mauritius Anthology of Literature in the African Context* (Port-Louis, 1977) and Armoogum Parsuraman, *From Ancestral cultures to National Culture-Mauritius* (Moka, 1988). The author was Minister of Education, Arts & Culture. More recently, the reader should note the rededication of the African Cultural Centre, which is funded by the Ministry of Arts and Culture, as the Nelson Mandela Centre for African and Creole Culture, following President Mandela's official state visit in 1998, as well as its continuing "Origins-Project" and "Family History Unit," which assists and advises individuals who seek to trace their slave ancestry.

70. See Alpers, "Dance and Society in Nineteenth Century Mogadishu," in Thomas J. Labahn (ed.), *Proceedings of the Second International Congress of Somali Studies*, II (Hamburg, 1983), pp. 127-144; Francesca Declich, "Identity, Dance and Islam among People with Bantu Origins in Riverine Areas of Somalia," in Ali Jimale Ahmed (ed.), *The Invention of Somalia* (Lawrencville, N.J., 1995), pp. 191-222.

71. Declich, "Coming Back from Southern Somalia to 'Zigualand' in Tanzania: What Matri-Kin Group do I belong to?," paper presented at the 38th Annual Meting of the African Studies Association, Orlando, Florida, 5 November 1995.

72. "Somali refugees claim Mozambican roots," *Mozambiquefile*, 258 (January 1998), pp. 19-20. For tufu, a coastal dance with Islamic origins, see Vasco Jacinto Nhussi, *A música tradicional de Moçambique: antologia das canções*, ARPAC, Colecção Embondeiro nº 9 (Maputo, 1996), pp. 20-21, and *Ilha de Moçambique: Danze e canti della costa settentrionale*, Folklore 7, Musiche dal nuovo mondo: Mozambico, Sudnord Records SN 0040, tracks 1, 5, and 11.

73. Clifford, *Routes*, p. 257.

CONTRIBUTION OF THE *MOZAMBICAN* DIASPORA IN THE DEVELOPMENT OF CULTURAL IDENTITIES ON THE INDIAN OCEAN ISLANDS

Eduardo Medeiros

Introduction

The social and cultural antiquity of the Indian Ocean was significantly greater than that of the Atlantic Ocean. A huge trade through maritime cabotage transport (whence the name of "scale civilization") to the Arab and Swahili littoral and adjacent islands' world), connected points from the east coast of Africa, south of Inhambane to Yemen, Persian Gulf, Gujarat coast and Sri Lanka, which explains the development of a chain of trading cities on those coastal regions, themselves a necessary link with the inlanders, who were sometimes in remote places. With the exception of Comoro, the islands of the Indian Ocean further east, such as the Mascarenhas and the Seychelles, were not inhabited by the continental Africans and Asians before they were occupied by the Europeans in the 17th century.

Islamism was, for many centuries, the main religion of the Indic littoral world. In spite of that, other religions and syncretisms always coexisted with Islam. In the eastern coast of Africa and nearby islands, the Kiswahili language and culture, besides Islam, characterized decisively the ethnic and commercial relations of all communities involved. In Madagascar, the context remained entirely Malagasy.

The European arrival entangled the same communities and neighbouring islands in the nascent Capitalist System, but only much later, during the modern colonization, were the local cultures profoundly affected. Due to the continental characteristic of Africa and the isolation of the more distant islands of the Indian Ocean, the rapid peopling of Mascarenhas and Seychelles was accomplished with slaves and individuals *contratados* (under a binding agreement), both from Africa and Asia.

In the above mentioned groups of islands, the religious, cultural and linguistic context became that of the African slaves and *contratados* brought by the Europeans in a late occupation, as much as by the presence of a large Indian working force and a limited Chinese immigration in the 19th century.[1] In the Comoro and some other islands close to Madagascar, that had experienced an early contact with Africa and whence slaves had been introduced before the arrival of the Europeans, the sociocultural context remained Islamic regardless of the colonial rule.[2]

With the exception of Yemen, where the abolition of slavery was completed only in the 20th century, on the islands of the Indian Ocean this took place at about the same time as that of the Atlantic world. However, different historical conditions and the lack of opportunities for the Africans to obtain a westernized education, similar to that in the Americas, inhibited, for a long time, the awakening of the Negro diaspora consciousness in the Mascarenhas and the Seychelles[3]. The constitution of a local identity took shape amidst a modern European colonial milieu, bringing about in these islands a process leading to the formation of a distinctive insular culture with considerably alterated aspects of what was still left of Swahili and continental African cultures of the 18th and 19th centuries, where a primitive plantation economy with slave labour existed.

Concerning the slave traffic to Mascarenhas and to other islands of the Indian Ocean, we have today enough information about the slave purchasing practices taking place on the Mozambican littoral at the time; in addition, an extensive literature exists relating to the maritime transportation of those human beings. Only recently, however, did we begin to acquire a more precise knowledge of the "organized" and "nonorganized" methods of capture (always forceful) of people in their townships. Nevertheless, in Mozambique, we still know very little about the conditions of life in captivity of those "forced émigrés". How did they live? How did they survive? How did they participate in the formation of an identity and culture adjusted to enslaved people in the places of exile? What remains today of these indigenous African communities taken away so long ago from the present territories of Mozambique and its neighbours?

We recognize the characterization of the *Diaspora*[4] as the transportation, as commodities, of a whole people and their descendents to the islands of the Indian Ocean, as an erroneous concept. We know that in this instance *Diaspora* does not mean the departure of a whole people to distant lands, for whatever reasons, while maintaining there the same identity nor of acquiring later a new identity with roots in the past. Here, the concept simply means the geographic transposition, most of the time violent, of people that "malgré-lui" ended at their destinations, resulting in the formation of new identities and, in the process, losing a great part of their social and cultural features of origin.Therefore, in this last sense, what we observe, strictly speaking, is not a diaspora of people from Mozambique settling in islands of the Indian Ocean, but the existence of insular societies with a feeble memory of their origins whose composition included several African cultural elements brought there, amongst others, by thousands of those whom we later would call "Moçambicanos". It is therefore due to the lack of a better term that we use this one.

1. The diaspora of the enslaved

Starting about 1720, thousands of Africans were kidnapped from their original social groups and transported to the more important islands of the Indian Ocean. Of course, before this date many other Africans had been taken away

not only to the Americas and Arab domains, in Asia -
mainly to the Persian Gulf - but also to the Comoro and to
the islands and lands bordering the northwest of
Madagascar. It is also known that, at the time, an Arab-
Swahili commercial route connected the African continent
with the Large "moon shaped" Island and with the Comoro.
But it was during the first quarter of the 18th century -
besides the much earlier Arab and Euro-American traffic -
that new sea routes of slave trade were opened; this time,
further east to the islands of the Indian Ocean recently occupied by the Europeans.

According to Alpers[5], the commencement of plantations of indigo and coffee - soon after to be replaced by
sugar cane in the Mascarenhas islands - date, coconut and
clove in Zanzibar and Pemba islands, grain in the Kenya
coast, date in the Persian Gulf, as well as building of ports
and urban development in Arabia, underwater harvest of
oysters for pearls in the Red Sea and Persian Gulf, cultivation
of grain in Madagascar and Somalia´s littoral, and the political expansion and consolidation in Yemen and Oman contributed greatly to the demand of a large quantity of African
labour force in the 18th and 19th centuries.

This increased search for labour in the geographical area
of today's Mozambique and in lands further to the west,
multiplied the processes of slave "production" and widened
the forms of servitude in the very heart of the local societies.
In relation to the Portuguese Crown, the traffic of slaves to
the French islands of the Indian Ocean was illegal, therefore,
smuggling was the way to break through, beyond the customs guidelines promulgated by Lisbon. At that time, Brazil
was the allure and the slave trade to these regions of South
America was a case for political and economic priority in
Portugal and Brazil. But to the slavers residing on the
Mozambican coast, Zambezi valley and elsewhere, this
state of affairs did not represent any sort of impediment or
worry, since they would find, repeatedly, subtle ways of pro-
ceeding with it, with the collution of the French, and even
of the Arabs and Swahilis. As to the African communities this
"problematic" legality or illegality only affected them to the
extent to which the diverse interests in securing slaves

increased the voracity of the domestic collaborators and the measure of violence applied in the methods of taking captives. We are driven to suggest that, during the major part of the 18th century and the whole of the 19th century, all ethnic groups, tribal units and families belonging to the present northern part of the Mozambican territory were involved in this enterprise, either as captives or captors, or both simultaneously.[6]

This commerce of human merchandise extended until the first decade of the 20th century. The slave traffic, as such, until 1854, and thereafter, the commerce of the so called *livres engajados* (free engaged) workers ensued. [7] Once more, such distinction was immaterial to the local communities; for them, the situation remained the same with regard to the kidnapping and exportation methods used towards their members. It is probable that at their destination some slight improvement may have occurred. However, the families at home had no knowledge of this and, anyway, it made no sense nor provided any consolation to those who were left behind or to those who were taken.

In short, as Edward Alpers points out, "although the African diaspora in the Indian Ocean had very old roots not totally as a consequence of the slave trade, essentially, it was the traffic of slaves and the enforced migration during the greater part of the 18th century and the whole of the 19th century that gave origin to the African insular communities, communities we are trying to study and understand".[8]

With the exception of the Mascarenhas islands - an European possession used for sugarcane plantation and, on this account, the only one where a record of its working force and its acquisition was kept - the accurate evaluation of slavery on the Indian Ocean's other dominions for this period is today an impossibility. What seems transparent is that the slave traffic to this region amounted to many hundreds of thousands of displaced individuals and that the intensity and duration of this trade sufficed to promote the growth of communities with the considerable magnitude of an African diaspora.[9]

Fillot wrote that "the Mozambican folk music and dance announce joy and strength. But the fear of the unknown and the conduct of the ship crews turned these men and women into despairing beings. Rebellion was a constant danger to the slaver"[10] at sea, and a permanent peril in the fields at their destination.

The syncretism that soon ensued locally, due to the great diversity of the slaves' origin, their disparate ethnic music and dance, which resulted in increasing confrontation, the reworking of a local magicoreligious mental disposition, that under-rated the blow endured through the loss of freedom, the mythic construction of heroism of the rebellions and "maronages", all this became new elements of cohesion in the African diaspora in those islands.

One of the legendary versions that spread all over the insular Indian Ocean was about the rebellion that took place on the high sea and initiated by Bororo, a "mozambican". Filliot relates that at 10.30 am on 14th May 1780, the slaves started a rebellion on board the Portuguese boat "Santo António das Almas", en route from Mozambique to Mauritius.[11]

The boat, under the command of Joseph Caetano Rodrigues, carrying 237 slaves, of which 217 went on board on account of Pierre Antoine Monnerou - a businessman in Port Louis - and the other 20 were put on board "at the disposition" ("para seu governo") of the ship´s crew.

The signal for the uprising was given by a man, Bororo[12], when the crewmen were dispersed all over the ship in their maintenace duties.

Bororo, who was on the poop deck, grabbed Le Bel, the pilot, by the neck while the other slaves took hold of whatever they could find at hand and proceeded to the poop and started to destroy everything. Le Bel, meanwhile, succeeded in freeing himself from Bororo, ran to his quarters, grasped his sword, sprang back to the deck, and there Le Bel and the other sailors killed and injured a large number of slaves, while some others, in desperation, jumped overboard. The pilot's rage must have had the effect of silencing the revolt, and the slaves hastened to take refuge in the hold. The captain ordered the closure of the hatchways on them. Soon after, 23 of the most energetic men had been put in chains and the rest tied with ropes. He then, wanted to know who had been the leader of the uprising and Bororo volunteered to admit the responsibility.

To his brothers in captivity, Bororo had ignited a vague feeling of hope. Many considered him a witch doctor, who was able to face, bravely, the slave lords.

The captain, after what had happened and knowing the numerical size of his crew, summoned the "officers" and decided to execute the leader of the revolt. Bororo was tied to the foremast's top and was shot in the presence of the remaining slaves. His body was thrown to the sea.

"Santo António das Almas" proceeded on her route and on 28th June arrived in the Maldives. On 4th July, she anchored at Tranquebar. The captain decided to disembark the remainder of the slave cargo, since the majority were not in a condition to continue the voyage to Mascarenhas.

The investigation and study about the edification of an African (and Malagasy) identity and the attainment of a self consciousness was initiated in a unique Indic-oceanic context, distinct from that of the Altantic. Besides, the absence - or backwardness in the formation - of an educated class among the diaspora's population due to the lack of schooling, opportunities and other historical circumstances[13] (if we disregard a few recent cases) was in contrast to what happened in North America.[14]

Although free migration for the purpose of commerce, sedentariness or work, represented obviously a subsidiary phenomenon in the whole diaspora of the Indian Ocean, which requires further investigation, this fact denotes a significant difference in relation to that of the Atlantic, as, with the exclusion of the Cape and the Mascarenhas, the worlds into which the Africans had been introduced were not, in its majority, either European or Christian, but Islamic.[15]

In Madagascar, the conjuncture was entirely Malagasy. In the Mascarenhas and the Seychelles, the religious, cultural and linguistic contexture was "Atlantic", notwithstanding, the addition of a massive Indian labour force and a limited Chinese immigration in the 19th century.[16]

2. The Diaspora in the Comoros Archipelago

The Comoro, located at the upper north of the Mozambique Channel, has been, since ancient times, part of the Swahili cultural space and played a noticeable role in the slave traffic to Madagascar, Seychelles and Mascarenhas.

The Archipelago comprises four islands, each being termed by its toponym: Ngazidya (the Large Comoro), Inzanam (Anjuane), Mehéli (Muali) and Motu (Mayotte). The word Comoro is derived from the Arab name "el-Komor" (the Moon). In the past, this name was also used to designate Madagascar.

In Comoro, there were no proper plantations. There, slavery was a political institution of the sultanates. It also constituted a significant element of commerce stimulated by the powerful *Ajojo* (singular *Mujojo*) shipowners. As a matter of fact, due to its localization, the Comoro formed the fundamental *pivot* of the slave commerce between the East African coast and the Indian Ocean islands. Mozambique has been, since very early times, a privileged region for the provisioning of this "merchandise" to the Archipelago. The Arab slave traders with their small boats (*pangaios* and *zambucos*) facilitated the comings and goings between the Mozambican coast and the Comoro, while slavers of French and other nationalities arrived there in their sailing ships and loaded the slaves. In 1869, most of the slaves arriving at the isle of Mayotte came from Cabo Delgado. The Comoranians and the Antalonians, too, were engaged in the slave transportation to Madagascar's Sakalava kingdoms, and in the shipment of macua (written there makoa) people. The last landings occurred, in secrecy, around 1906 at Besalampy and Soalala, in the large Island.[17]

In Comoro, the slave owners regarded slaves as "luxury goods" and as domestic servants. The exiguity of the soil for cultivation did not permit the development of a plantation economy, and therefore, the utilization of large contingents of labour power in agriculture or even for artisanal production was unnecessary.The great Muslim dignitaries in

Comoro, endowed with innumerable clientele - submissive and disposable - in the international market, made use of them as pawns in their political strategies inside the city-state. Slavery was one of their main occupations.

Even so, the subsistence of the cities was, in great measure, secured by the activities of farmers and fishermen of slave ancestry, mostly residing outside the boundaries of the city in distant towns. This spatial occupation marked literally and clearly on the terrain the irreducible, social cleavages existing, at the time, between these disparate societies.[18]

As the decades went by, almost all the Africans of the present Mozambican territory that were taken away converted to Islam. Then, due to the dynamic web of sea links woven between Comoro and the Mozambican coast, chiefly to the north of the Zambezi, the emergence of lasting relationships between the peoples of both sides of the sea grew in strength, through commercial routes, marriages and the work of islamic sisterhoods and, more recently, due to the colonist occupiers. The religious fraternities in Angoxe, Mozambique Island and Querimba Islands, had been in permanent contact with their insular congeners. The islamic hierarchy and the formation of their religious personnel had a secure base in the Comoro.[19]

The Mozambican's "idiomas da praia" (seashore idioms) or *Kiswahili* had - and still have - common points in concordance with the Comoranian dialects. According to Marie-Françoise Rombi, many songs, intoned nowadays in Mayotte during the narrating of a popular story, have the same literary form and texture as these at the time when the slaves were transported there. The Mozambican linguist, José Mateus Katupa, points out that many of the songs were expressed in one of the "emakhuwa" dialects.[20]

3. Diaspora in Madagascar

The slave traffic to Madagascar, namely to the island's northwest, was very ancient and practically only ended at the beginning of the 20th century. The first transports were made to Mejunga, a location in the island's west coast, initiated by the Arabs. In the beginning of the 17th century, the

Portuguese trade was so intense, in the northwest, that the Netherlanders, who settled in the Antongil bay, felt themselves victims of the trading activities carried out by Malagasy agents working for the Portuguese. During the French period, in the second half of the 18th century, an increase in the traffic occurred, because the slaves were, then, taken away eastwards to some other islands of the Indian Ocean. In addition to that, the Malagasy pirates of Sakalava origin ravaged, frequently, the islands and the coast of Cabo Delgado during the last years of the 18th century and the first decade of the 19th century.

In spite of the Anglo-Malagasy treaty, forbidding the traffic of slaves to Madagascar, the island not only continued with the importation, but also went on reshipping slaves to the Mascarenhas. By this time, the Malagasies were already interested in direct trade with the Mozambican coast. The slavers were active in carrying out incursions on the Comoranian coast and nearby islands, as well as on the northern islands and coast of Mozambique. The Querimba Islands were also a chosen region for their incursions. Even after these incursions had ceased, Madagascar went on receiving many slaves from Mozambique. A great number of small vessels (*pangaios*) were used, by 1859, for smuggling all over the Mozambican coast, which resulted in the introduction of textiles to the little ports and loading slaves (some were bought, others looted), who were transported to Madagascar and Comoro. In 1859, the commander of the steamship Lyra seized and burnt a number of *pangaios* found on the Mozambique channel, as they were involved in the slave trade.[21] In 1866, a Mauritian newspaper announced the existence of a slave traffic from Mozambique to Madagascar and adjacent islands.[22]

Due to the banning of slavery by England, the French traffickers halted the transportation of slaves from the African coast on large steamers and turned instead to their rendezvous on the western coast of Madagascar, where *pangaios* of various sizes could load from 60 to 180 Negro slaves each time.[23] Even in 1870-1880, the slave traffic from Mozambique to the French possessions in the Indian Ocean were made through Madagascar. However, a substantial number stayed in the island. In 1875, the British admiralty estimated that two hundred thousand "Mozambicans" were settled on the highlands of Madagascar.

In 1877, the Queen of Tananarive issued a decree emancipating the *Masombiky* slaves, but on the Sakalava monarchies - that stayed out of her jurisdiction - the abolition remained just an unkept promise.

In these monarchies, the captives, people more prone to be herdsmen than farmers, were reserved for the cultivation of cassava on the lands belonging to the Sakalava aristocracy. On this account, the slave descendents - during the French colonial occupation at the end of the last century and the beginning of this one - became "owners of the lands and *machambas*" (relatively small tracts of cultivated soil) that had first been tilled by their forefathers in captivity.

In the 19th century, the French tried, apparently without success, to cultivate sugarcane in Nosy-Bé, an islet northeast of Madagascar, whose workers consisted of "Mozambicans". One letter sent by the General-Governor of Mozambique to the Portuguese Consul in Nosy-Bé, dated 27th January 1888, mentions that "unfortunately, even now, from some unoccupied regions of this extensive coast, Negroes are shipped to the ports of Madagascar, Marambity, Salye and Tonhalalah, and from there some are sent to Nosy-Bé".[24]

According to a document from the last quarter of the 19th century (1888), the workers in the plantations were badly fed and harshly treated by the local authorities.[25] In 1890, the Portuguese Consul in Nosy-Bé informed the Governor of Mozambique that the Mozambican workers, at that time, had the benefit of a more stable situation than in the previous years: some working in the plantations under legitimate contracts, while others were already in possession of resident documentation in Nosy-Bé, had a family, a house and land ceded by the colonists. Many others escaped to the Malagasy "continent" to avoid the plantations. These were numerous and resided in the towns of Ankissumane and Bênomevi, in Bassandava's bay, either self employed or working for the Havas.[26]

When the traffic was declared illegal by the rulers of Tananarive under the reign of Radama I, the "Masombika" slaves were set free by orders of the Queen, in 1897. However, their bondage continued in the independent northeastern monarchies of Sakalava until the arrival of the French, in 1896.[27]

"In Madagascar, the hierarchical character of the Malagasy society represented a matter of political sensibility by imposing the slave *status* to the descendents of slaves, an issue only very recently voiced by the national intelligentsia. To these east Africans enslaved in Madagascar, who were referred to by the Malagasies as 'Mosambika' and 'Makoa', the status of slaves and of African origin were closely linked, and the stigma persisted until today. The Malagasy term *Zazamanga*, used for those Africans, makes this fact unambiguous, since 'zaza' means 'child' and 'manga' means 'blue', and that, according to the intelligentsia of Madagascar, is the Malagasy way of making reference to a black person".[28]

"Mozambican" communities of the so called Makoa origin have preserved until very recently their ancestor's customs, mainly in Nagazidja and Maintirano.[29]

Noel Gueunier suggests "that at least some of the Makoas in Maintirano's surroundings claim having arrived in Madagascar, in the 19th century, as merchants and not, questionably, as slaves".[30] And according to Pierre Sômany Talata; a 'Makoan' old man, called Morasy, from Menabao town, and born in Morima (a word originating from the Kiswahili *mrima*, referring to coast, littoral), on the other side of the sea (meaning the other side of the Mozambique Channel) met some African soldiers stationed on the island, who displayed some facial scarifications similar to his own, could communicate with them in the Emakhuwa tongue, since the soldiers were from his home town(!). According to the storyteller, when they departed, they said: "we could take you back home, but you see, we are on duty and are not allowed to do that. However what we can do is to tell our story when we return to town and affirm how we saw you with our own eyes".[31]

Even if these descriptions are a little beyond credibility, they, nevertheless, show the extent to which the popular consciousness kept its ties with Africa, and the role played by the African troops in the diaspora of the Indian Ocean. [32]

Molet wrote[33] that the ethnological identification of these "Makoa" is relatively transparent: it deals with Africans, being taken away to Madagascar at the time of slavery, stayed there, and grew roots there, mainly after the abolition of slavery on 20th June 1877 and its effective implementation in 1897.

Anthropologically speaking, we are dealing with people of Negroid race with crisped, or "*grão de pimenta*" (pepper berries) hair that, upon becoming Malagasyophone, those in the islands of Saint-Marie and Nosy-Bé, in Sambirano and cape of Saint-Sébastien, retained only few African words, but maintained, through their music, their customs and material culture, many of the vestiges from the Old Continent, at least, until the fifties of this century. In spite of large-scale miscegenation, it is apparent that they belong to an African stock, by facial features, stature, hair, etc. and the elder ones did not conceal, in 1950, their *Masombikiness*, that is, they recognised their non-Malagasy ancestry.[34]

Later, Edward Alpers,[35] added that the "Makoa had the propensity to reside in settlements away from their Malagasy neighbours, even after their emancipation in 1877. This state of affairs resulted in the formation of two main residential areas, concentrated around Nosy-Bé and Tambohorano, between the Sakalavas, and more isolated groups in Imerina. The fact that they were living in segregated villages seems to have facilitated the preservation of the "Makoa" language, at least until the twenties of this century, when many "Macuas" gave up teaching the language to their children as a token of assimilation into the Malagasy society, a process that was neither easy nor totally accomplished. Even in those instances, where the "Macuas" attained total integration, their status as descendants of former slaves served as barriers that were difficult to surmount. For example, in a community near the country's capital, where, in the last century, men were employed as masons in the construction of the more important palaces - a people representing only one quarter of the population - were almost literally forced to continue with their endogamic marriages, even when one of them had been appointed head of the regional autarchy. This restriction, as a result, caused the persistence of some African traits, clearly visible, that had an inhibitory effect towards a comprehensive social integration. Moreover, the Malagasy epithet used to designate the "Makoa" or "mosambica": "Zazamanga" underlines the separation, when "zaza" means child, and "manga" means blue, the Malagasy way of naming the African Negroes.[36] The inconvenience, not surprisingly, is a heavy burden for the "makoa" obliged to go on speaking both languages: Malagasy and "Makoa".[37] In both cases, it is evident that the upper "makoan" social stratification continues, likewise, to function unfavourably for the Africans in Madagascar; even the stream of jokes spread in the Sakalava region amongst the "Makoa" and amongst their Malagasy neighbours about both groups is symptomatic of the social remoteness between them.[38] Thus, the preservation of African culture varies, and yet, as recently as in the last two decades, researchers could gather a number of folk narratives and "Makoa" words among the eldest members of the population.[39] Lastly, a different kind of African consciousness is present in the island of Nosy-Bé, where the black inhabitants are poetically known in Kiswahili as "maganja", an ambiguous name, stemming probably from one of the major ethnic groups of the southeast of Niassa lake, that as slaves, may have given origin to the largest African populational group in Madagascar.[40] Surely, the eponyms "makoa" and "maganja" represent, more properly, eventual origins than ethnicities.

4. Diaspora in the Seychelles Archipelago

The Seychelles stood, under French domination, in the 18th century, as the privileged port of call for the slaver vessels sailing from Madagascar to the African east coast and from there to the neighbouring islands on the way to India.[41] The Archipelago served as a haven for the sailing boats; there they watered the vessel and awaited the monsoon. However, the Archipelago had, in various periods during slavery, another function: to "Frenchify" the African and Malagasy slaves before their arrival in the Mascarenhas. The trick was to write down the slaves in the registers of the Seychelles residents before taking them, legally, to Mauritius and Réunion.

However, besides the mercantile aspect that the Seychelles had to the slave traders, the development of a small plantation economy took shape in the main islands of the Archipelago. The plantation of clove, cotton and coffee, among others, was made possible due to the labour of workers who were former slaves.

From 1803 to 1810 - war years in Europe - the slavers in the Mascarenhas could not meet the demand of slave labour necessary for their plantations. Therefore, the traffic in the Seychelles was seen as a source of wealth to the Archipelago, in spite of the perils it entailed. On acccout of this increase in traffic, many slaves stayed on in the Archipelago.

In 1811, the Seychelles, as well as Mauritius, came under British domination. Soon after the British occupation, it was decided to make a survey of the slaves in the islands and the obligatory registration of all arrivals and departures of that particular "merchandise". However, the English project was not concluded because of the complexity of such a demographic survey, and due to the fact that both English and French residents, who continued to trade in slavery, were not in the mood to reveal their "stocks".

Notwithstanding this, the traffic was banned *(Abolition Act of 1807)* and the English authorities proceeded with the eventual confiscation of those slaver ships they happened to seize. We can state that, only as late as 1830, was the commerce of slaves fought with a measure of vigour in the Seychelles, however, without its complete elimination.

In 1818, due to all that, the swift decline of the Seychelles began. Because of soil depletion, the production of cotton declined and the indifference of the landlords towards this crop also had its say, in view of the fact that American cotton was being sold at a much lower price on the international market than that of the islands of the Indian Ocean. Another cause for the soaring prices of the

Seychelles' goods was its compulsory passage through Mauritius. It was during this period that a huge emigration of colonists from the Seychelles was registered as well as the relocation of slaves to the sugarcane plantations in Réunion and Mauritius.

In 1835, by the deliberation of the British Government, all registered slaves were declared "apprentices", and they were to stay at their owners service until 1841, when emancipation was to be conferred. Yet, the "servile population" could not stand the hardships any longer: they broke their fetters and revolted, in 1839.

In that same year of 1835, the estimated number of slaves was 6521, distributed, according to their origin, as follows: *Mozambiques*, 3924, *Creoles*, 2231, *Malagasies*, 282, *Indians*, 38, *Malayans*, 3 and, of unknown provenience, 43. The total population in the Archipelago, at the time, was 7500 inhabitants, and it reveals that the "non-slaves" didn't even total five hundred. [42]

From 1861 till 1870, close to 2500 African *libertos* (freed) were sent anew to the Seychelles. Thanks to this additional workforce, the Archipelago was able to transform its agriculture and expand coconut plantations that became the principal source of wealth to the islands. In 1871, the Seychelles was in such a standing, that it could request an end to the Mauritian tutelary management and simultaneously demand its autonomy and the immigration of a greater number of African *libertos*.[43]

The "Moçambicanos," with a small population and diverse origins, could not retain their languages and cultures of birth. Even today, we hear them speak about their forebears: *macondes, macuas* and *maraves*. Under insular and micro-societal conditions, the African, European and Asian intercultural relations gave rise to the creation of Seychelles Creole language and to unique culture with African roots.

As mentioned before, one of the cultural elements that contributed to the formation of local identities was the epic on rebellions and "quilombos". Let us review a case in the Seychelles with reference to Mozambique.

During slavery in the Seychelles, as in the other islands of the Indian Ocean, the escape of slaves from the plantations or from their owners' homes in search of freedom was not infrequent either in the deep woods or in distant and quasi-inaccessible places. Those who succeeded in this way were nicknamed in all the Indian Ocean islands with the term *marrons,* and, the self phenomenon, by the adverbial locution of *marronage.*[44]

One of the more famous and popular *marrons* in the Seychelles Archipelago was Castor.[45] A document from 1832, found in the National Archives of that insular country, describes Castor as a *Maconde,* about 44 years old, 5 feet and 4 inches tall, and a face marked with tattoos. The document discloses also that Castor worked as a cutter and flayer of cattle for meat and, occasionally, as a sawyer in the forest. The same source of information adds that Castor was chief of a group of *marron* slaves, and together with his companions managed to enjoy their freedom for three or four years. Then, for completely unknown reasons, he surrendered. It is not known which immediate causes turned Castor into a *marron.* In all the countries where slavery existed, *marronage* existed, i.e. the obtaining of freedom through escape, followed by survival in hidden and inhospitable places. At least, two reasons led the slaves to running away or trying to run away. These were to earn their freedom or to escape the maltreatment to which they were subject.

In Seychelles, where the slaves were in general humanely treated, as the document suggests, it is almost certain that Castor became a *marron* due to the simple desire for freedom. Undoubtedly, he managed to flee when sawing timber in the forest. Yet, what sounds astonishing is how Castor and his companions managed to stay free for three or four years, considering the difficulties that they had to surmount. In fact, there were not many places in Mahé island where one could hide oneself. Likewise, food was not easy to find, either in the forests or on the rocky hills. At the time, the island's tortoises were already extinct, and they could only hunt birds, such as pigeons, and turtle doves, and some varieties of bats. It is true, however, that edible crops were in abundance, and they could be obtained fugitively at night. *Marronage* was not easy, and a *marron's* life in Seychelles was certainly an arduous one.

The question as to why Castor surrendered remains unanswered. Could it have been due to ill-health? Another document in the archive, however, reveals that the doctor who examined him, soon after he gave himself up, found him in good health and with no signs of illness.

Did Castor get tired of his wandering life, all these years, with no prospects of escaping from the island? It is probable though there is no evidence to substantiate it. Subsequent events he was supposed to be associated with also seem rather strange. After giving up his vagrant liberty, Castor is reputed to have collaborated in the fight against the *marrons*, which may have (re)made his fame.

Finally, an old record of deceased people, also from the Seychelles National Archives, mentions the death of a man named Castor in the village of Anse Royale. The death registration date is 29th August 1854. It is almost certain that this refers to the old *marron*, Castor, who would have been 60 years old at the time of his death.

If this is the case, Castor, then, died 146 years ago. However, the story of his *marronage* is alive in the collective memory of the people of Mahé and the other islands of the Archipelago. A location, even, exists with his name: a small village in Anse aux Pins, a wild place with its enormous and frightful rocks. Castor found his refuge here at the time of his short-lived freedom in these remote regions of the Indian Ocean.

5. Diaspora in the Mascarenhas Islands

It was, certainly, in the southwest islands of the Indian Ocean that the greatest economic plantation development occurred and, for the same reason, the largest contingent, of all the slave traffic to the French East Islands, was directed there. Between 1773 and 1840, 143 expeditions took place to the Mozambican coast with boats from Mascarenhas. However, vessels from other provenances also took the same slaver route.

During the French occupation of Mauritius (1715-1810) and Réunion (from 1665), in both islands, coffee and some spices represented the main profitable (agricultural) activity. And yet, in the 19th century, sugarcane plantations occupied almost all the island's arable soil.

Let us examine some statistics on population evolution in Mauritius: in 1787, it was evaluated at 40,439 inhabitants, 33,832 of which, were slaves; in 1827, the number of inhabitants increased to 92,997, of which 68,962 were slaves. [46] Under the category "slave", in the second quarter of the 19th century, between 40 and 45 per cent of Mozambicans could be registered, from 30 to 35 per cent Malagasies, and 10 to 15 per cent Indians. In 1834, Mauritius and the Seychelles had a joint population of about seventy thousand people. In 1848, in Réunion, sixty thousand were slaves. However, these numbers, in relation to the servile population, represent but an insignificant percentage of the individuals uprooted from their communities. According to Filliot, of the 620 Mozambicans who embarked in 1739 en route to Mascarenhas, 360 perished during the voyage. The same researcher adds that, between 1777 and 1808, the mortality rate of the slaves on board the ships rose to 21%. [47]

Gaétan Benoit considers that Mauritius island was the grave to more than one million Africans since the beginning of slavery until 1869. [48]

Today, in Mauritius, out of a population of about one million inhabitants, over two hundred thousand can claim African descent. [49]

The Mozambicans came mainly from the ethnic groups, Marave (Cheua-Nianja), Senas, Maconde, Macua, Machona and Yemvane (Inhambanes). [50]

As the slaves were sent ashore to the Mascarenhas, the slaves were apportioned to plantation owners. With this method of distribuition, it was not possible to bring together people of the same ethnic lineage, sufficient to establish a community able to maintain and transmit the respective language and culture to future generations. This was, certainly, one of the reasons we cannot find many specific cultural traces of today's Mozambican communities in the islands of Mauritius and Réunion, where many of their sons and daughters were taken. We know, through some trade registers, that in the particular "Moçambicanos" case, the majority of slaves came, originally, from the matrilineal societies of northern Mozambique. Moreover, in these communities, the unilateral principle of filiation is determined through the female line and the transmission of the elders wisdom and culture was, and is, even today, promoted essentially within sororal groups. Since the probabilities for men in captivity to get married were slim, and more so, for women of the same cultural extraction, the appearance of groups structured according to the tradition of each tribal cluster was virtually impossible. To these men, who established families with women of a different ancestry, their progeny - that, by the way, continued to be slaves - was considered as belonging to the wife's group. The mother, was the pivotal person in cultural transmission.

All the islands of Mascarenhas and Seychelles share common cultural traits, such as the intelligibility of "French Creole" or, simply, *Kreol* and the *séga*, a dance of slave origin with a musical structure with Afro-Malagasy roots. Notwithstanding the significant number of Africans sent to these islands as slaves, or as 'free emigrants', in the 18th and 19th centuries, if we consider language, few evident signs of Bantu influence exist in these Creoles and, certainly, no extant member, speaking any of the east African languages, such as we can witness among the Makoa in Madagascar. [51] According to Baissac, well known scholar in Creole of the 19th century, at that time, it was possible to distinguish a dialectal variant called Mozambique Creole, a kind of 'patois' spoken with a peculiar Mozambican accent. On the other hand, Baker has identified in Baissac's collections a significant number of enigmatic expressions of African origin. [52] In Réunion's Creole, however, some references about Africans lean towards a pejorative tone as the following sayings translated into French illustrate: *"Au bout de cent ans dans le pays, le 'cafre' mange toujours les patates douces avec la peau"* 'At the end of one hundred years in the country, the Kaffir continues to eat sweet potatoes with the skin' // *"Parole de noir, pet de chien"* 'Word of black, puff of dog'// *"Un noir, un chien, deux cousins germains"* 'One black, one dog, two first cousins'// *"Le cafre a sept peaux"* 'The Kaffir has seven skins'. [53]

The Malagasy influences are also equally important in number, yet they are not pejorative.[54]

Nevertheless, this state of affairs was not static. Evidence abounds pointing to the fact that both Africans and Malagasies in the Mascarenhas were conscious of their roots. In the 1840's, the French ethnographer Eugène de Froberville, during his tours, interviewed over 300 east African natives, among them approximately 50 who had just departed from their countries. In search of information on their customs and traditions, he collected 60 masks and models. 50 portraits were drawn containing the characteristic tattoos that these races preferred to embellish their faces and bodies with, and 31 terms in their language. Amongst those he gathered information from were included Macuas and Niambanas (so called because they came from the Inhambane's region), Mozambique, and Ngindos from the inner south of the present Tanzania.[55] Ten years later, a British missionary and pioneer noticed that the freed slaves retained the characteristic superstitions and engaged in pagan rites of their country of birth, including reverence for their forefathers. They used to supposedly throw magical objects that could predict the future and usually carried a talisman by the name of *grisgris*. Referring, particularly, to the Malagasies in Mauritius, the author emphasized that their liaison with the ancestral land was not simply emotional, but one that embodied their religious beliefs. They believed that, at death, when the soul departed, the body would return, not to God, but to the place of birth where a new existence would begin under another form. The wish that their bodies should be buried in the native lands was, perhaps, as important to them as much as their love of freedom, which could induce them to commit suicide, for example, by jumping into the sea. This yearning is probably connected with their religious beliefs, which continues to prevail among Madagascar's inhabitants. [56]

"In the course of the last century and a half, these sort of beliefs had been effectively stifled in Mauritius through conversion to Christianity (Catholicism), and the stand of the Church in refusing to accept, in its institutions, some of their significant cultural features, although Benjamin Moutou

asserts that, "in the Creole context, practices which originated in Madagascar or even in Africa continue to take place
at some funeral ceremonies".[57]

Whatever the role of the religious organization in the
Mascarenhas might be, popular religion is a whole area
where Afro-Malagasy and Indian influences can and do survive. In Mascarenhas, the relative consistency of Malagasy
culture, compared with the fragmented ones of African
origin, and the enormous development of witchcraft among
the Malagasies, grants them a genuine prominence in this
space of social discourse. On her part, Réunion, due to the
faith's strong influence, that can be traced to rural France,
delights herself in that rich and well researched popular religious culture that flows significantly into the Afro-Malagasy
beliefs and superstitions.[58] Some of them have deep roots,
others have a recent appearance, such as the devoted cult to
Sitarane, the nickname of a Mozambican worker called
Simicoudza, who came to Réunion in 1889, together with
some accomplices, terrorized the Island during the first
decade of this century, and was hanged for alleged theft,
murder, incitement to murder and witchcraft.[59] Although few
had the preoccupation to analyze seriously similar practices
in Mauritius, a recent popular study, however sensationalist,
suggests that such beliefs exist, and are very alive, and that
the Malagasy effigy has both meanings: higher spirit and fol-
lower.[60] In this respect, anthropologist Linda Sussman's
paper on medical pluralism in Mauritius suggests that the
popular tradition of specialized witch doctors "may represent
one sample of what exists in Europe of herbalist and
Christian practices and even in Madagascar and Africa,
such as those in Réunion. They treat various diseases, particularly *tambave*, a syndrome well known in Mascarenhas
and Madagascar, the name derives from the Malagasy word
for "woman" and is treated by "appointment".[61]

No doubt, the better known example of African cultural
influence in these islands is a dance called *sega*, also called
"maloya" in Réunion, and "moutia" in Seychelles. Rooted in
the experience of slavery, *sega* is a combination of African
and Malagasy dance forms and musical instruments, though
the instruments used today may be considered modern as

compared with the earlier ones. Mauritians assume that *sega* represents the only living example of the Afro-Malagasy culture in the Island and that, in some respects, its survival and popularity has functioned as a painful reminder to the Mauritian Creoles of Afro-Malagasy descent, and hence of their second class status in society. *Sega's* history has still to be written in its entirety. However, until its "rediscovery" and titling "African" by the Creole intellectual Jaques Cantin - himself a composer of *sega* lyrical music - it was despised for its slave origin and was not very popular. Its approbation is related with Alphonse Ravaton's (known popularly as Ti-Frère) unforgettable career, whose image has become a symbol of *sega's* culture.[62] The Mauritian *sega* has now entered into the wider orbit of world's rhythms, whereas the more recent variation of its evolution is known as *seggae* by its incorporation in the Caribbean patterns of *reggae*. In reality, the Mauritian Creoles, today, face more serious problems than the *sega* accommodation. The economic and political dilemmas they confront, originated in the usually described "Creole calamity", already officially recognised by means of a written report, concluded last year, about what is locally denominated the "exclusion". On the 150th anniversary commemoration of the abolition of slavery in 1835, a movement was created among some members of the Creole society to defend the right of their identity as Afro-Mauritians, which, in this context, is a highly political issue. In this African invocation, as in the calls for recognition of Creole as the official language, *sega* identifies itself.[63] While Mauritius is aiming at an identification closer to the African continent, with which, presently, it pretends to maintain fresh economic relations, it would be interesting to study to what degree the raising of a popular and cultural consciousness with Afro-Malagasy roots is being revitalized or confined.[64]

References concerning Africa also occur in nonmusical contexts. For example, people religion and the healing arts in Mauritius and Réunion, that have no musical associations, that arouse, evidently, both "the Malagasy spirits" and other followers. In the two islands, and even in the Mascarenhas, a syndrome exists known as *tambave*, derived from the word "woman" in Malagasy. In Mauritius, the same convultions take the name of "crises malgasses". A notable cult in Réunion is the one devoted to Sitarane, nickname of a known renegade from Mozambique, in the beginning of the 20th century. [65]

Karl Kugel states that warlike dances, "more or less violent" and often "with spiritual or holy connotations" in which two dancers or two groups take part, are familiar in the Indian Ocean Islands; in Madagascar, under the name *morangy,* in Comore, as *m'rengue* and, in Réunion, as *moringue*.[66] All of them have a certain resemblance to the Brazilian *capoeira* which has an African origin.

In conclusion, it can be stated that the Creole culture in the southwestern islands of the Indian Ocean was the product of the fusion and the new elaboration of European and African cultures, together with the cultural inputs originating from a large Indian work force and a limited number of Chinese immigrants in the 20th century. [67]

Notes & References

I am much obliged to my good friend, Adelino Simões, at Gothenburg, Sweden, for translating the Portuguese version of this paper.

1. ALPERS, Edward A.- *Recollecting Africa: Diasporic Memory in the Indian Ocean world.* Paper presented at the conference "African Diaspora Studies on the Eve of the 21st Century". Department of African Studies. University of California, Berkeley. April 30 - May 2, 1998, p.3
2. *Idem,* p.9
3. ALPERS, Edward A.- *The African Diaspora in the Indian Ocean: a comparative perspective from the other hemisphere.* Paper presented at the conference on Black Diaspora in the Western Hemisphere. Humanities Research Centre. Australian National University, 7-9 April, 1998, pp.19-20.
4. A short version of this paper was published with the title "Diáspora moçambicana nas ilhas do oceano Índico, 1720-1910" in *Tempo* (Maputo), Nr. 774, August 11,1985, pp.46-48, Nr. 775, August 18, 1985, pp.45-46 and Nr. 776, August 25, 1985, pp.46-48.
5. ALPERS, Edward A.- *Recollecting Africa: Diasporic Memory in the Indian Ocean world.* Op. cit., p.3.
6. MEDEIROS, Eduardo - *As etapas da escravatura no norte de Moçambique.* Maputo, Arquivo Histórico de Moçambique,1988, (Col. Estudos,04).
7. CAPELA, José and Eduardo Medeiros - *O tráfego de escravos para as Ilhas do Índico, 1720-1902.* Maputo, INLD/ UEM, 1988.

8. ALPERS, Edward A.- *Recollecting Africa: Diasporic Memory in the Indian Ocean world.* Op. cit., p.2
9. *Idem.*
10. FILLIOT, Jean-Michel - communication quoted.
11. ASGARALLY, Issa - *Les révoltes d'esclaves dans les Mascareignes où "l'Histoire du silence".* Paper presented at INTERNATIONAL SEMINAR ON SLAVERY IN THE SOUTH-WEST INDIAN OCEAN; Mahatma Gandhi Institute, Maka-Mauritius, 26th February-2nd March 1985.
12. The term Bororo was occasionally used to indicate the population lómwè in Chire's valley; see G.T.Nurse, The people of Bororo: a lexicostatistical enquiry, in: *The Early History of Malawi* (Edited by B.Pachai). London, 1975, p. 123-135.
13. ALPERS, Edward A.- *The African diaspora in the Indian Ocean: a comparative perspective from the other hemisphere.* Op. cit., pp. 19-20.
14. ALPERS, Edward A.- *The African diaspora in the Indian Ocean..*, Op.cit, p.10
15. *Idem,* p. 9
16. *Ibidem*
17. VERIN, Pierre - *Les séquelles de l'esclavage aux Comores et a Madagascar, 150 ans aprés première abolition dans l'Océan Indien.* Paper presented at INTERNATIONAL SEMINAR ON SLAVERY IN THE SOUTH-WEST INDIAN OCEAN; Mahatma Gandhi Institute, Maka-Mauritius, 26th February-2nd March 1985.
18. *Idem*
19. MEDEIROS, Eduardo - *Irmandades Muçulmanas No Norte de Moçambique.* Maputo, S/d, Raízes culturais,nº 5.
20. ROMBI, Marie Françoise - *Le shimaore (Ile de Mayotte, Comores). Première approche d'un parler de la langue Comorienne.* Paris, SELAF, 1983 (Langues e Cultures Africaines, 3).
21. ARQUIVO HISTÓRICO DE MOÇAMBIQUE. From the General Governor to the Sultan of Zanzibar, 13th October,1859. Códice 11-118 Fls 57 vs.
22. ARQUIVO HISTÓRICO DE MOÇAMBIQUE. From the General Governor António de Canto e Castro to the Overseas Minister, 9th August,1866. Códice 11-49, fls 4.
23. *Idem.*
24. ARQUIVO HISTÓRICO DE MOÇAMBIQUE. From the General Governor of Mozambique to the Portuguese Consul in Nossi-Bé, 27th January, 1888. Códice11-316, Fls 36.
25. NIRMA, Rosoarifetra B. - *L'esclavage dans le Sud-ouest de l'Océan Indien.* Paper presented at INTERNATIONAL SEMINAR ON SLAVERY IN THE SOUTH-WEST INDIAN OCEAN; Mahatma Gandhi Institute, Maka-Mauritius, 26th February- 2nd March 1985. In the sixties of last century, Nosy-Bé served as an important slave entrepôt (Christpher Lloyd, *The Navy and the Slave Trade.* London, 1908, pp. 207-228).
26. ARQUIVO HISTÓRICO DE MOÇAMBIQUE. Nineteenth Century "Fundo", General Governorship, box 27, bundle 2(3), nr.5, From the Portuguese Consul in Nossi-Mé to the General Governor, 30th June, 1890, in José Capela and Eduardo Medeiros, *La traite au*

départ du Mozambique vers les îles de l'Océan Indien, 1720-1904, paper presented at INTERNATIONAL SEMINAR ON SLAVERY IN THE SOUTH-WEST INDIAN OCEAN; Mahatma Gandhi Institute, Maka-Mauritius, 26th February-2nd March 1985.

27. VÉRIN, Pierre - *Reminiscences Portugaises de Madagascar.* Maputo, 1970, MONUMENTA'S off print, nr.6.

28. ALPERS, Edward A. - *Recollecting Africa: Diasporic memory in the Indian Ocean world. Op. cit.* , p.4, which quotes: Michel Razafiarivony, Les zazamanga D'Antanetibe Ambato: de la servitude à la lutte continue pour la reconnaissance réelle, In: *Fanadevozana où esclavage: Colloque international sur l'esclavage à Madagascar* (Antananarivo, 1996), pp. 548-559; Malanjaona Rakotomalala and Célestin Razafimbelo, Le problème d'intégration sociale chez les Makoa de l'Antsihanaka, *Omaly sy Anio,* 21.22 (1985), pp. 93-113; Lesley A. Sharp, *The Possessed and the Diapossessed: Spirits, Identity, and Power in a Madagascar Town* (Berkeley, 1993) 1993), pp. 59, 68, 77.

29. VERIN, Pierre - Communication quoted. See also MOLET, L. - Quelques Mokoa e Antaimoro, in: *Bulletin de l'Academie de Malgacge,* XXXIII, 1955, P.29-31.

30. GUEUNIER, Noel - Documents sur la langue makhuwa à Madagascar et aux Comores (fin XIXe - début Xxe siècles), in *Fanadevozana ou esclavage.* Quoted in ALPERS, Edward A. - *The African diaspora in the Indian Ocean.. .* op.cit, p.9

31. Quoted in ALPERS, Edward A. - *The African diaspora in the Indian Ocean...* op. cit, pp. 10-11.

32. *Idem,* p.11.

33. MOLET, Luc - Presénce d'éléments mokoa à Sainte-Marie de Madagascar, in: *Bulletin de l'Académie Malgache,* n° 53, XXX, 1951, p. 29-31

34. Idem

35. ALPERS, Edward A. - *The African diaspora...* op.cit. pp.13-14

36. RAZAFIARIVONY, Michel - Les Zanzamanga d'Antaneitibe Ambato: de la servitude à lutte continue pour la reconnaissance réelle, in *Fanadevozana où esclavage: Colloque international sur l'esclavage à Madagascar* Antananarivo, 1996, pp. 548-559.

37. RAKOTOMALALA, Malanjaona and Célestin Razafimbelo - *Le problème d'intégration sociale chez les Makoa de l'Antsihanaka.* Omaly sy Anio, 21-22 (1985), pp. 93-113.

38. RAJAONARIMANANA, Nrivelo - Les parents à plaisanterie des Makoa, in: Études Océan Indien, 8 (1987), pp. 119-123.

39. GUEUNIER, Noél - *Contes de lacôte ouest de Mdagascar.* Antananarivo et Paris, S,d. pp. 78-96; *Histoire du peuple* (les gens qu'on avait vendus comme esclaves). Récit enregistré en Avril 1977 par M. Schrive à Mandrosomiadana près de Sajôavato (Diego-Suarez). *Personal* communication.

40. GUEUNIER, Noél - *Les poèmes de Maulidi Manganja: Poèmes swahili recueillis à Nosy-Bé,* in: *Bulletin des Études Africaines de l'Inalco,* 3/6 (1983), pp.7-76.

41. NIONNET, Guy - *The abolition of slavery and its aftermath in Seychelles.* Paper presented at INTERNATIONAL SEMINAR ON SLAVERY IN THE SOUTH-WEST INDIAN OCEAN; Mahatma Gandhi

Institute, Maka-Mauritius, 26th February-2nd March 1985.

42. *Histoire des Seychelles* (coord. Jean-Michel), Ministère de l'Education et de l'Information,1982.

43. LY-FANE PINCO, Huguette - Aperçu d'une immigration forcée: l'importation d'africains libertés aux Seychelles, 1840-1880; in: (Institut d'Histoire des Pays d'Outre-Mer / Univ. de Provence Ed.). *Minorités et gens de mer en Océan Indien. xix e xx siècles.* Sémanque, 1979, p. 7384 (Etudes et Documents, n°12.)

44. According to the French researcher Jean-Michel FILLIOT, the vocable *marron* itself derived from the Castilian "cima", meaning "forest" and all the domestic animals that took refuge there (in *History des Seychelles*, 1982, P.60).

45. Portuguese version of the text originally written in the *Seychelles Creole language*, and translated into French by Guy LIONNET. Personal communication.

46. LU-TIO-FANE PINCO, Huguette - *Food production and plantation economy of Mauritius.* Paper presented at INTERNATIONAL SEMINAR ON SLAVERY IN THE SOUTH-WEST INDIAN OCEAN; Mahatma Gandhi Institute, Maka-Mauritius, 26th February-2nd March 1985.

47. FILLIOT, Jean-Michel - *La traite vers l'île de France- Les Contraintes maritimes.* Paper presented at INTERNATIONAL SEMINAR ON SLAVERY IN THE SOUTH-WEST INDIAN OCEAN; Mahatma Gandhi Institute, Maka-Mauritius, 26th February-2nd March 1985.

48. BENOIT, Caetan - *The Afro-Mauritius-Ar Essay.* Moka Mauritius, Mahatma Gandhi Institute, 1985-59. Paper presented at INTERNATIONAL SEMINAR ON SLAVERY IN THE SOUTH-WEST INDIAN OCEAN;Mahatma Gandhi Institute, Maka-Mauritius, 26th February-2nd March 1985.

49. MOUTOU, Benjamin - *Tares et séquelles de l'esclavage a l'île Maurice et a l'île Rodrigues.* Paper presented at INTERNATIONA SEMINAR ON SLAVERY IN THE SOUTH-WEST INDIAN OCEAN; Mahatma Gandhi Institute, Maka- Mauritius, 26th February-2nd March 1985.

50. REDDI, Satasivan - *Aspects of the British Administration.* Paper presented at INTERNATIONAL SEMINAR ON SLAVERY IN THE SOUTH-WEST INDIAN OCEAN; Mahatma Gandhi Institute, Maka-Mauritius 26th Februry-2nd March 1985.

51. For the lack of significant African linguistic influence in Réunion Creole see Chaudenson, *Le lexique*, II, pp.1093, 1106-1109; but cf. Baker and Corne, *Isle de France Creole*, pp.100-101, nr.3, and *passim* for evidence of significant West African language influence as a consequence of the presence of "Senegalese" slaves imported by the Compagnie des Indes when Mauritian Creole was forming during the middle decades of the 18th century.

52. FAINE, Jules - *Le Créole dans l'univers: Études comparatives des Parlers Français-Créoles*, I: Le Mauricien (Port-au-Prince, 1939), pp. 61-63; Philip Baker, On the origins of the Mauritian Creole Riddles in Baissac 1880, *Journal of Mauritanian Studies*, 2/2(1988), pp.40-85.

53. CHAUDENSON, *Le lexique, I,* p. 323; see also p. 108.

54. *Idem*, pp. 1082-1086.

55. FROBERVILLE, Eugène de - Notes sur les coutumes e traditions des

amakoua, sur le commerce et la trait des esclaves das l'Afrique orientale, in *Bulletin de la Société de Géographie*, 3e Série, 8 (1847), pp.311-329; Notes sur les Va-Ngindo, et tribus nègres bégayeurs au nord de la cafrerie, *Bulletin de la Société de Geographie*, 4e Série, 3 (1952) pp. 425-443, 517-519.

56. BEATON, Patrick - *Creoles and Coolies; or, Five Years in Mauritius*. For Washington and London, 1971, 2nd ed. (1st ed. 1859), pp. 78, 79-80 (Quoted by Edward A. ALPERS, *The African diaspora...* op. cit. p.16)

57. MOUTOU, Benjamin - *Les Chétiens de l'Île Maurice* (Port-Louis, 1996), p. 272

58. EVE, Prosper - *La religion populaire à la Réunion*. 1985, 2 vols.

59. SAM-LONG, Jean-François - *Sitarane où le jeu des malefices*. Quoted by Edward A. ALPERS, *The African diaspora...* op.cit., p 16.

60. SELINY, Pierre-Edmond Pulvenis de - *Vrais et extraordinaires aventures de ...chez les sorciers de l'Île Maurice: 'Traiteurs' et 'Longanistes' au travail et des Scènes terrificantes d'exorcisme*. Port-Louis, 1996, pp.42, 44, 45, 57, 77, 79, 83, 101, -1o2, 139, 143, 147.

61. SUSSMAN, Linda Kaye - *Medical pluralism on Mauritius: a study of medical beliefs and practices in a polyethnic society*. Washington University - St. Louis, Ph.D. dissertation, pp 152-154, 160.

62. RICAUD, Claudie - *Séga-Lae: aspects of traditional music in Mauritius*. B.A. thesis, University of Sydney,1986.

63. BENOÎT, Gaetan - *The Afro-Mauritanians: An Essay*. Moka, 1985. DIDIER, Marcel - *Pages africaines de l'Île Maurice*. Bell Village, Mauritius, 1987.

64. ALPERS, Edward A. - *The African diaspora in the Indian Ocean: a comparative perspective from the other hemisphere*. Paper presented at the conference on Black Dispora in the Western Hemisphere. Humanities Research Centre. Australian National University, 7-9 April, 1998, pp. 14-18

65. SAM-LONG, Jean-François - Sitirane où le jeu des maléfices, in *Revue Grand Océan* (Réunion), 4; *Les Âmes errantes: sorcellerie et magie dans les Mascareignes* (n.d., but mid-1990s), pp. 78-86. Quoted by Edward A. ALPERS, *recollecting Africa: Diasporic memory in the Indian Ocean world...op.cit.,p.10*.

66.Karl Kuguel, personal communication. Letter from Le Port, Réunion, 28th, May, 1998.

67. ALPERS, Edward A. - *Recollecting Africa: Diasporic memory in the Indian Ocean world...op.cit.* , pp.3 and 4.

MADAGASCAR AND THE AFRICAN DIASPORA

Malyn Newitt

Introduction

The coast of eastern Africa is subject to the regime of the western Indian Ocean monsoons about as far south as Inhambane. This has meant that, in spite of the hurricanes, swiftly running currents and dangerous shoals and reefs of the Mozambique Channel, the whole of this coast has been relatively easy to access for the maritime peoples of Arabia, the Gulf and India. For more than two thousand years there has been a steady flow of cultural influences along this maritime route, influences which have included architecture, crops, weaving, ships, music, language and religion. North-eastern and north-western Madagascar and the Comoro Islands lie well within the area affected by this cultural Gulf Stream, though southern Madagascar has always been more remote and more difficult of access. Madagascar has also probably had direct links across the Indian Ocean with Indonesia which has contributed to its peopling and to the distinctive language of the island. However, it has been argued that Indonesian influences did not come from Java directly across the ocean but may have followed the more conventional route around the northern shores of the Indian Ocean reaching Madagascar by way of the Comoro Islands, and that at one time Indonesian influence, today so clearly present in Madagascar, affected all the east African littoral.

Migration from Africa to Madagascar by way of the Comoro Islands has probably always been the most important route by which people have settled the island and this process has continued unbroken for two thousand years. African influences in Madagascar are arguably as strong if not stronger than the Indonesian. The Malagasy language owes 20 per cent of its vocabulary to the Bantu languages of the continent and the physical appearance of many Malagasy strongly suggests an African origin. Strong cultural links have been found between some Malagasy groups, like the Bara, and the cultures of central Africa while it has been argued that the Anteimoro of the south, with their semi-literate culture, have their origin in migrants from Somalia. Although at all periods some Africans would have arrived as slaves, there was also free migration and a strong possibility that at different times chiefly lineages and elite groups moved across to the island.[1]

In the flow of people and cultural influences between Africa and Madagascar, the Comoro Islands have played a crucial role. The islands lie like stepping stones between Madagascar and the mainland, shortening the sea voyage and facilitating regular access between the great island and the continent. These stepping stones are the route by which Bantu and Swahili culture reached the northern shores of the island and by which the settlements that were established there maintained their contacts with eastern Africa; they are also the route by which, from time to time, Malagasy influences have travelled to Africa, for relations between Africa and Madagascar have always been a two way process.

At the time of the arrival of the Portuguese in 1498, the Comoro Islands and the northern coasts of Madagascar were fully integrated into the maritime commercial culture of eastern Africa. Along the north-eastern and north-western coasts were numerous port-cities similar in structure and culture to those of eastern Africa. The coastal elites, the Antalaotra, speaking a dialect of Swahili, recognised kinship with the clans of eastern Africa, claimed the same origin in Shiraz or the Hadramaut and enjoyed a common islamic culture. The Comoro Islands also developed urban sultanates whose economy was based on trade with Kilwa and the other east African cities, and whose rulers built elegant stone towns and married into the ruling commercial elites of eastern Africa.[2]

However to the south of about 18 degrees on the western coast and below the Bay of Antongil on the eastern coast, the Swahili, islamic culture dies out. Partly this is due to the inaccessibility of much of this coastline and the lack of natural harbours, but more important is the regimen of the winds that makes regular contact difficult for those coming from the north.

Trade and Slaves

At the time of the arrival of the Portuguese, exports from the ports of northern Madagascar were *"commodities that were lacking in eastern Africa (rice, copal resin, chlorite schist (soapstone)) or in Arabia and the Persian Gulf (mangrove stakes and rice; slaves to be taken into harems)"* Imports consisted of pottery, porcelain from China, silver, textiles and beads.[3] From the early sixteenth century Madagascar was regularly visited by Europeans and the commercial and social life of the coastal areas of the island was reflected in European maritime narratives. A picture emerges of small scale but regular seaborne commerce between western Madagascar and the African mainland and continuing cultural contact and intermarriage of the coastal elites of Madagascar, the Comoro Islands and East Africa. Europeans report a slowly growing trade in slaves which was probably becoming the principal item of commerce.

During the 16th century there was relatively little contact between Europeans and Madagascar. The Portuguese explored and mapped the coast from 1500 and raided two of the northern towns in 1506. Other plundering expeditions are known to have taken place in 1527 and 1543. Occasional documents then refer to trade in carved stone objects, masts, bark cloth and provisions - always, it seems, between Mozambique Island where the Portuguese had their principal port and the northern ports of the island. The trade in foodstuffs assumed some importance for the Portuguese settlers in Mozambique and in the early seventeenth century small boats regularly plied the route via the Comoro Islands to the ports of the north-western coast. Dutch and French visitors found the Portuguese language to be well known at

least in the islands. However, what impresses one most is
the extremely limited extent of these contacts. Madagascar
had no commodities that interested the Portuguese Crown
which clearly did not think that the trade of the northern
Malagasy towns in any way threatened the important
monopoly in gold or ivory.[4]

During the first century of European contact there is little
record of slave trading. The Portuguese owned a few slaves
who served their forts or were drafted onto the Indiamen to
supplement the crews. Slaves were also sent to the
Portuguese settlements in India and the Far East, usually as
household servants, concubines or soldiers, or as rowers for
the galleys. Sometimes the Portuguese bought Malagasy
slaves at Boina or Ampasindava in the extreme north while
en route for India, but for the most part they took their
slaves from eastern Africa.[5]

However, in the 17th century Europeans began to visit
Madagascar more often. English, French and Dutch,
excluded from the use of Portuguese ports in eastern Africa,
explored the coasts of Madagascar in search of anchorages
where water and fresh provisions could be obtained and
began also to establish links with the Comoro Islands.
These European ships showed little interest in the trade of
Africa and were determined on rapid voyages to the East
Indies. For this reason a port of call in southern Madagascar
was of particular importance and St Augustine's Bay on the
south-west coast became a popular place to take on water
and provisions. By the 1630s these European powers were
looking to establish their own permanent way stations; the
Dutch occupied Mauritius in 1638 and the Cape in 1652 and
the French established a settlement at Fort Dauphin on the
south-east coast of Madagascar in 1642. The English took St
Helena in the South Atlantic and experimented briefly with
settlements at St Augustine's Bay and Nosy Bé on the coast
of Madagascar between 1645 and 1650 before settling for an
alliance with the sultan of Anjouan in the Comoros.[6]

The interest shown by the Europeans in Madagascar and
the Comoro Islands is reflected in the published accounts
which give a great deal of detail about the maritime trade
between Madagascar, the islands and the mainland. From

these accounts it is clear not only that there was regular trade between the African coast, the Comoro Islands and the ports of western Madagascar but that one of the commodities being traded was slaves. The slaves were being obtained in eastern Africa and shipped to the islands, partly for local use but partly also for onward shipment to the Gulf. Fragmentary as these accounts are, they indicate that the trade involved comparatively low numbers.

From the 1660s, and probably earlier, slaves were from time to time bought in Madagascar for sale in the West Indies and towards the end of the century this trade grew extensively with the establishment of European pirate traders at Sainte Marie and other places on the east coast. The pirates took part in slave raids launched from the coast against inland peoples and they acted as brokers in the trade selling slaves to any buyer that turned up. The South Sea Company was one such buyer, purchasing Malagasy slaves for sale in South America, while New York-based slavers were active on the coast buying slaves captured by the Sakalava chiefs in their wars[7]. However, the European settlements in the Indian Ocean also required slaves as workmen, field hands and crew and in the early days of the Dutch settlements in Mauritius and the Cape, Madagascar was a favoured place from which to obtain slaves. The Dutch even maintained a permanent slave trading station at the Bay of Antongil between 1642 and 1647. The slaves bought were paid for with silver dollars or with firearms.

European accounts of the seventeenth century make it clear that slaves were being imported into Madagascar as well as exported from it. Some of the slaves imported were destined for re-export but domestic slavery existed in Malagasy society where the shortage of population often dictated that slaves should be retained for agricultural purposes. The physical appearance of the Malagasy suggests strongly that many of these slaves became fully incorporated into the Malagasy population, though in Imerina there was no mixing between the Merina ruling elite, the Hova (or freemen), and the *andevo* (slaves). Ex-slaves would remain a distinct element in the population even after slavery was formally abolished at the end of the 19th century. This two-way movement of slaves was to characterise the slave trade in Madagascar until the end of the 19th century and makes a clear understanding of the significance of this trade and the pattern of migration that it represents difficult to grasp.

The French Trade in the Indian Ocean

The early French settlements in Île de Bourbon (later La Réunion) from 1649 and Fort Dauphin in Madagascar had not flourished, but in 1721 French settlers occupied Mauritius, renamed Île de France, and began to grow indigo, tobacco and sugar. By the middle years of the century both Mauritius and Réunion were thriving plantation colonies and French settlers were beginning to occupy the scattered islands of the Seychelles. A second Caribbean was being created in the Indian Ocean. The demand for slave labour in the islands grew along with the tobacco and sugar industry. Initially the French sought to buy slaves in the nearest market and developed contacts with suppliers on the eastern coasts of Madagascar. Although they subsequently opened up contacts with the Omani controlled coastal ports of East Africa and with the Portuguese in Mozambique Island, Madagascar remained their principal source of slaves. It has been estimated that over the whole period from 1610 to1810 a total of 160,000 slaves were imported into the islands and that 70,000 of these came from Madagascar[8]. The peak period for the trade appears to have been 1760-1793 when a total of 80,000 slaves were taken to the islands.

Slaves were paid for in a number of ways, though by far the most important was payment in firearms. The import of guns into Madagascar, which began in the 17th century, had the predictable effect of enlarging the scale of warfare and of leading to the emergence of more powerful state systems. By the second half of the 18th century, northern Madagascar, with which region most of the trade was carried on, had seen the emergence of the powerful Sakalava, Betsimisaraka and Merina kingdoms.

In 1750 the French from Île de France acquired sovereignty over Sainte Marie and, using that off-shore island as a base, established slave trading stations along the eastern coast of Madagascar[9]. Most of the trade was carried on through the ports which lay between Antongil and Taomasina (Tamatave) on the north-east coast and the slaves were captured on the thickly populated plateau of the northern interior and brought for sale by Merina traders. In 1792 there were alleged to be 22 French slave traders established in Taomasina[10]. The French traders concentrated on the east coast and seldom visited the ports on the north-western coast which remained the preserve of the muslim Antalaotra[11].

The high price fetched by slaves and the seemingly insatiable market for them soon brought others into the trade, so that by the last quarter of the eighteenth century the rulers of the north-eastern and north-western coastlands, the Betsimisaraka and the Sakalava were also seeking slaves to sell to the French. Although they, like the Merina, captured slaves in the Madagascar interior, they soon turned to raiding the Comoros and the coasts of Mozambique to supplement the supply. Between 1785 and 1823 large fleets of ocean going war canoes, numbering 300 vessels and carrying up to 5,000 men, set out from the northern ports to raid the Comoro Islands and the coasts of East Africa from Kilwa to Ibo and Mozambique Island[12]. The years between 1795 and 1830 were years of recurrent drought in eastern Africa and the supply of slaves was swollen by starvation and the movement of warlike migratory groups like the Nguni. The slaves captured on these raids were brought to the coastal ports of Madagascar where they were sold on to French traders from the Mascarene islands, some of them being marched overland from the west to the east coast.

The Napoleonic Wars and the Rise of the Merina Kingdom

From 1793 the British and the French embarked on a prolonged struggle for control of the Indian Ocean which culminated in 1810 when British forces captured Île de

France/Mauritius and received the surrender of Île de Bourbon/Réunion and the Seychelles. Britain had already ended the slave trade, though not slavery itself, in 1807 and began to enforce a policy of suppression in the Indian Ocean. This policy might have been relatively easy to carry out had not the decision been taken to restore Réunion to France in 1815. With the return of the French, the western Indian Ocean once again became the scene for intense rivalry. The French wished to continue to import slaves for their plantations, as did the plantation owners of Mauritius and the Seychelles who were under British rule, and the British feared the growth of French influence in Madagascar through their connection with the slave trade.

The result was the formulation of a British policy to lend direct support to the Merina king in Madagascar in return for his co-operation in suppressing the export slave trade and, by implication, in securing the exclusion of the French[13]. Embassies were sent to Imerina in 1816 and 1817 and a treaty was signed in the latter year recognising Merina sovereignty over the whole of Madagascar and providing money and military aid. In 1817 the Merina conquered Taomasina and for the first time obtained direct control of a port from which large numbers of slaves were exported. A further treaty signed between Britain and the Merina king, Radama, in 1820 offered the king a subsidy of 20,000 dollars a year in return for a ban on the export slave trade which was duly implemented. This treaty and the conquest by the Merina of the Betsimisaraka and Sakalava of Boina between 1820 and 1824 effectively ended the raids on the Comoros and eastern Africa as well as the *export* of slaves from northern ports.

The French responded to the threat posed by the Anglo-Merina alliance in three ways. First they intensified their attempts to purchase slaves from eastern Africa both directly and via Swahili agents in the Comoro Islands; second they began to open up new slave trading operations in central and southern Madagascar; and third they sought to counter British influence by establishing new colonies in the Comoro Islands and at Nosy Bé on the north-west coast of Madagascar. Another consequence, largely unforeseen at the time of the Anglo-Merina treaty, was the rapid growth of the demand for slaves within Madagascar itself and a great growth in the *import* of slaves into the island as opposed to the *export* of slaves from it[14]. It was one of the great ironies of the British anti-slavery campaign in Madagascar that the treaties that were designed to end the slave trade had the effect of stimulating the very trade they were intended to suppress. After 1820, therefore, the demand for slave labour was focused in two main areas, the rapidly expanding Merina kingdom in Madagascar and the European island plantations.

First were the planters of Mauritius and Réunion with their offshoots in the Seychelles, in Nosy Bé (after 1840) and Mayotte (after 1843). The reduction of duties on Mauritian sugar in 1825 created a strong demand for labour and when the institution of slavery was abolished in 1835 in that island and the former slaves began to leave the plantations, the demand for labour became ever more insistent. In this context, to prevent a revival of the slave trade Britain allowed the Mauritians to import contract labour from India. The French in Réunion, however, did not have access to Indian labour and scarcely deigned to conceal the continued import of slaves until the French government also abolished slavery in 1848. This had exactly the same consequences as had occurred thirteen years before in Mauritius and stimulated the demand for labour still further. However, as Britain refused to allow the recruitment of Indians, the French began to develop the trade in *engagés* (contract labourers), from the Comoros, Mozambique and southern Madagascar. Between 1848 and 1859 an average of 7,500 *engagés* per annum were imported into Réunion, a figure which would need to be considerably enlarged if the other French plantation islands were added to the total[15].

One place where slaves, thinly disguised as contract labourers, could be obtained was the Comoro Islands. Dhow owners operated from the islands, which are only two or three days sail from the African coast, during the hurricane season when the Royal Navy's ships were not on patrol[16]. They imported cargoes of slaves from the small Muslim controlled ports on the Mozambique coast (like

Angoche) which after a short stay could be re-exported as
engagés to French agents who found the ports of northern
Madagascar closed to them[17]. The French recruiters also frequented the ports of central and south-western Madagascar
which were outside Merina control, to buy Malagasy slaves.
Numbers by the mid-1850s from this region may have been
as high as 5,000 per annum, made up partly of native
Malagasy and partly of slaves imported from Mozambique
for onward shipment.

At the same time the enlarged, and still expanding,
Merina kingdom in the north began to import slaves in large
numbers. The demand for slaves in Merina had risen with
the successful conquests undertaken in the 1820s. The
Merina population was small and as more and more of the
men were required in the army or to garrison forts in the
captured regions, slaves were imported to perform agricultural tasks and to provide head transport. It has been estimated that the population of the capital, Antananarivo,
rose between 1820 and 1833 from 10,000 to 50,000 and that
two thirds of these were slaves[18]. Many of these slaves were
Malagasy war captives but increasing numbers were also
imported through the ports of north-western Madagascar
north of Baly Bay, the area of traditional Swahili (Antalaotra)
influence. While the slave trade into and out of the western
Madagascar ports continued to grow, trade on the eastern
coast largely ceased. In 1829 and again in 1845 the French
tried to force their way back into the trade of Taomasina but
the result was that the Merina rulers closed this port almost
totally to European commerce and adopted a policy of economic self-sufficiency, which also had the effect of stimulating the internal demand for slaves[19].

The Madagascar Slave Trade in the 19th century

In the middle years of the 19th century, c 1830-1860, the
ports of north-western Madagascar developed rapidly in
wealth and importance. By this time largely under the control of Merina governors, they became the principal ports for

the Merina kingdom. The traditional Antalaotra merchant elite of towns like Mahajanga were now reinforced with Zanzibaris and Indians who had established commercial contacts with the Omani sultanate in eastern Africa and with the trade of the Gulf and north-western India. Although 'legitimate' trade was coming to play an increasingly important role in the commerce of this region, the trading communities of these ports were still deeply implicated in the slave trade. They exported some Malagasy slaves, bought from the independent Sakalava chieftaincies to the south, as *engagé* labour to the French, while buying slaves from eastern Africa for service in the Merina kingdom[20].

The demand for slaves in the Merina kingdom resulted in part from the shortage of manpower resulting from the wars of conquest but principally from the emergence of a strong market economy. The state required labour for military purposes, for construction, for road building and even industrial development, while the growth of crops for the market also stimulated the demand. Much of this labour was supplied by a forced labour system imposed on the king's own subjects, but slave labour was always in high demand, and had the added attraction that the slave could be sold on to the French if he or she were no longer needed. It was reported that an imported slave in 1824 was valued at 40-50 head of cattle and in the 1830s at 30 silver dollars. Such prices were well able to tempt rich trading houses from Bombay to invest in the trade to the exclusion of other forms of commerce. Profits on a slave sold in Réunion could represent 1000 per cent profit[21]. In practice the slave trade to Madagascar seems to have been carried on in conjunction with 'legitimate' trade, most of the slaves being transported in relatively small numbers on ordinary trading dhows. Slave imports from eastern Africa, which may have run at an annual average of 3-4000 a year during the 1820s, had risen to 10,000 in the 1830s[22].

This growth in the demand for slaves within the Merina kingdom exactly parallels the growth in the demand for slaves among many of the coastal kingdoms and chieftaincies of Africa. Most of the slaves imported into Madagascar, whether they were destined for onward shipment or local employment, came from eastern Africa south of Kilwa. In the early part of the century most of them were shipped from the main trading ports of the coast - Kilwa which was loosely under Zanzibari influence, and the ports under Portuguese control - Ibo, Mozambique Island, Quelimane, Sofala and Inhambane. Important also was the independent sultanate of Angoche on the coast between Quelimane and Mozambique which was not brought under Portuguese control till the 1840s.

Although the area from which the trade drew appears fairly wide spread, it is perhaps important to distinguish between the areas north and south of the Zambesi. South of the Zambesi slaves were obtained as a result of the Nguni wars which led to the rise of the kingdoms of Nxaba and Soshangane dominated by a cattle owning military elite. The Nguni raided for slaves largely for their own purposes but considerable numbers were sold from time to time to Portuguese dealers on the coast, particularly when drought increased the numbers of slaves on the market. These slaves came from the patrilineal societies of Shona, Tsonga and Chopi, and were principally traded to the ports of southern Madagascar, many of them destined for the French islands. The pattern of winds in this southern part of the Mozambique Channel meant that slaves could be shipped all the year round, while further north the monsoons limited sailing to only six months of the year.

North of the Zambesi slaves were obtained from the Portuguese *prazo* warlords of the interior and from the Yao. Most of them came from the matrilineal peoples of the Shire Highlands and the northern Zambesi region between the Shire and the Luangwa. During the middle years of the century the flow of slaves was stimulated by the movement southwards of a number of Yao chieftaincies into the Shire Highlands (a process documented by Livingstone and his companions) while the Afro-Portuguese expanded up the Zambesi to the Kafue and along the Luangwa valley[23].

From 1836 onwards the Portuguese authorities began gradually to squeeze the slave trade out of their main ports, and after 1842, when the Portuguese signed a bilateral treaty with Great Britain, there were even joint patrols aimed at suppressing the trade. So from the mid-1840s onwards slaves were increasingly shipped from the smaller ports and river mouths of the coast. Portuguese involvement in the trade itself gradually declined and the trade became increasingly concentrated in the hands of the Muslim sheikhdoms of the coast[24]. In 1855 the Portuguese also began to take action against the trade in *engagés*. However, this was rudely interrupted in 1857 when, following the arrest of the French slaver *Charles et Georges*, the French government had demanded the vessel's release with compensation. So the trade in *engagés* continued as did the import of slaves into Madagascar for local use.

In 1865 a new treaty signed by Britain with the Queen of Madagascar formally outlawed the importation of slaves, just as the treaty with Radama in 1820 had outlawed their export from the island. Nevertheless the trade in slaves (or *engagés* when they were destined for Réunion) was still very much alive in 1867 when G.L.Sulivan was appointed to command the anti-slave trade cruiser *Daphne*[25]. An open trade in slaves with the ports of north-eastern Madagascar was impossible and the British consul in Taomasina, the main port for the Merina kingdom on the eastern side of the island, reported any slave cargoes landed to the Queen who then had them released to the British. However, Sulivan admitted "detection is rare, and the trade is very extensive". However, the situation in the Mozambique Channel was complex. The French sugar planters of Réunion had for twenty years been spreading plantation capitalism to the islands off the western coast of Madagascar. In 1840 they had occupied the island of Nosy Bé and in 1843 had obtained a treaty giving them control of Mayotte, one of the Comoro Islands. Initially the French found that the wars in Madagascar between the Merina and the Sakalava provided large numbers of slaves or contract labourers but as these islands were much closer to Mozambique than Réunion, the development of the plantations led to a great expansion of the trade in *engagés* from mainland Africa as well. Slaves and *engagés* were imported into the islands either for local use on plantations, or for onward shipment to Réunion or to feed the clandestine trade to Madagascar.

From Mayotte plantation agriculture gradually spread to the other Comoro Islands. Sugar plantations were established on Anjouan, some owned by the sultan and one by the British Consul, Sunley, until he lost his commission for employing slaves. So it was, as Sulivan explained, that "there is a very extensive slave-trade carried on to and from these islands, from the Portuguese settlements to the West; indeed, it forms the staple trade with them here". The slaves were brought from the Mozambique coast "with the designation of 'passengers' or 'engagés'" [26].

However, Sheppard has argued that most slaves imported into the Comoros at this time, if they were not exported again, were retained as a sign of the wealth and status by their Comorian owners and were not employed as agricultural labour. The name *wamakwa* was applied to these slaves which, like the Malagasy name *Makoi*, was derived from the 'Makua' language spoken by most of those who came from Mozambique north of the Zambesi[27]. However, there was another attraction in slave ownership, one which the Comorian elites shared with the chiefs and headmen of the matrilineal peoples of Mozambique. Where, as in the Comoros or among the Yao of Mozambique, children were considered as belonging to the mothers lineage, men often sought to establish families more directly dependent on themselves by obtaining slave wives whose children would belong to the father's rather than the mother's lineage[28]. Acquiring slaves, particularly female slaves, therefore, helped build up the strength of patriarchal family units.

The other major trend in the period after 1850 was for European labour 'recruiters' and dealers to operate increasingly from ports on the south-western coast of Madagascar which were not under Merina control and where the commercial alliance of Antalaotra and Indian capital was not so well entrenched. In these southern ports, which previously had not participated to any great extent in the trade, the French introduced firearms and stimulated a final phase of internal warfare before their own take over of the island as a colony in the 1890s.

The End of the Slave Trade to Madagascar

Thus the trade in slaves continued into the final decades of the century. In 1873 Sir Bartle Frere, in his report to Parliament on the East African slave trade, thought that 10,000 slaves a year were still being landed in Madagascar[29].

Captain Colomb, whose account of the slave trade in Madagascar waters was also published in 1873, was emphatic that there was still an extensive import of slaves into Imerina. Although, he wrote, *"very little in the way of work seems to be done or doing in the centres of population in Madagascar, there is always a vast superabundance of negroes ready to do it; and there is reason to believe that the importation of slaves from Africa is as brisk as ever it was"* [30]. The slaves, he was certain, came from Mozambique and not from Kilwa further north. The general pattern of the trade was as follows - *"across from the mainland to Cape St Andrew or to ports south of it, and then a coasting voyage northwards, disposing of the slaves as markets offers. If circumstances militate against a sale in Madagascar, the traders take their wares across to the Comoro Islands where...there is usually a demand for the article"* [31].

In 1877 private slavery was formally abolished in the Merina kingdom and former slaves became a government labour reserve. This caused shortage of labour in the private sector and provided a continued incentive for the continuation of the clandestine trade. When H.W. Little published his classic *Madagascar its History and People* in 1884, which he dedicated to the prime minister, Rainilaiarivóny, and the "People of Madagascar", he was able to say with considerable confidence, but also with a certain naivety, that *"in the friendly cooperation in time to come of themselves and the English government, we have doubtless the key to the solution of that perplexing problem - the effectual and complete suppression of the slave traffic in East African waters and the South Indian Ocean"* [32].

In the 1880s the French established protectorates over the other three Comoro Islands, Mohéli, Anjouan and

Grande Comore, and in 1896, following their conquest of the whole island of Madagascar, they formally abolished the institution of slavery. However, it was not until 1913, when the last of the independent coastal sheikhdoms of Mozambique came under Portuguese rule that the shipment of slaves from the mainland finally ceased.

When slavery was abolished in 1896, 500,000 persons officially designated as slaves were freed. Most of these were Malagasy slaves but the French census in Madagascar and the Comoro Islands in 1928 separately categorised the population of slave origin that was still distinct from other ethnic groups, the *Makoa* or *Makois*. The census counted 48,067 *Makois* in Madagascar proper as well as an unspecified number in the population of the Comoro Islands which were then under the Madagascar government[33]. In 1956 the *Makoi* were said officially to number 58,934. The status of slave continued long into the era of emancipation. In many areas of Madagascar, particularly those where there was a considerable Merina population, former slaves remained a distinct element in the population which was still expected to recognise and perform certain obligations towards their former Merina owners[34].

Under colonial rule the phenomenon of immigration to and emigration from Madagascar continued. The largest single group of immigrants were the Comorians who left their cramped islands in large numbers and took advantage of French colonial rule to settle in Majunga and the other port-towns of the north west. There was also recruitment by French plantation owners of contract labour (still called *engagés*) in various parts of Africa. At the same time Malagasy labour continued to be recruited by the planters of Réunion[35].

Conclusion

African migration, both free and enforced, to Madagascar has taken place over the best part of two millenia and has contributed substantially to the physical and cultural formation of the people. Of the slaves who were brought to Madagascar from the end of the 17th century to the end of the 19th, most were absorbed into existing communities. However, in some areas, particularly in Imerina where no intermarriage occurred, the numbers were sufficiently great for them to form their own ethnic communities, the *Makoi*, which remained distinct throughout the colonial period.

Notes & References

1. For a summary of the early history of Madagascar see Pierre Vérin, *The History of Civilisation in North Madagascar,* Balkema (Rotterdam and Boston, 1986); Mervyn Brown, *Madagascar Rediscovered,* David Philip (Claremont SA, 1978). For the most detailed account of early African influences in Madagascar see R.Kent, *Early Kingdoms in Madagascar,* Holt, Rinehart and Winston (New York, 1970).
2. For the early history of the islamic settlements in northern Madagascar see Vérin, *The History of Civilisation...*
3. Vérin, *The History of Civilisation...* p.4.
4. Vérin, *The History of Civilisation...* p.104-6 and M.Newitt, 'The Southern Swahili Coast in the First Century of European Expansion', *Azania,* 13 (1978) pp.111-126.
5. J-M.Filliot, *La Traite des Esclaves vers les Mascareignes au XVIIIe siècle,* ORSTOM (Paris, 1974), p.115.
6. Brown, *Madagascar Rediscovered* and M.Newitt, 'The comoro Islands in Indian Ocean Trade before the 19th century' *Cahiers d'Etudes Africaines,* 23 (1983) pp.139-165.
7. Vérin, *The History of Civilisation...* p.109.
8. Gwyn Campbell, 'Madagascar and Mozambique in the Slave Trade of the Western Indian Ocean 1800-1861', in W.G.Clarence Smith ed., *The Economics of the Indian Ocean Slave Trade in the Nineteenth Century,* Frank Cass (London, 1989), p.166.
9. Brown, *Madagascar Rediscovered,* p.102.
10. Brown, *Madagascar Rediscovered,* p.104.
11. Filliot, *La Traite...,* p.151.
12. James Prior, *Voyage along the Eastern Coast of Africa to Mosambique, Johanna, and Quiloa... in the Nisus Frigate,* (London, 1819), p.64 and Vérin, *The History of Civilisation...* pp.122-130.
13. Campbell, 'Madagascar and Mozambique...', pp.168-9.
14. Gwyn Campbell, 'Madagascar and the Slave Trade 1810-1895', *Journal of African History,* 22, 1981, pp.203-227.
15 Campbell, 'Madagascar and Mozambique...' p.170.
16. R.W.Beachey, *The Slave Trade in Eastern Africa,* Collings (London, 1976), p.30.
17. Gill Shepherd, 'The Comorians and the East African Slave Trade', J.L.Watson ed. Blackwell, *Asian & African Systems of Slavery,* (Oxford, 1980) pp.100-134.
18. Campbell, 'Madagascar and the Slave Trade' p. 209.
19. Campbell, 'Madagascar and the Slave Trade', p.211.
20. Campbell, 'Madagascar and Mozambique...', pp 172-3.
21. Campbell, 'Madagascar and Mozambique...' p.179.

22. Campbell, 'Madagascar and Mozambique...' pp.184-5.
23. For the Mozambique slave trade north of the Zambesi see, Leroy Vail and Landeg White, *Capitalism and Colonialism in Mozambique*, Heinemann (London, 1980) chapter one and E.A. Alpers, *Ivory and Slaves in East Central Africa*, Heinemann (London, 1975).
24. The classic contemporary account of the Mozambique slave trade is F.L.Barnard, *A Three Years Cruize in the Mozambique Channel*, Bentley (London, 1848).
25. G.L.Sulivan, *Dhow Chasing in Zanzibar Waters and on the Eastern Coast of Africa*, (London, 1873), reprinted Dawsons of Pall Mall (London, 1967).
26. Sulivan, *Dhow Chasing...* p.138.
27. Shepherd, 'The Comorians...', pp. 85,92.
28. Shepherd, 'The Comorians...', pp.90-91.
29. Beachey, *The Slave Trade in Eastern Africa*, p.36.
30. Captain Colomb, *Slave-catching in the Indian Ocean*, (London, 1873), reprinted Dawsons of Pall Mall (London, 1968), p.308.
31. Colomb, *Slave-catching in the Indian Ocean*, p.309.
32. H.W. Little, *Madagascar its History and People*, Blackwood (London, 1884), p.25.
33. André You, *Madagascar Colonie Française 1896-1930*, Sociétés d' Editions (Paris,1931), pp.14-5.
34. Maurice Bloch, ed., Modes of Production and Slavery in Madagascar: Two Case Studies', *Asian & African Systems of Slavery*, J.L.Watson ed. Blackwell (Oxford, 1980) pp.73-99.
35. You, *Madagascar...* chapter xviii.

FROM FRENCH SLAVES TO FRENCH CITIZENS: THE AFRICAN DIASPORA IN REUNION ISLAND

Helen Hintjens

Woven into the entire fabric, is the slave trade, its antecedents, its fate, its reality and its myths, and the influence it had – and maybe still has – on the economy, on people's perceptions, on human relations. [1]

Introduction

Today, the legacy of slavery remains a part of the creole cultural landscape and social mentalities in Réunion island, located in the South-West Indian Ocean, 800 km to the east of Madagascar, and 200 km west of Mauritius. Until the 7th century, the island was uninhabited. Today it is inhabited by almost three-quarters of a million people. Of these, roughly one third are descendants of the former African and Malagasy slaves brought into the island from the 17th to the mid-19th century. Although there has been a profound deracination of the African-Malagasy population of the island (compared with the elements of cultural resilience among the population of Indian-origin, for example) many aspects of Réunionnese creole culture carry the traces of the African and Malagasy past of many Réunionnese. Local place names include 'Manapany', which means 'bat' in Malagasy, and *Plaine des Cafres,* literally Black slaves' Plain. In the mountainous interior, one of the former volcanic craters, now inhabited by poor whites and descendants of freed slaves, the Cirque of Mafate, is reputedly named after a maroon, or run-away slave leader known as Maffate. [2]

Together with Mauritius and Rodriguez, Réunion forms part of the Mascarenes group of islands, named after the Portuguese explorer who first charted the area in 1514. The volcanic origin of the island has created a spectacular, though inhospitable, terrain, with narrow coastal plains. It was on these plains, vulnerable to erosion, flood and cyclones, that the plantation economy of the island emerged from the late 17th century onwards. The plantation economy was based from the start on slave labour, introduced initially from Madagascar, and then increasingly from Mozambique and Zanzibar. Settlements along the coast were often isolated, and some towns like Le Port were not accessible by boat until the late 19th century. In spite of images of earthly paradise, Réunion was not a particularly easy territory to colonise or to exploit.[3] Being of recent volcanic origin (with a live crater at La Fournaise) there are few bays, and no natural harbour. The steep gradient and poor quality of much of the soil, means that less than one third of the total surface area is suitable for cultivation. The best soils are on the arid leeward side of the island, where high yields are only possible with irrigation.

Given the difficulties of traversing land that is criss-crossed by ravines and crevices, plots have traditionally been divided "from the shoreline to the summit of the mountains". In many areas plots have been subdivided over generations, with examples by the 1930s of properties stretching up to 8 km downhill, but only a few metres wide.[4] To this day, the physical features of the island continue to have an impact on socio-economic and political realities in Réunion. This was even more so during the era of colonisation and the slave-based plantation economy.

Variations in the intensity and nature of human settlement in the island, themselves in part due to the complex and diverse terrain, have produced a persistently uneven spatial distribution of Réunion's population. Although more than half the population could now be said to be 'mixed', in terms of colour, there is some concentration into different regions and sub-regions. Map 1 from Jean Defos du Rau's seminal thesis on Réunion island, shows the distribution of the population of predominantly African origin, with which this chapter is concerned, during the post-war era. Defos du Rau simply refers to the categories 'white', 'black' and 'mixed', but even this gives us a clue as to the historic patterns of colonisation in Réunion. [5] Colonial legacies linger on in other ways, both in images and in the arts, and not just in Réunion of course. [6] Images of the Réunionnese as bare footed stereotypically 'negro' types persist in the French press as well (see for example Map 2 and Cartoon 1).

The colonial past weighs heavily in Réunion, and terms dating back to the days of slavery remain widespread in the creole language. The term *cafres* (originally from the Arabic *kaffir*) is still commonly used in everyday speech to refer to the population of predominantly Afro-Malagasy descent, who account for around 30-40 per cent of the population. The term used for the mainly Hindu Indian creoles is *malbars*, deriving from the region where Indian contract labourers and slaves had originated during the colonial era. Another term is *zindous,* which is used synonymously with *malbars*, and simply means Hindus. *Tiblancs* is an abbreviation for *petits blancs* and refers to the poor whites who make up roughly one third of the island's population. More recently, *zarabes*, meaning Arabs, is the term used to refer to Indians of muslim origin, mainly more recent immigrants. The other groups in Réunion are *chinois* (Chinese), traditionally small grocers, and the *zoreils* (literally ears), the metropolitan French whites, who predominate in the public sector. All these creole identity-markers continue to be widely used up to the present.

There have also been changes since the colonial era, however. One example is the use of the term creole, which now refers to anyone from Réunion who speaks creole. During the colonial era, the term creole referred only to the population of European origin born in the colony. Creole itself was previously considered a *patois*, a dialect, of French, tainted by its association with slavery and the plantation. Today it is recognised as a language, which is both a product of colonial society and a living means of expression which has survived the integration of Réunion into France since 1946. [7]

Réunion's History: an Overview

From its earliest colonisation, Ile Bourbon was part of the old empire of France, a colony of settlement and a sign of the prestige and grandeur of the French state. The lack of indigenous inhabitants made this *terra nullius*. The emptiness of Réunion before colonial settlement helped to create the image that persists today, which is that Réunion does not have any problems of 'racial conflict'. More accurately, and perhaps more to the point:

> …before being French, (Réunion) was nothing: there was no one there, no one was chased out, nor had it been exploited by anyone. [8]

After being discovered in 1514, the Mascarenes islands were to remain uninhabited for a century and a half. The first human settlement was in 1664, when a handful of French settlers arrived along with some Malagasy women. These men and women were the first settlers in the island, and until the Revolution, *Ile Bourbon* (as Réunion was known) was populated only very gradually, with a free population of 538 and 633 slaves by 1713. Hunting and gathering were still possible, and made life relatively comfortable in what was described by many as an 'earthly paradise'. [9] Before plantation production started in earnest in the 19th century, the slave population did not outnumber the free population of settlers by much. The island was a staging post for the French fleet on their way to the East. From 1665 to 1767, Ile Bourbon was controlled by the *Compagnie des Indes*, which then passed the island to the monarchy.

Coffee production started in the 1720s, and by 1744 the island produced 2.5 million tons of coffee. The *Compagnie des Indes* had a monopoly over land allocation and over purchasing and marketing of coffee. Coffee was never a monocrop, however, and the island remained more than self-sufficient in foodstuffs. As the age of self-sufficiency, this has for some become the historic 'golden age' for the island. The number of people was still relatively small, and it was possible for Ile Bourbon to be self-reliant. This situation did not persist, as in 1744-49 a crop disease halved coffee exports, and alternative exports had to be found. There followed a period of experimentation with various other crops, mainly food crops.

The introduction of sugar cane and the establishment of large plantations in the late 18th and early 19th century eventually provided a replacement for coffee. Suddenly there was a huge increase in the demand for labour, and slavery was seen as the only solution. The mainly African and Malagasy (but also a small number of Indian) slaves in the island increased from 4,500 out of a total population of 6,950 in 1735, to 37,000 of a total population of 45,000 by 1788. This had the effect of significantly intensifying the slave trade in East Africa through Zanzibar.[10]

After 1789, the Jacobinism of the French state affected all the French colonies. The revolutionary ideology of republicanism implied the assimilation of all the colonised into France, slaves and freed alike. This ideology proved highly unpopular among the white creoles of Réunion. Even the island's name being changed from *Ile Bourbon* to Réunion was resented. The name *Ile Bourbon* was adopted during the restoration, and the island only finally became known as Réunion in 1848. After the revolutionary and Napoleonic era, the Mascarenes were under British control from 1811-1815. *Ile Bourbon* was then returned to France, being considered less valuable than Mauritius, which remained under British control.

The Illegal Slave Trade and the Sugar Boom

There are some useful studies which include accounts of the abolition of slavery in Réunion and the position of freed slaves in the society after 1848.[11] It is more difficult to find accurate accounts of the period of slavery itself. As Andre Scherer noted in his study of Réunion's historical Archives, much of the key documentation on the era of slavery was destroyed in the early 19th century. Details of escaped slaves (*declarations de marronnage*), for example, and letters related to the slave trade, have been lost forever. The documents of the *Compagnie des Indes* nonetheless reveal that escaped slaves organised themselves into *maquis* (bands) in the 18th century, carrying out raids on the coastal areas. For the most part, archival evidence about the era of slavery and its legacy have been obliterated by cyclone damage, neglect, carelessness, vandalism and paper-eating insects.[12]

Slavery was formally abolished in 1794. Yet the slave trade and the institution of slavery continued, albeit not under that name, until 1860, twelve years after the abolition decree of 1848. The decree of 1794 was never implemented in Réunion, and there was reportedly little reaction from the slave population. Only one major slave revolt was documented in the island's history, and this took place during the British occupation of 1811-15.[13]

The Indian Ocean remained isolated, remote from slave revolts in the Caribbean colonies, especially in St Domingue and Guadeloupe.[14] Slavery was not abolished, but even so a few poor whites started to emerge in Réunion, with no slaves or land of their own.[15] Larger plantation owners continued to feel quite secure, and fiercely resisted republican efforts to impose the 'fatal decree' of abolition. The *Assemblee Coloniale* (colonial local government) both in Réunion and neighbouring Ile de France (later Mauritius) both refused to abolish slavery, even threatening to declare independence if Paris insisted on implementation.[16]

Recognising that the colonial economies were only profitable if labour supplies were cheap and plentiful, Napoleon restored slavery in all the French colonies in 1802. In Réunion, since nothing much had changed, there was little response. Abolition in the Caribbean was indirectly to affect Réunion's economic fortunes quite dramatically, however. The loss of St Domingue in 1803 meant the loss of France's most profitable colony. This created new opportunities for Réunion's planter class, as did the take-over of Mauritius by Britain. The French sugar market experienced shortages which were met from elsewhere in the Empire. Very soon after the island returned to France in 1815, the planters of *Ile Bourbon* started to clear huge tracts of the island to plant cane.[17]

Réunion started cultivating sugar cane almost one hundred years after the French Caribbean colonies.[18] The boom years for the sugar plantations lasted from 1815-1860, starting at around the time that the Treaty of Vienna outlawed the slave trade. From 1817 to 1830 the slave trade into Réunion was carried out illegally, some 38,500 slaves being imported mainly from Mozambique, and some from Zanzibar and Madagascar. Hubert Gerbeau has shown that this illegal trade continued until at least the late 1830s. A later estimate by the same author puts the number of illegal slaves brought into the island after 1817 at 45,000.[19] The mortality rate of the slaves was high, and male slaves significantly outnumbered females, so that birth rates were very low. In 1788 there were around 37,000 slaves. In spite of at least 40-50,000 new slaves being brought in up to the late 1830s, the slave population was estimated at only 62-65,000 at the time of abolition in 1848.[20]

There followed a period of rapidly increased profitability. Payments of a 'colonial indemnity' were made to all planters whose slaves (their former property) had been emancipated. After emancipation, sugar exports increased dramatically, from 19,000 tons in 1850 to 73,000 tons by 1860. Sugar mills were constructed on all the largest properties, with an increase from 10 mills in 1817 to 189 in 1830.[21] Final processing of cane sugar took place in France, and there were substantial profits at both ends of the trade.

Heavy capital investments were needed to increase yields; soil had to be cleared of stones, and irrigation channels had to be constructed. Increased production was utterly dependent on the labour power of Africans and Malagasy, and due to the abolition of slavery also on Indian and African contract labourers. From the early 19th century, but much more acutely thereafter: "the question of labour and immigration was the key problem in the life of the island", and preoccupied the entire planter class and colonial administration.[22] In the Indian Ocean at this time, just as in the Caribbean and the Americas, "direct slavery is as much the pivot of bourgeois industry as machinery, credit" and so on.[23] A steady and plentiful supply of enslaved Africans, even an illegal supply, meant that sugar planters could make sizeable fortunes. Concentration of production resulted in a decline in the number of sugar mills from 189 in 1839 to 110 by the time of abolition.[24] The availability of cheap labour tended to slow the pace of technological improvement on the plantations and in the sugar mills during the mid-19th century.

Unlike coffee, sugar cane led to a mono-crop economy in Réunion, promoting a concentration of land holdings, and the removal of tree cover on the coastal plains. Food crops suffered a decline, and foodstuffs had to be imported to make up the shortfall. In short, sugar was so profitable that it became economically viable to import foodstuffs rather than to grow them locally. Madagascar and the other French colonies started to provide the population of Réunion with rice and other staples.[25]

In many ways, the present economic, social and cultural norms of Réunion were formed during the sugar boom era. Population structures altered dramatically, and population increases through immigration and rising birth rates increased the number of people living in the island from around 60,000 at the turn of the century to 110,000 by 1848.[26] Wealthy *creoles* (during the colonial era, the term creole referred to locally born whites) became a small, defensive minority, as more and more poor whites fled into the mountainous interior. Until the 1860s, people of African and Malagasy descent were still in the majority in most parts of the island. In some areas, the Afro-Malagasy accounted for three-quarters of the total population.[27] The uneven distribution of the Afro-Malagasy population, as shown in Map 1, dates from the period of emancipation.

Abolition could have meant the end of the sugar boom, if other sources of labour had not been found. A clandestine trade in African and Malagasy 'workers' continued until 1860 or so, but the main source of labour after 1860 was India. An estimated 35,000 Indian contract labourers and around roughly the same number of African contract labourers were recruited during the 1860s and 1870s.[28] The arrival of Indian labourers altered the demographic and socio-cultural profile of Réunion significantly, as most Indian indentured labourers remained in the island after the end of their contracts. They rarely made common cause with the African-Malagasy population, whether indentured or former slaves. According to Fuma, the Indians tended to consider themselves above the African and Malagasy in the 'pecking order' of colonial society.[29] Yet ironically, Indian labourers received the same humiliating and punishing treatment as the slaves had received in the past, and which freed Afro-Malagasy were now no longer willing to accept. In turn, the contract labourers who replaced the slaves came to value the same ideals of self-employment and land ownership that the former slaves had striven to attain after leaving the plantations.

The Flight from Slavery

The archival material remaining suggests that the African people in Réunion were mainly transported from Mozambique and Zanzibar, and some from Madagascar. From the start, some managed to escape into the interior and organised raids on the coastal plains. *Marronage*, the flight of enslaved Africans out of the plantations, remains today a symbol of freedom for the population of African descent, still known as *cafres* in everyday parlance in Réunion island.[30] The 19th century Réunionnese-born poet Auguste Lacaussade dedicated these lines to a legendary African *marron*, known as Anchiang or Anchian.

> To this awesome, wild, inaccessible mountain
> Came one miserable Negro, in his despair
> Demanding back his liberty
> which had been grabbed away.
> He made these rocks blossom;
> he brought them alive [...]
> An African exposed upon these deserted slopes.[31]

After slavery was abolished, all slaves were given new family names, and their marriages were legalised. Yet it is significant that until the early 20th century, the only deaths recorded were those of white people of European origin.[32]

Freed slaves were French citizens, but were economically and politically marginalised within the colony. Very few had purchased their liberty prior to abolition, and even they were treated as second-class citizens.

Once the 62,000 slaves in the island gained their freedom, the tendency was for the *affranchis* (freed slaves) to flee the plantations. According to Sudel Fuma, in his definitive study of the condition of emancipated people in Réunion:

> The act of emancipation released the need for independence among the former slaves. Having lived in a closed community, constrained by the controlling authority of the master, in their behaviour and in their hostility to work, the freed person asserted their right to their own individualism.[33]

A few African and Malagasy people started to establish themselves as small holders, moving into the areas where land was still available. A few settled in the mountainous interior of Réunion, which also became the refuge of the poor whites, or *petits blancs*, increasingly outnumbering the planter class of whites. "Becoming a property owner was the ideal that the freed slaves struggled to attain".[34] The land they bought, however, could not usually produce enough to support an entire family, and most adults were obliged to travel to the main towns seeking work to supplement their incomes. A few remained on larger properties as contract workers (*engagees*) alongside those contract labourers recruited from India during the early 1860s. Vagrancy and labour laws, obliging those without a fixed address to work, were used to try and prevent the Afro-Malagasy population from moving around. But they could not prevent them from leaving the hated plantations.

Freed slaves had to work for a living, or else they would starve. But direct dependence was too reminiscent of their recent slave status to be attractive to them.[35] During the 1850s and 1860s, the former slave population increasingly congregated in a precarious freedom around the capital St Denis, and other main towns of Réunion. On the whole, they preferred even the most insecure forms of petty trading and self-employment, and later office and shop work to manual labour for a single, personal employer.[36] Salaries on the plantations remained derisory after emancipation, and free labourers were not willing to work at these rates of pay. Planters had great difficulty recruiting labour, and complained that the African population had become lazy and a danger to public order. A few hours of work a day as a carpenter, mason, seamstress, office clerk, blacksmith, baker, or selling goods on the road, could yield a better return for the former slaves and their children than a month's hard plantation labour. Control over one's own working time was not possible on plantations.[37]

Few freed slaves resisted the lure of freedom; of 45,700 who had been working on plantations in 1848, only an estimated 15,600 remained four years later. Most of these were employed as contract labourers, often at near starvation wages.[38] Despite severe labour shortages, planters continued to treat workers badly, and freed slaves continued to flee the plantations. For both sexes, manual labour was equated with slavery, and various strategies of escape were employed.[39] Freed women had their own professions, including craft and sack-making; they also resorted to prostitution in order to survive. At the same time, sanitary conditions were neglected for this rapidly growing and impoverished urban population, and diseases such as smallpox and cholera broke out in the early 1850s, particularly affecting the African and Malagasy population of the island. There was an epidemic of malaria in the island in 1865, which was to become the main cause of mortality until after the Second World War.[40]

Crisis and *Colonage*

The late 19th century was a period of crisis. With the sugar economy boom, production increased from 15,000 tons in 1815 to 73,000 tons by 1860. Thereafter, the economy went into recession and increasing numbers of small landowners were forced out of business. The crisis of profitability became perennial and land ownership became progressively more concentrated. Cane started to monopolise the best arable land. By 1860 it covered two-thirds of all

land under cultivation. As the sugar economy entered an era
of crisis, the sugar industry went into rapid decline, and by
1870 production had fallen by two-thirds. In spite of this, the
population of Réunion continued to grow for a while, from
178,000 in 1860 to 211,000 by 1869. Thereafter, it declined
by 1880, to around 170,000, as Réunion entered a period of
recession which lasted until the 1930s. [41] Former slaves
could have been recruited for plantation work if they were
paid adequately, but the wage levels did not attract them.
The planters were obliged to find various forms of tied
labour for the plantations in order to maintain production
and profit levels.

By the last few decades of the 19th century, various
forms of enforced labour as were introduced in order to
ensure that agricultural production continued. Labour was
tied through a share-cropping system, known in Réunion as
le colonat partiaire. This roughly translates as tribute farming, in which the direct producer, or sharecropper, retained
a share (usually two-thirds) of the product of the land, and
the remainder was handed over to the land-owner. As
Auguste Brunet stated:

> In order to secure labour for its exclusive services (the plan-
> tation) had somehow to ensure that for the mass of the popu-
> lation there was no other way of making a living.[42]

The main reasons for the decline in the sugar economy
in Réunion were changes that took place elsewhere in the
Empire. Trade liberalisation immediately reduced profit
levels as preferential pricing structures were dismantled
for the sugar exports of the French colonies. The gradual
replacement of cane sugar with beet was another factor.
Many plantations ceased to be viable during the 1860s and
1870s, and ownership of land became increasingly polarised
between a handful of vast estates and a multitude of small
properties. The largest estate at the end of the 19th century
belonged to the Kerveguen family, and covered one third of
all arable land.[43] The role of *colonage partiaire* was to rein-
tegrate underemployed labour into the plantation system in
order to maintain production. The arrangement gave the

colons the feeling of independence, in exchange for basic equipment, transport and a market being provided by the landowner. For the plantation economy, the *colons:* "played the part of 'shock absorbers' by bearing part of the risks incurred in sugar production".[44]

From 1860 to 1918, Réunion suffered an unprecedented economic eclipse. Thereafter, the German occupation of beet-growing areas in Alsace and Lorraine created a renewed demand for cane, and a new sugar market agreement came into force in 1934. Réunion was allocated an annual quota of 62,000 tons at a favourable price, and production recovered, reaching 110,000 tons during the 1930s. The population had stagnated since the 1870s, but started to increase once again, and reached 220,000 in 1941 (roughly the same as in 1869). At the end of the Second World War most of the island's infrastructure dated back to the era of brief prosperity and mass immigration between 1848 and 1860. Mortality levels were among the highest in the world, with deaths outnumbering births until the 1930s; in 1931 the population was the same as in 1865.[45] At the end of World War II, almost half the cane grown in Réunion was still cultivated under *colonage*. The social and political implications of this were the perpetuation of the dominance of the small plantocracy that controlled most of Réunion's economic assets. But this dominance was soon challenged by moves towards full French citizenship and departmental status.

The Afro-Malagasy population in the 20th century

Réunion's African and Malagasy population was largely urbanised by this time, with a pattern of concentration around the major towns, as illustrated in Map 1 which was discussed earlier. The map is particularly valuable and unique, as the last official census of Réunion's population which included the category 'racial' or 'ethnic' origin was in 1848. It should be noted, however that the general urbanisation of the island's population in the post-war era has

resulted in a break down of some of the tidy compartmen-
talisations identified by Defos du Rau's research.

There is a rough three-way split of Réunion's population
between poor whites, people of Indian-origin and Afro-
Malagasy. This has generally meant that a single group could
not dominate in electoral terms, and has undermined any
simple correspondence between colour and class. The
creole society which existed in Réunion was more complex
than that in most Caribbean creole societies, for example.
Political conflicts and social identities did not tend to crys-
tallise along either colour or class lines. Instead, there was
a strict colonial pecking order based on a combination of
status and colour, with lighter colour denoting higher status,
but wealth able to compensate for darker colour, and
poverty resulting in loss of status for any colour. Philip
Mason describes the stratification typical of most Caribbean
creole societies in the following terms: "it seemed natural
that men should be graded in ranks or degrees....and that
the grading should take account of colour".[46] This image is
too simplistic for the case of Réunion, however.

There are few shared religious symbols, and few cultural
traits associated with African culture that remain clearly iden-
tifiable in creole culture. The main exceptions are the *sega*
and *maloya* dances, which retain elements of African and
Malagasy traditions, some foodstuffs and elements of the
creole vocabulary itself. In comparison with 'Indianness',
which has remained a recognised element in local
Réunionnese folklore, it has been relatively difficult to form
any sense of distinctive 'African' identity in the island.[47]

Ethnic politics has surfaced periodically since 1946, but
usually in subliminal ways. No sense of popular Réunionnese
nationalism could develop above the sharp social and class
cleavages that divided the islanders. Instead, a sense of
elite distinctiveness persisted among the numerically insignificant, but economically dominant, *Grand Blancs* creole
elite. Until the law of departmentalisation in 1946, this small
group of families continued to act as if Réunion was a private
company. Their preference was for maximum local control
over economic and political affairs in the colony. Increasingly
this desire for control was confronted with popular demands

from the Left for integration into France. Demands for equal citizenship and full social rights were particularly well supported among the mixed, Indian and Afro-Malagasy population.

Demands for Equal Citizenship

In the first half of this century, most of the population of Réunion faced appalling social conditions and few opportunities for economic security.[48]

> "Nowhere is there a greater contrast between the wealth of a few and the misery of the many. It is as if the island were created in order to illustrate the Marxist view of colonialism".[49]

Increasingly, they looked to France for a solution to their problems. The inter-war years were a period of agitation, with strikes, protests and demands for legal assimilation being made. Such demands were resisted both in Paris and among the local planter class. In 1936 twenty people died during elections, when widespread violence followed the decision not to extend Popular Front labour reforms to Réunion and the other *vieilles colonies* (old colonies).[50]

Illusions of grandeur prompted the elite to dream of colonising neighbouring Madagascar, and many poor whites were helped to settle in the island, hoping to make a new life. Colonial policies were overtly discriminatory during the inter-war years, with much more attention being given to impoverished whites than to impoverished people of mixed, African or Asian origin. Poor whites were 'rescued' from decadence as people of European origin. Those in Madagascar were eventually relocated to mainland France.[51]

In terms of electoral rights, 1848 also marked the birth of a very short-lived Republic. Colonial representation was withdrawn in 1849, and not restored until 1870. In the late 19th and early 20th century, elections were generally characterised by violence and intimidation. In the election of 1912, for example, twelve people were killed, and 150 injured.[52] The plantation elite retained almost exclusive control over political representation.

This started to change prior to World War I when Radicals were elected in 1914, in spite of violence and intimidation of the electorate.[53] The Socialist and Communist parties started to organise the electorate in the inter-war years. Former slaves, who, in 1848 had been converted overnight from property to part of the electorate, and full citizens, thus remained in a shadowy no-man's land until at least the 1930s. The creole population of local-born whites resisted all moves to integrate the island's non-European population into politics. In 1946, as in 1794 and 1848, the local elite came into conflict with the French central authorities over the issue of legal reform in Réunion.

The segregationist attitude of the plantocracy towards the mixed, African and Asian population helped recruit supporters for the Socialist and Communist parties, both of which favoured integration into France and full French citizenship for all Réunionnese.[54] A *Comite Republicaine de l'Action Democratique et Sociale* (CRADS) was created during the years of the Popular Front. At least outside the plantations, the opposition between the haves and have-nots was largely unmediated by ethnic or colour divisions.[55] The argument of supporters of the law of departmentalisation, proposed in 1946, was that the inhabitants of Réunion (and also Martinique, Guadeloupe and French Guyana) were already fully French in cultural, linguistic and religious terms. They should therefore be accorded the full benefits of legal, social and administrative assimilation into France. Full French citizenship and departmental status were desirable because they implied the end of the local plantocracy's stranglehold over economic and political life. As one Socialist deputy remarked of the French Caribbean colonies:

> "the main concern of the proponents of the law was to promptly obtain the benefits of social and labour laws for the workers of the colonies".[56]

The same scenario occurred in Réunion. The infrastructure of the island was in an advanced state of decay, and the sugar economy had collapsed, being cut off from its main market during the War. In Martinique, Aime Cesaire explained "We need roads, docks, airports, running water and drainage systems. We need hospitals and schools".[57] The demand for departmental status and full French citizenship thus responded to the urgent material needs of the majority of the population, and was widely supported. The law of 1946 was also presented in the French Assembly as the final stage in the liberation of the former colonised people of Réunion and the Caribbean colonies.[58] Those descended from the former slaves of African and Malagasy origin were simply part of the mass of the dispossessed, with no particular claims of their own.

The law was passed, and CRADS was supported by 55% of the electorate in Réunion. The Communist Party obtained an unprecedented 37% of the vote in 1945.[59] After 1946, there was little recognition from the Communist Party of any distinctively African element among the electorate of Réunion. The unifying factor of creole identity was to rally *le peuple Réunionnais* to the party and to the cause of equal rights and integration. This contrasted with the situation in the French Caribbean colonies, where the demand for integration was accompanied by the ideology of *negritude*, which simultaneously advocated "a return to African roots".[60] This ideology has had only a faint echo in Réunion; even the leader of the Communist Party of Réunion (PCR), Paul Verges, described Réunion as "a French department which suffers from no racial problems, and which has always been inhabited by Frenchmen". A more realistic appraisal follows from the geographer, Dupon who says "If Réunion is not entirely French, it is not for that matter entirely Malagasy, African or Asiatic".[61] In the specific context of Réunion, it certainly seems that "rather than encouraging the demand for independence, as it did elsewhere, the racial factor prevented it from emerging".[62]

Conclusion: echoes of the past

Réunion's population today is much more diverse than previously: the island is displayed in tourist brochures as a multicultural paradise, a 'tiny Eden', where people of mixed origins intermingle in peace and harmony.[63] The reality behind the appearance is more problematic and complex than could be guessed from the gushing phrases of the tourist brochures. Réunion is indeed a beautiful, harmonious place if one chooses to ignore the continuing discrimination, poverty and deprivation of part of the population.

The Afro-Malagasy population remains predominantly affected by this poverty and social exclusion. Sharp distinctions continue to be made, and are particularly apparent, for instance, in inter-personal relations, on the basis of colour and 'features' associated with African origin. African features are still regarded as generally less desirable than Asian or European-type features, in relation to hair, skin and shape of face. Persistent and sometimes harsh discrimination continues to take place in terms of marriage, employment and social status, based on these features. In many families of light-skinned mixed people, physical manifestations of African features are treated as a form of disability; darker members of the family may even be kept out of sight and socially ostracised.[64]

In recent years, signs of a crisis of state legitimacy in Réunion have been emerging. There is widespread disillusion with both local and national governments, and complete alienation among a large part of the electorate from European-level politics. There has been an accompanying reassertion of a distinctively politico-cultural creole identity, and an increasingly vociferous debate concerning the implications of ignoring creole as the first language of most Réunionnese people.[65]

In recent years, the poor and marginalised in Réunion have started to express their discontent with their position by demanding, sometimes violently, the enforcement of equal rights. In the early 1990s, riots and protests arose concerning the Radio-TV station Free-DOM, whose director Camille Sudre became a symbol for much of the discontented 'black' creole population of the capital, St Denis.[66] Demands were made for greater equality, especially for unemployed young creole men, who felt excluded from the mass consumer society emerging in Réunion.

On the whole, these signs of discontent were concerned with frustrated demands of the marginalised for
equal treatment and a decent standard of living; there was
virtually no support for independence or greater autonomy
from France. Most Réunionnese people, including those of
Afro-Malagasy origin and the most impoverished, adopt
both creole and French identities depending on the context.
They demand equal treatment in terms of state provisions
and policies, and simultaneously demand that their speci-
ficity be recognised and accommodated with regard to the
creole language and local cultural identity. As Aldrich and
Connell stated, the Réunionnese "move easily between the
metropolitan and Creole worlds".[67] On the walls of Réunion,
especially following riots in 1991 and 1992, and more
recently in 1998, it was common to see slogans in creole
demanding equality with France. *Egalite comme de Moun de
Frans*, in creole, means Equality with French people.[68]

The whole post-emancipation history of Réunion might
be regarded by some as an unusual and interesting colonial
experiment in enlightened emancipation, were it not for the
fact that moves towards greater equality were demanded by
the former slaves and contract labourers themselves. Today,
as in 1946 and prior to that in 1848, popular sentiments are
entirely behind the emancipatory strand within official state
policy emanating from the 'centre'. To this extent, the lib-
eratory discourse lurking within the Republican project,
and so often contradicted in practice, has been fully internalised by most Réunionnese, including the descendants of
people of African and Malagasy origin brought to the island
by force.

References and Notes

1. Hubert Gerbeau (1986) "La Réunion et le temps: une respiration
    insulaire", in *La Réunion dans l'Océan Indien,* CHEAM, Paris, pp.
    18-41, p. 20, author's translation.
2. Michel Robert (1976) *La Réunion: combats pour l'Autonomie,* IDOC-
    France/L'Harmattan, Paris, p. 15.
3. Auguste Toussaint (1966) *History of the Indian Ocean,* Routledge &
    Kegan Paul, London, p. 109, and also see Jean-Luc Bonniol (1995)
    "Généalogie du Paysage Réunionnais (1650-1950), *Annuaire des*

Pays de l'Océan Indien, Vol. XIII, 1992-94, pp. 151-81.

4. Andre Scherer (1980) *La Réunion*, Que Sais-Je No. 1846, Presses Universitaires Françaises, Paris, p. 32.

5. The map is reproduced from Jean Defos du Rau (1960) *L'Ile de la Réunion,* Doctoral thesis (Geography), Université de Bordeaux, published CNRS, Bordeaux, p. 298.

6. See the excellent study by Jan Nederveen Pieterse (1992) *White on Black: Images of Africa and Blacks in Western Popular Culture*, Yale University Press, New Haven-London. For Réunion, one recent study stresses the lack of positive role-images for Réunion's non-white population, and stresses that history of the island has largely been written by whites, both local-born and French, see Rose-Mary Nicole (1996) *Noirs, Cafres et Créoles: Etude de la représentation du non blanc réunionnais. Documents et littérature réunionnaise (1710-1980)* , L'Harmattan, Paris.

7. For further details on Réunion's recent history, see Helen Hintjens (1988) *Réunion, France and the EU: the State in North-South Relations*, PhD thesis in Politics, University of Aberdeen, and Helen Hintjens (1995a) *Alternatives to Independence: Explorations in Post-Colonial Relations*, Dartmouth Publishers, Aldershot, pp. 49-78.

8. Quotation from Elie Romaro (1972) "La Réunion: entre le Département et la Nation", *Revue Française d'Etudes Politiques Africaines,* No. 77, May, pp. 38-50, p. 40 and see also Paul Vergès (1993) *D'une ile au monde,* interviews with Brigitte Croisier, Ed. Harmattan, Paris who holds a similar position.

9. Details on numbers of slaves and freed population, from Scherer (1980) op. cit , p. 111. On the idea of an earthly paradise, see Bonniol (1995), op. cit.

10. Population figures from Scherer (1980) op. cit., pp. 13-14, 21. Also see Defos du Rau (1960), op. cit., pp. 142-4. On the relation between the Mascarene Islands and the slave trade in East Africa, see Roland Oliver (1991), *The Africa Experience*, Weidenfeld and Nicolson, London, p. 164.

11. Sudel Fuma (1982) *Esclaves et citoyens: le destin de 62,000 Réunionnais,* Fondation pour la Recherche et le Développment dans l'Océan Indien, St Denis (Réunion); see also Scherer (1980) op. cit. and Hai Quang Ho (1995) "Le Colonage Partiaire à la Réunion: Emergence et Evolution jusqu'en 1914", *Annuaire des Pays de l'Ocean Indien,* Vol. XIII, 1992-94, pp. 183-96.

12. Scherer, Andre (1974) *Guide des Archives de la Réunion*, Imprimerie Cazal, St Denis (Réunion), pp. 4-7; 12.

13. On abolition and the decree of 1794 see Scherer (1980) op. cit., pp. 40, 65. The slave revolt is documented by Auguste Brunet (1948) *Trois Cents Ans de Colonisation à la Réunion*, Editions de l'Empire Français, Paris, p. 158.

14. The definitive study on the revolutionary period in Réunion is the doctoral thesis by Claude Wanquet, *Histoire d'une révolution: La Réunion 1789-1803*, Thèse de doctorat, Université de Provence, 1977.

15. See Hintjens (1988) op. cit., p. 74 and Scherer (1974), p. 32.

16. Henri Cornu (1976) *Paris et Bourbon: la politique française dans l'Océan Indien*, Académie des Sciences de l'Outre-Mer, Travaux et

Mémoires No. 4, Paris, p. 33 and Fuma (1982) op. cit, p. 102.

17. See Ho (1995) op. cit., p. 184.
18. Hintjens (1988) op. cit., p. 77.
19. Figures from Fuma (1982), op. cit., p. 12 and Scherer (1974) op. cit., p. 28. Gerbeau's two estimates, the first in Hubert Gerbeau (1972) "Quelques aspects de la traite illégale des esclaves à Bourbon au XIXe siècle" unpublished conference paper presented to the Fourth Congress of the International Historical Association for the Indian Ocean, St Denis (Réunion), p. 38 and the second estimates in Gerbeau (1986) op. cit., p. 30.
20. Scherer (1980) op. cit., pp. 21, 60.
21. Scherer (1974) op. cit., p. 32 and Scherer (1980) op. cit., p. 56.
22. Quote is from Defos du Rau (1960) op. cit., p. 155. See also Ho (1995), p. 187.
23. Quotation from Karl Marx (1978) *The Poverty of Philosophy*, Foreign Languages Press, Peking, p. 105.
24. See Scherer (1980) op. cit., p. 56.
25. Information from Scherer (1980) op. cit., p. 54 and Defos du Rau (1960) op. cit, pp. 237-8.
26. Scherer (1980) op. cit., p. 57.
27. Population data by commune detailed in Fuma (1982) op. cit., p.101.
28. For discussion of the contract labourers' position, see Ho (1995) op. cit.
29. Fuma (1982) op. cit., p. 63.
30. Scherer (1974) op. cit., p. 12 and Robert (1976) op. cit., pp. 13-16
31. Quote from Bonniol (1995) op. cit., p. 168, translated by the author. On the same story see also Robert (1976) op. cit., p. 15.
32. See for this Scherer (1974) op. cit., p. 31 and Scherer (1980) op. cit., pp. 18-19.
33. Quotation from Fuma (1982) op. cit., p. 91.
34. ibid. p. 41.
35. ibid. p. 21.
36. ibid., pp. 41, 75.
37. ibid. pp. 39-40.
38. ibid., p. 32.
39. Scherer (1980) op. cit., pp. 73-4.
40. ibid., pp. 68-73 and Gerbeau (1986) op. cit., p. 34.
41. Scherer (1980) op. cit., pp. 71, 74-5.
42. Brunet (1948) op. cit., p. 148.
43. Defos du Rau (1960) op. cit., p. 196.
44. On colonage see Ho (1995) op. cit., p. 193 on colonage and quote is from Roland Lamusse (1980) "Labour Policy in the Plantation Islands", *World Development*, Vol. 8, No. 3: pp. 1035-50, p. 1036.
45. Hintjens (1988) op. cit., p. 105.
46. Philip Mason (1971) *Patterns of Dominance*, Oxford University Press, Oxford, p. 277.
47. The importance of reinserting Réunion's non-white population into mainstream accounts of local history has been noted in Nicole (1996) op. cit.
48. Scherer (1980) op. cit. pp. 88-91.
49. André Blanchet, *Le Monde*, 29.1.1949, trans. in Hintjens (1988) op. cit., p. 163.

50. Defos du Rau (1960) op. cit., pp. 483-5
51. Brunet (1948) op. cit., p. 162, and on Malagasy settlers from Réunion being relocated to France, see Alphonse Techer (1983) *Le BUMIDOM et la Migration Réunionnaise*, ANT (Agence Nationale pour le Travail) circular, Paris, p. 21.
52. Details on elections, violence and plantation politics in Scherer (1980) op. cit., pp. 86-7 and Brunet (1948) op. cit., pp. 150-54.
53. Robert (1976) op. cit., p. 21.
54. Fuma (1982) op. cit., pp. 44-46.
55. Defos du Rau (1960) op. cit., p. 483.
56. Paul Valentino, deputy of Guadeloupe, in the Constituent National Assembly Debates, 14.3.1946 author's translation. For a more detailed discussion of this period, see Helen Hintjens (1995b)"Constitutional and political change in the French Caribbean", in R. Burton & F. Reno (eds) *French and Caribbean: Martinique, Guadeloupe and French Guiana Today*, Macmillan, London: pp. 20-33, p. 23.
57. Aimé Césaire, deputy of Martinique in Constituent National Assembly Debates, 29.11.1945, author's translation. See Hintjens (1988) op. cit., p. 107.
58. Hintjens (1988) op. cit., p. 112.
59. Sylvie Jacquemart (1983) *La Question Départementale Outre-Mer*, Presses Universitaires Francaises, Paris, p. 211.
60. ibid. p. 29.
61. First quotation from *Le Monde*, 26.4 1962, see also Verges (1993) op. cit. Second quote from Jean-François Dupon (1977) *Contraintes Insulaires et Fait Colonial aux Mascareignes et aux Seychelles*, (4 vols.), Doctoral thesis (Geography), Universite Aix-Marseille II, published Librairie Honore Champion, Paris, p. 1207.
62. Jean Boyer (1978) *Le Passe Réunionnais: un Passe Francais*, La Pensée Universelle, Paris, p. 224.
63. Article in *The Sunday Times*, 1.10.1989. Also Gerbeau (1986) op. cit., pp. 21-2.
64. Hintjens (1995a) op. cit., p. 78ff.
65. ibid., pp. 59-64.
66. An interesting study on recent demands of the marginalised creoles in Réunion is Arnaud Pontus (1995) *Le Phénomène Free-DOM à l'Île de la Réunion*, Editions Simone Sudre, Rochemaure.
67. Robert Aldrich & John Connell (1992) *France's Overseas Frontier: Départements et Térritoires d'Outre-Mer*, Cambridge University Press, Cambridge, p. 177.
68. Hintjens (1995a) op. cit., p. 60 and also Pontus (1995) op. cit., pp. 118-119.

CREOLISATION AND DECOLONISATION IN THE CHANGING GEOPOLITICS OF THE INDIAN OCEAN

Jean Houbert

'Creolisation' is derived from the word 'Creole', which in the original Spanish, *criollo*, was used for: 'committed settler...one native to the settlement though not ancestrally indigenous to it.'[1] This definition fits quite well in the Indian Ocean islands of Mauritius, Réunion, Seychelles, Rodrigues, and the Chagos. None of these islands had indigenous inhabitants; willing and unwilling immigrants peopled them all. Creolisation will thus be taken to mean a variant of settler colonisation. The originality of this variant of settler colonisation was that most of the immigrants were slaves of various non-European origins who were brought together by Europeans and regimented in work on plantations in uninhabited oceanic islands. In the process new societies - Creole societies - came into being and new languages - the Creole languages - were born. The Creole societies and the Creole languages came into being, maintained themselves and grew under European colonial rule. The white slave-owners and the slaves, born in the islands under slavery, were 'native to the settlement though not ancestrally indigenous to it'. The descendants of these slave-owners and those of the slaves are the Creoles of the islands today. However, all persons who were subsequently born in the islands are not considered to be Creoles. Are Creoles only the descendants of those who were born - master or slave - in the islands in the context of slavery?

More recent immigrants from Asia or Europe, even when born in the islands for more than one generation, are not considered to be Creoles.

The islands were colonised in the context of the struggle between European states for hegemony over the Indian Ocean and trade monopolies in Asia. Decolonisation was a policy of the West as well as a process reflecting the changed configuration of political power in the global international system of the Cold War. What is the significance for the Creole islands of the redeployment of power in the changing geopolitics of the Indian Ocean? What can be the meaning of decolonisation in Creole societies? Does decolonisation amount to decreolisation? Or, on the contrary, does decolonisation mark the further integration of the societies as Creole societies?

The Indian Ocean islands that are covered in this paper are usually classified geographically as African islands, Africa being the nearest continent. A number of the slaves brought to the islands were from the African continent. In the geographical sense then the 'African Diaspora' would be an intra-African one: from the continent to its offshore islands, so to speak. Indeed, when seen on a globe or a world map, the islands look like small offshoots of Madagascar, which itself appears as an appendage of Africa.[2] The significance of geographical location for a particular country changes with the technology of transport and with the configuration of political and economic power in the international system. As will be argued, in historical terms and in their present structures, these islands form a little New World in the Indian Ocean, a world away from Africa: they have more in common with the distant West Indies than with their non-Creole neighbours.

Creolisation

The Mascareignes, the Seychelles and the Chagos - the Creole islands of the Indian Ocean -are unique in the region in being entirely creations of the colonial phenomenon. The societies, the economies, the polities, the very flora and fauna of these islands are the direct results of colonisation during the past four centuries. Distant Europe, rather than Africa or Asia, colonised these islands precisely because of their location in the middle of the Indian Ocean; for although the sailors of the littoral had navigated the Indian Ocean for countless centuries before the arrival of Europeans, they had usually kept to the northern part of the ocean, where the seasonal reversal of the monsoons facilitated navigation.[3] When the sailors and merchants of the littoral ventured south of the equator it was along the coast of Africa into the Mozambique Channel, seldom into the cyclone-prone region full of reefs and sand banks to the east of Madagascar. Moreover, the uninhabited islands of that perilous part of the ocean had no attraction for the merchants. Arab and Swahili-speaking migrants from the coast of East Africa peopled the Comoro islands and frequented the northern part of Madagascar. The Indonesians who peopled Madagascar, before the arrival of Islam in Southeast Asia, might have crossed the Indian Ocean to the south of the equator. If they did they probably saw some of the Seychelles islands, but there is no evidence that these proto-Malagasy landed in the Seychelles on the way to the Great Island. It is more likely that the Indonesians crossed the Indian Ocean to the north, perhaps in stages, using the monsoons, stopping for long in East Africa, and mixing with the local peoples, before settling in Madagascar. This will account for the African phenotype of many Malagasy. What is certain is that the Seychelles, the Chagos and the Mascareignes were uninhabited when the European colonisers arrived.[4]

European colonies can be divided into two categories: 'settler colonies' and 'non-settler colonies'. In its original meaning, in Greek antiquity, a 'colony' was a group of settlers who left their parent city-state to settle in an uninhabited land and form a new city-state. Cultural and sentimental links were kept with the parent state but no political domination was involved. In modern history this form of colonisation is not found in its pure form because two important elements were present: indigenous inhabitants already occupied the land where the colonists settled and the parent state kept its political rule over the settlers. The Creole islands of

the Indian Ocean formed an exception to the first but not to
the second of these factors. The dynamics of European settler colonisation-decolonisation overseas, and, in the unique
case of Russia, overland, has radically changed the course of
modern history and transformed the world. When the
European settlers were numerous and powerful, decolonisation overseas, without exception, took the form of transfer of sovereignty from the parent state to the settlers. This
could be brought about by the settlers using force, as was
the case for the United States, or peacefully, as was the case
in Australia or Canada. Decolonisation did not put an end to
the domination of the settlers over the indigenous inhabitants. On the contrary, once the restraint imposed by the
parent state had gone, the powerful settlers were free to find
a 'final solution to the native problem'. The settlers thus
became the new natives, so to speak: Americans,
Australians. In the unique case of the territorially immense
European settler colony overland in Eurasia, decolonisation
was through integration with the Russian parent state.[5]

Power at sea was the precondition of Europe's overseas
colonial expansion. The age of discovery was first and
foremost the European 'discovery of the sea'.[6] The discovery that all the seas of the planet are interconnected, forming one global body of salt water on which it was possible
for Europeans to sail to all parts of the world. This took
place very rapidly: when Columbus embarked on his historic
voyage in 1492, Europeans had not crossed any oceans, yet
only thirty years later, in 1522, one of Magellan's ships
returned to Europe, having gone right round the world and
crossed all the oceans. Almost as rapidly as the Europeans
discovered the sea, they imposed their hegemony over all
the oceans of the planet. Innovations in maritime technology, most notably the building of artillery into the hull of
ships, thus transforming them into floating fortresses, rather
than being just platforms for the infantry, gave the
Europeans a compelling advantage over the maritime activities of other civilisations. The gunned-sailing ships of
Atlantic-Europe drove the ships of the non-Europeans out of
the seas of the world.[7] As the sea makes up over two-thirds
of the surface of the planet, the Europeans, through the

exercise of sea power, acquired a global reach early on in modernity. Europe in effect extended its frontiers to the shorelines of the other continents. The sea power that the West acquired in these early days of modernity has been retained to the present day, with one of Europe's erstwhile settler-colonies, the United States, now playing the leading part.

European hegemony over the sea was translated immediately into colonial power over the land in the Americas. In Asia, when the Europeans first arrived on the coast, the indigenous civilisations were much too powerful on land to be conquered by a handful of *conquistadors,* thousands of miles from Europe. At first, the Europeans seldom ventured inland in Asia beyond the reach of their naval guns. In Asia, and likewise in Africa, unlike America, it was the Europeans who had no resistance to the local diseases. Besides, the objective of the Europeans in Asia and in Africa, initially, was trade rather than conquest and colonisation. Power at sea, plus a few fortified enclaves on the coasts, were sufficient. Europe, however, was not one political entity but was subdivided into sovereign states frequently at war with one another. Wars in which, increasingly, hegemony over the seas and trade monopolies in Asia and Africa became important stakes. The erosion and eventual collapse of the indigenous authorities also drew the Europeans into political involvement in Asia and Africa. The time came when, with industrialisation, the power of Europe became irresistible. The only choice left to the non-Europeans was to adopt the institutions which had made Europe rich and powerful, in particular the modern state and the capitalist mode of production, or have modernity imposed through European colonial rule. Japan was the only non-European state which succeeded in modernising itself rapidly enough to join the ranks of European colonial powers and, indeed, eventually to defeat them in Asia.[8]

The word 'colony', from its original usage of settler colony, came to be applied to this altogether different phenomenon: the imperial rule of European states over the peoples of Asia and Africa. In Africa, some European settlers were present, but they were not sufficiently numerous, rel-

ative to the indigenous inhabitants, to make settler colonisation irreversible in the long term. On the whole, in Asia
(with the major exception of Russia in Eurasia, and the very
special case of Israel) and in Africa, the 'colonies' were non-
settler colonies. In this kind of colony, a few European
administrators, soldiers, and entrepreneurs exercised political and economic power with the collaboration of indigenous elite groups. The term 'decolonisation' has come to be
used primarily for the ending, since the Second World War,
of that form of rule by foreigners in Asia and Africa.

The European colonisers did not just rule in Asia and
Africa; they also performed the function of transferring elements of the two outstanding institutions of modernity to
these continents: the capitalist mode of production and
the modern state. This function was accompanied by an ideology of 'progress': Asia and Africa were to be transformed
in the image of Europe. Through the 'civilising mission' of
Europe, modern nation-states resting on prosperous capitalism would eventually come into being in Asia and Africa.
In this respect the European left was as 'colonialist' as the
right. Marx was if anything even more certain of the 'progressive' role of Europe in Asia and Africa than the colonisers on the ground.[9] With decolonisation, the United States
and the Soviet Union took on the 'white man's burden' by
vying with each other for 'developing' the new states in Asia
and Africa.

The Creole islands were settler colonies, but they were
a very distinctive variant of settler colonies in the middle of
an ocean that eventually came to be surrounded by non-settler colonies. Born of the expansion of maritime Europe, like
other settler colonies, the Creole islands were original, *sui
generis*, in two fundamental respects: there were no precolonial indigenous inhabitants and they were peopled
under European colonial rule but largely by non-European
settlers. Unlike other European settler colonies, the Creole
islands of the Indian Ocean had no indigenous hunter-gath-
erers to be hunted down to extinction,[10] no subsistence
peasantry to be displaced and their lands appropriated by
settlers. No genocide marked the birth of the Creole islands.
On the contrary, the European colonisers were only able to

conquer the natural environment and make permanent settlements by bringing in 'unwilling immigrants'. Africans were among the slaves who were brought to the islands. It is in the context of slavery and the slave trade that the 'African Diaspora' entered the Creole islands.

The European colonisers did not invent slavery; it was endemic in Africa and in Madagascar.[11] The Europeans articulated this indigenous institution with mercantile capitalism, which gave rise to a massive movement of populations over long distances. The vast bulk of the Africans who were shipped out as slaves went across the Atlantic to people the New World.[12] Africans had also been shipped out as slaves in a much older trade in the Indian Ocean. This was part of the age-old monsoon trade system between Africa and Asia in which the Arab merchants had a leading role.[13] The Europeans tapped this ancient trade in African slaves to get a labour force for the Creole islands of the Indian Ocean. The little New World, however, gave rise to a new slave trade in the Indian Ocean, similar in some respects to that of the Atlantic.

The wind systems over the oceans determined the trade routes in the days of sail. Shipping slaves across the Atlantic from West Africa to America was relatively easy with the trade winds. In the Indian Ocean it was not difficult, at the right time of the year, to take slaves from East Africa to the Middle East and on to India with the monsoon. It was much more difficult to get the slaves from Africa to the Mascareignes islands. Although they are relatively near Africa, these Creole islands were isolated from that continent by the prevailing winds and currents. The sea route from Europe to Asia which the Portuguese pioneered took the ships out in the Atlantic well off West Africa, almost to the coast of Brazil, before turning to round the Cape of Good Hope, then up the Mozambique Channel and to catch the monsoon off Mombassa to India.[14] It was not necessary for this route to touch the mainland of Africa, although the ships did call to take ivory, gold, and sometimes slaves, on the way to Asia. Some islands in the Atlantic and in the Mozambique Channel became convenient watering places on that route, but not the islands to the east of Madagascar.

It was on the return journey from Asia to Europe that the ships followed a route that took them close to what became the Creole islands. The wind system of the Indian Ocean made it easier to go from Asia to the Creole islands and from these islands to Africa, than the other way round. The reasons why it was Madagascar and Africa, and not Asia, that initially provided the bulk of the slaves for the islands have to do with the shipping policy of the French East India Company, the attitude of the local indigenous authorities and the proximity of Madagascar. On the return journeys to Europe, the Company wanted to maximise profits by filling the ships with valuable Asiatic goods, thus leaving no space for slaves.[15] The Company also had existing slave trading posts in West Africa, where the indigenous authorities were more co-operative than in Asia. Above all, the French succeeded in developing a profitable source of slaves on the east coast of Madagascar.

The Dutch and the French, who were the first Europeans to attempt to colonise the Creole islands, did not always take the traditional route through the Mozambique Channel on the way to Asia. To go to Indonesia after rounding the Cape, the Dutch found that it was easier to go round the south of Madagascar. This route took them near the Creole islands and they made two attempts at settling Mauritius.They first landed on the island in 1598 but occupied it in 1638, naming it after their *stadhouder* Mauritz of Nassau, but abandoned the island twenty years later. In 1664 the Dutch tried again to settle Mauritius but in 1710 they abandoned the idea. The principal reasons why the Dutch did not succeed in making a permanent settlement in Mauritius are that the Cape, which had been occupied in 1652, proved a better half-way station for them between Europe and Indonesia. The Creole islands were too far north for the 'roaring forties'; the westerly winds that the Dutch increasingly used to get to Indonesia after rounding the Cape. Moreover, the Dutch never had sufficient European settlers and slaves to cope with the natural environment; although they did succeed in cutting down and exporting the more accessible ebony trees. The Dutch East India Company gave priority to settling the Cape and wanted the slaves they obtained from

Madagascar to be transported to the Cape rather than to Mauritius. The Dutch introduced slavery and the sugar cane to Mauritius; when they abandoned the island definitively, two runaway slaves were left behind. Unlike the dodo, which did not survive the Dutch, the two maroon slaves did. These two maroons can thus be said to have started the human occupation of Mauritius on a permanent basis. Meanwhile, the French had begun to colonise Réunion in 1663.[16]

The French, like the Dutch, and unlike the Portuguese and the British, used the route to the east of Madagascar, rather than the Mozambique Channel, on the way to Asia. From very early on, 1601-1604, the French were interested in Madagascar and at one point, in 1642, made an attempt at starting a settler colony at Fort Dauphin, on the east coast of the Great Island. In 1638, on the way to Madagascar, an expedition of the *Compagnie Particulière de Navigation* had ' taken possession' of Réunion and Rodrigues.[17] The settlement at Fort Dauphin was a disastrous failure and the survivors were taken to the then uninhabited Réunion - known at first as Mascarin, then Bourbon and finally Réunion. A few Malagasy came with these first French settlers. In 1664, Colbert created the French East India Company with the intention of reinvigorating French trade in Asia. The Company was, according to its charter, to have a monopoly of French trade with Asia but was not to trade in slaves. Réunion was idealised in Europe at the time, as an example of what the uncorrupted 'state of nature' was like.[18] Yet Réunion was the first of the islands in which 'creolisation' took place. Unlike Madagascar, Réunion proved well suited for a settler colony: there were no 'unfriendly natives' and no diseases. The Europeans and the slaves, who were sometimes near death on arrival, recovered rapidly. This was attributed at the time to the climate of the island. In fact it was the fruits and vegetables which restored those suffering from scorbutic illnesses after a long sea voyage. The island had plenty of fresh water and food crops, including European varieties, which grew well. Réunion therefore would have been a good watering place for the ships of the French East India Company on the way to or from India, except that it did not have a good harbour. Réunion was also to the leeward of Mauritius and that, in the hands of an enemy power, could present a threat to the colony. Therefore, as soon as the Company knew that the Dutch had departed, the French took possession of Mauritius in 1715. From Mauritius, the French explored the other uninhabited islands of the region and occupied the Seychelles in 1742.

The French succeeded, where the Dutch had failed, in making permanent settlements in the Creole islands, because they had more settlers and slaves. Under the pressing need to get a labour force for the islands the prohibition to trade in slaves was discarded. The islands also became more important to the French than to the Dutch, in that they were their only halfway station to Asia. For the European powers, and for their respective monopoly companies, the oceanic islands were less ends in themselves than logistical means on the way to the fabulous riches of Asia. The real goals were trade monopolies in Asiatic goods and hegemony over the Indian Ocean.

The French colonised the Creole islands in the context of the long duel with Britain for empire in India and control of the Indian Ocean.[19] When the fortunes of war turned against France in the Indian subcontinent, the islands became the principal French military base in the Indian Ocean. First under the French East India Company, with Mahé de Labourdonnais as Governor-General of the islands from 1735 to 1746, a real insular system was organised in a bid to regain control in India and over the Indian Ocean. In 1764, the Company being ruined by the wars, the French government took over and the successive authorities of the Ancien Régime, the French Revolution and Napoleon continued the policy of using the islands as their military stronghold in the Indian Ocean. Mauritius was the centrepiece of the military insular system, ideally suited for a naval base because of its two natural harbours, Port Louis and Grand-Port (Mahebourg). Within that system the function of the other islands was to supply the central base in Mauritius. Réunion and Rodrigues provided food, while the Seychelles and the Chagos provided timber for shipbuilding and repairs, as well as acting as forward bases giving early warning of the presence of the English fleet. A strategy based on oceanic islands called for superior sea power, however, and France never achieved this. The corsairs based at Port Louis and the occasional larger ship sent over from France, were an irritant but made little difference to the position of Britain in India and to Britain's command of the Indian Ocean. Without a superior French fleet in the Indian Ocean, the base in Mauritius was ultimately at the mercy of British sea power. The battle of Grand-Port, shortly before the decisive British assault on Mauritius in 1810, was the only sea battle that the French won against the British during the Napoleonic era. This victory had no consequence for the final outcome of the confrontation between Britain and France in the islands, but is commemorated by a plaque under the *Arc de Triomphe* in Paris. The long–delayed capture of the Creole islands by the British put an end to the French threat in the Indian Ocean, but not to the presence of France in the islands.[20]

The period of almost 150 years under French rule (1663-1810) was critically important not only because all the Creole islands were under one authority but also because these were the crucial years when the Creole societies emerged and the Creole language was created. These essential features have remained, in spite of the successive dismemberment of the insular entity, and of Britain's replacement of France in all the islands except Réunion. The Seychelles had capitulated to a British squadron in 1795 but the opportunist local administrator flew the French or the English flag, depending on the war ships that visited the islands, until news of the fall of Mauritius was received.[21] Rodrigues and Réunion were taken by the combined land forces of the British East India Company and the Royal Navy shortly before the final assault on the base in Mauritius in December 1810. Britain had captured Mauritius for a negative military strategic reason: to deprive France of a base from which it had harassed British shipping. In control of India and the Cape and with dominant sea power, Britain had little need of Mauritius as a base. Indeed at the end of the Napoleonic wars, hegemonic Britain was quite reluctant

to acquire any more colonies. Sri Lanka and, after hesita-
tions, the Cape were annexed but Indonesia was returned to
the Dutch. After Waterloo, and the restoration of the monarchy in France, Britain was anxious to see the legitimacy of
the Bourbons accepted; French colonial possessions judged
not to be of significance could be returned. Réunion did not
have a good harbour and, being to leeward of Mauritius,
presented no danger in the days of sail to the British position in the islands, and so was returned to France. In 1715,
France had annexed Mauritius for the security of Réunion.
Now, one hundred years later, in 1815, Réunion was
returned to France because it posed no threat to the security
of Mauritius. All the other Creole islands, including the
Seychelles, Rodrigues and the Chagos, then became parts of
the British Crown colony of Mauritius. The insular strategic
system had lost its *raison d'être*, however, with the British
conquest. From a naval base and commercial entrepot of
Asiatic goods captured on British ships, Mauritius became a
sugar plantation. The 'dependencies' of Mauritius:
Seychelles, Rodrigues, Chagos, Agalega, Saint Brandon lost
their roles of supplying the base in Port Louis and, not being
suited to growing sugar, fell into almost complete oblivion
for over a century.

By the time of the British take over it is estimated that
some 160,000 slaves had been brought to the islands.[22] Of
these 45 % came from Madagascar (mostly shipped out of
the east coast); 40 % from the East African coast
(Mozambique and the Arab trading posts: Kilwa, Zanzibar,
Mombassa, in particular); 13 % were from the Indian sub-
continent; and 2 % from West Africa (mostly shipped out of
Goree in Senegal). It appears from these figures that an
equal number of African and Malagasy slaves arrived in the
islands during the crucial French period. It is not only the
numbers that are important for understanding creolisation,
however, but also the time of arrival in the islands. Many
more Malagasy than Africans came in the earlier part of the
period, under the East India Company. A good proportion
of these Malagasy slaves, however, probably had African
antecedent.[23] The descendants of the Malagasy and those of
the Africans have largely merged forming the black Creoles.

The East India Company brought a few slaves from West Africa during that early period. The French had trading posts in West Africa for slaves shipped out to the West Indies. Occasionally a ship bound for the Indian Ocean was diverted to West Africa to take some slaves. This was not economical because the mortality rate of the slaves was high due to the long voyage. The French acquired a virtual monopoly of the slave trade on the east coast of Madagascar. Not only were prices kept low but also slaves could be paid for with cloth, beads, trinkets, above all with guns, thus saving the scarce *piastres*.[24] On the East African coast, the Portuguese as well as the Arabs, insisted on receiving monetary payments. Because of the prevailing winds, getting back to the Mascareignes from the East African coast, meant a long journey via the Seychelles or, alternatively, after exiting the Mozambique Channel, going well to the south of Madagascar. In the latter part of the French period, and after the British had taken over, the proportion of slaves arriving from the coast of East Africa increased.

Creolisation was significantly affected but was not transformed by the French Revolution and the British conquest of the islands. These two events took place at the time when the demand for labour in the islands was increasing as the plantations developed. The fate of the indigenous inhabitants has often been a cause of conflict between settlers and their parent states in settler colonies. In the Creole islands this conflict was over slavery and the slave trade. At first, the French Revolution had had an extremely enthusiastic response in the islands. The white settlers, who were soon dominated by the local Jacobins, elected a Colonial Assembly and the powers of the Governor from the *Ancien Régime* were practically eliminated. The islands were virtually independent under this Assembly until Bonaparte reinstated colonial rule in 1803. In February 1794, Paris declared the abolition of slavery in all French colonies and two Commissioners of the Republic arrived in Port Louis in June 1796 to impose the abolition decree. Although the Commissioners had arrived on a war ship and were accompanied by an armed guard they were forced to sail away having totally failed in their mission. Three years before the capture of the islands, the House of Commons had voted for the cessation of the slave trade under the British flag. From the point of view of the slave-owners this was not as bad as the French Revolution's project of ending slavery itself. The treaty of capitulation of 1810 stipulated that the inhabitants would keep their properties, their religion, their customs, and their laws. The major and most valuable part of the properties of the inhabitants was their slaves. The *Code Noire* was a core element of their laws. The first British administrators were keen to win the collaboration of the French-speaking settlers and did not manifest any zeal in preventing the importation of new slaves. Mauritius having lost its seafaring military and commercial roles, the British administrators encouraged the ex-corsairs and merchants to turn to the land. Sugar plantations would make the island pay for itself and provide the revenues for the maintenance of the British administration and the British troops garrisoned there. Sugar plantations called for a large labour force and this required more slaves. Although the white settlers were never to regain the autonomous power they had enjoyed with their Colonial Assembly, they were not too dissatisfied with British colonial rule so long as it guaranteed their properties, a market for sugar, plentiful and cheap labour, and did not interfere with their customs and their laws.

Any hope that the slaves might have entertained that the French Revolution meant their liberation was dashed when, unlike what happened in Saint Domaingue, the power of the white settlers was reinforced under the Colonial Assembly. The arrival of the British likewise, on which the slaves had put great store, was a bitter disappointment. The British forces crushed a slave uprising in Réunion soon after they arrived. Indeed, during the five years, 1810-1815, that the British occupied Réunion, they formed a regiment, the Bourbon regiment, which specialised in putting down 'slave unrest'. The Bourbon regiment, in which young white Creoles enlisted as officers, at times with some of their slaves, who served in the ranks, was active not only in the Indian Ocean islands but also in the West Indies. Lieutenant-

Colonel Keating, who had taken Réunion in 1810, and who was supposed to stop the entry of new slaves into the island, was himself a slave-owner who later came back to Réunion, after it had been returned to France, and settled as a planter. In Mauritius, the first British Governor, Sir Robert Farquhar, an old hand of the East India Company, not only turned a blind eye to the importation of slaves but is reputed to have personally invested in the trade. After Réunion went back to France the pretext could be used that as the ships bringing in the slaves flew the French flag they could not be arrested. The prohibition of the slave trade, although there was no eagerness to enforce it, was significant nonetheless in modifying the relative importance of the regions from which the slaves were imported and the type of ship used as well as the prices paid for the slaves.

The slave population of the islands was not selfsustaining. Slave-owners in the islands did not engage in slave breeding on any scale. Before the ban on the slave trade it was cheaper to import new slaves rather than breeding them in the islands. There was always a shortage of women as mainly male slaves were imported. Although the shortage of white women was even more marked and resulted in a good deal of interbreeding between the white masters and their female slaves, the ensuing children being the property of the slave-owners, these children were often freed. The British navy at sea was keener than the administrators in the islands to enforce the prohibition of the slave trade, not least because there was a bonus paid for capturing slavers. An Admiralty court was set up in Mauritius that frequently condemned the ships found guilty of bringing in slaves. The Admiralty court was one of the rare means of bypassing the judicial system of the islands that had been left almost unchanged. Manned by white Creole judges, who were themselves slave-owners, the local courts interpreted the capitulation terms of 1810 extensively and stood firmly by the *Code Noire.* Slaves were brought in and landed at night on deserted beaches and rapidly taken to the *habitations* where the British soldiers were reluctant to go and search. Much smaller ships were used so that if caught by the Royal Navy fewer slaves would be lost. The ships built locally did not cost much and could easily be replaced; in some cases the owners succeeded in buying the ships back after they had been found guilty of slaving by the Admiralty court.

More significantly, the slave trade moved away from the east coast of Madagascar to the Mozambique Channel. In Madagascar, the British had succeeded in reinforcing the 'nations' of the interior of the island against those trading in slaves on the east coast. Under Radama I, the Merina nation extended its hegemony over large parts of the Great Island. Radama was persuaded to curtail the number of slaves reaching the coast. As a result prices increased and it became economical for the Creole slavers to buy in East Africa, despite the much longer and difficult voyages for the small ships. In East Africa, the Portuguese as well as the Arabs could not be persuaded to halt the very lucrative slave trade. One method used to mitigate the ban on the trade was to take slaves from East Africa to Seychelles, which was on the route that the slavers had to take because of the winds; from Seychelles (then a part of Mauritius) the transfer of the slaves to the Mascareignes was said to be an internal one and therefore did not come under the illegal slave trade. Large numbers of slaves were thus taken to Mauritius and to Réunion via Seychelles. Sometimes the newly arrived Africans would be kept in Seychelles and in exchange slaves already creolised in Mahe would be taken to the Mascareignes. Endeavouring to curtail the introduction of new slaves, London had ordered Farquhar to open a Slave Registry in which all the slaves already in the islands would be registered. But the Slave Registrar became very popular with the slave-owners for interpreting his duties as doing nothing. It is estimated that some 43,000 slaves were taken illegally into Réunion before abolition in 1848. British abolitionists of the 1820s held that some 40,000 illegal slaves had been introduced in Mauritius since 1810. One abolitionist went as far as saying that the slave population of Mauritius, standing at 60,000 when the British took over, had all been worked out and replaced illegally several times over by the time of abolition in 1833-4.

It is probable that most of the slaves brought in illegally in the islands were Africans. These slaves were shipped from

East Africa, but many had reached the coast after long forced marches from widely separated regions deep in the interior of the continent. The dispersed places from which the Africans originated, the small size societies in which they had lived, their young age, the fact that they were enslaved as single individuals and not as family groups, and the relatively late stage of slavery in the islands by the time that they arrived, all made it unlikely that much of their cultures of origin would survive in creolisation. There was no call for genocide in the little New World of the Indian Ocean but the process of creolisation was an effective ethnocide. This was thoroughgoing at the linguistic level and less so in some other aspects of culture. Under the *Code Noire* slaves had to be baptised in the Catholic faith. To this day Creoles with slavery antecedents are among the most fervent Catholics. Music and dancing were not detrimental to the interests of the slave-owners and were encouraged, even on board the slave ships. Elements of the music of Africa, combined with music of other origins, have survived in the islands. In the more material aspects of culture, the European settlers were, in the very early stage in the *habitations*, in some respects, more dependent on the slaves, who were familiar with tropical environments, than the slaves were on them. The Malagasy in particular but also the Indo-Portuguese have left their marks in early Creole houses, which were built entirely with vegetal materials, in basketry, in cooking, in food preservation, in the techniques for fishing in the rivers and the lagoons. These and other elements of material cultures in the islands can be traced back to non-European milieus. However, these elements have been transformed through creolisation and do not bear much resemblance now to the cultures from which they originated.

Creolisation as a variant of settler colonisation was an aspect of early capitalism. Whereas in Asia and Africa the capitalism that the Europeans brought at first was purely trade-capitalism, in the settler colonies capitalism came as a mode of production. The plantation, although initially based on a slave labour force, was an early form of the capitalist mode of production.[25] In the islands, unlike in Asia and in Africa, where capitalism only engaged in trading at first and not in production, capitalism had to start in production simply because no other modes of production were present. The modes of production, which had structured the societies from which the slaves originated in Madagascar, in Africa, could not be reconstructed in the islands under plantation slavery. Likewise the kind of political formations which the slaves had known before being captured and transported could not be recreated in the islands under European colonial rule. The two outstanding institutions of modernity, the capitalist mode of production and the colonial variant of the modern state, which in Asia and Africa colonialism eventually superimposed on pre-existing modes of production and political formations, these institutions found virgin soil in the islands and grew unencumbered.

There is a controversy in the literature about the islands regarding Creoles as languages. Some linguists, such as Philip Baker, argue that there was an important African input, particularly from West Africa, in the origin of the Creole language of Mauritius. Also that the Creole language of Mauritius developed independently of that of Réunion. Robert Chaudenson, on the other hand, provides a more plausible argument for the Creole language originating in Réunion and then being transplanted in Mauritius and Seychelles[26]. There is no space here for more than a brief summary of Chaudenson's rich thesis. At first, for some fifty years in Réunion, the French settlers - lower class, mostly males, from the western provinces of Brittany and Normandy - were as numerous as the slaves. The slaves, males and females from Madagascar, were all very young - 10 to 15 - and settlers and slaves lived very closely together, isolated on the *habitations*[27] and experienced a common poverty in the new raw environment, for long periods without any contact with distant France. At that early stage of colonisation, the only language in use was the *langue d'oil*[28] variant of French spoken by the illiterate settlers. The young slaves were rapidly acculturated in this poor French culture. Sexual relations between male settlers and female slaves produced a number of children of mixed race some of whom were freed. The language of the white settlers in being imitated by the slaves was creolised to some extent but it was still recognisably French. Had the colonial circumstances remained the same, Creole as a language would not have become autonomous from French.

With the development of the plantations, however, a large labour force was required and the slaves gradually outnumbered the settlers. Unlike the *habitations*, the plantations created a marked distance between the masters and the slaves. Contacts between the French and the large number, but culturally very heterogeneous, newly arrived slaves - called *Bossals*[29] – were few, when compared with what had been the case in the earlier period on the *habitations*. The slaves of that earlier period, including the children of the settlers with the slaves, played a decisive part in the emergence of Creole - the society as well as the language. The *Bossals* adopted as their model not the masters, with whom they had little contact, but the *habitation* slaves. The elements of the French language which the *habitation* slaves had assimilated from the settlers, and which they used in directing the *Bossals* on the plantations, were further modified in being copied by the *Bossals*. The language that the *Bossals* came to speak was thus twice removed from the French spoken by the settlers on the *habitations*: an imitation of an imitation. In the process, the French language was restructured and became a new language: Creole. Creole is thus a language that has crystallised out of French in two stages: the *habitation* stage and the plantation stage.

Chaudenson also points out that Creole is not a language that developed out of a pidgin.[30] A pidgin is a contact language which eliminates intercommunication problems between two groups which have, outside the specific context in which they interact, usually the market place, their own language and culture. To argue that a pidgin had preceded the Creole language in the islands it is necessary to assume that the slaves formed a group or groups with their own language(s) and culture(s) that they were able to keep in the colonial situation. This was manifestly not the case. On arrival in the islands the slaves were linguistically and culturally extremely heterogeneous. What is more it was in the interests of the newly arrived slaves to be creolised as rapidly as possible. This was not only in order to be able to understand what was required of them in their new environment but also to become part of Creole society.[31] The slave plantation was an organised 'total institution' in which the white master was dominant in every respect: legal, economical, sexual even, and those who could not speak Creole were at the bottom of the hierarchy. To remain 'African' in that context would be to have the worst of the tasks on the plantations with their concomitant punishments. Of course, there always were maroons, but they were seldom *Bossals*. The slaves who left the plantations and took to the forests and mountains were Creoles who had a good knowledge of the country. Maroon life was not sustainable for long: lack of food and the relentless pursuit of the maroon-hunters soon brought back those who had not voluntarily returned to the plantations. The story of newly arrived Africans taking to the forests and presenting a real challenge to the plantation system of the islands is a present day myth. The maroons, perhaps a maximum of 10% of total slave population, never had an alternative project and an ideology to replace that of plantation slavery.

When Mauritius was colonised by the French, the East India Company insisted that a number of Creole white-settlers and Creole slaves from Réunion be sent to the new colony to teach the new settlers arriving from France and the *Bossals* how to cope with their new environment. The Réunionais brought with them to Mauritius their Creole language that had already been formed. The new colony could thus go straight into the plantation stage of creolisation with the advantage of an already existing Creole language. Initially then the Creole of Mauritius was much closer to the Creole of Réunion than it is today. In Réunion, enough of the *habitation* stage of the language has survived to make its Creole closer to French than is the case for the Creoles of the other islands. The French language has itself been standardised so that today it is quite different from the *langue d'oil* spoken by the illiterate settlers of Réunion in the 17th century.

In time the new Creole language became the language spoken by all, from the white planter at the top to the Creole slaves, to the *Bossals* on the plantations. The French language did not cease to exist in the islands, however. The masters, and some of the *habitation* slaves, in particular the children of the white settlers with the slave women, became bilingual in French and Creole. Thus language in the Creole society became closely associated with legal status in the period of slavery and, when slavery was abolished, with the class and colour hierarchy. To this day, monolingual Creole speakers are at the bottom of the hierarchy; all upwardly mobile Creoles in the social hierarchy become bilingual speakers of French. French is highly valued as the language associated with wealth, power and prestige; while Creole, associated with its origin in slavery, and with the lower class, is despised - although it is the language spoken by all, and one of the few genuine cultural creations of the islanders. Only the Seychelles, under the one-party 'progressive' regime, have made Creole an official language. Perhaps this is a sign of 'real decolonisation'; an issue which will be discussed later on in this paper.

The slave-owners had succeeded, with the collusion of the colonial authorities, in limiting the effects on their way of life of the abrogation of the slave trade. The abolition of slavery itself, as the slave-owners saw it, was a threat not only to their property but to the only kind of life they knew. The colonial powers, Britain then France, pressed for abolition at the time when, with sugar booming, the plantations' demand for labour had become insatiable. The loss of Saint Domingue meant that a large share of the French market for sugar went to Réunion. Farquhar had exercised his influence in the House of Commons for the equalisation of duties on Mauritius sugar entering the British market with those of the West Indies. If it could be argued that abolition in the West Indies was in Britain's economic interest, as the soils of its sugar colonies there, after the long period of production, were exhausted; this could not be applied to Mauritius that was still fresh.[32] Moral considerations more than economics swayed the colonial powers over abolition. The abolitionists, good bourgeois moralists, took increasingly strong objections to the violence involved in slavery. At first it was thought that reforms could so ameliorate the conditions of the slaves that the institution could be kept for its economic benefits. If reforms meant the removal of violence then there were limits beyond which they could not go. It is not that the slave-owners were particularly violent and cruel but that violence was written in the economic logic of slavery. The master-slave relationship could be a paternalist relationship. It was the articulation of slavery within an over-all capitalist mode of production that made a certain amount of violence inescapable in plantation slavery. In his own interest the slave-owner had to feed, dress, and house his slaves. The slaves were perfectly conscious that their keep was secure. To maximise the extraction of labour out of the slaves, therefore, the owner had to use the threat of physical violence.

It is only when labour is 'free' that physical coercion becomes unnecessary; that is when the worker must sell the only 'commodity' that he possesses, his labour power, in order to get the means for reproducing that labour power.[33] Proletariat labour was not available in the islands and that is why slavery was institutionalised in the first place. The most difficult task of 'development' is to turn the peasants of a pre-capitalist mode of production into a proletariat. Slavery in the islands, as it has turned out, was a short cut in making the peasants of Madagascar, of Africa, of India, into a Creole proletariat. The peasants who stayed behind in their homelands, to this day, are still peasants and are thus behind in 'development' when compared to the Creoles. At the time of abolition, however, it was thought that a transition stage was necessary from slavery to 'free' labour: the slaves had to serve an 'apprenticeship' on the plantations after abolition. The exploitation of Indian indentured labour, however, proved so profitable that the planters raised no objections to the 'apprentices' deserting the plantations. Remarkably little concern was shown by the abolitionists for the fate of what had become in effect a redundant black proletariat in Mauritius and, to a lesser extent, in Réunion.

The slave-owners, particularly those in Mauritius, had put up a show of resistance to abolition. At one point there was even an attempt at a repeat performance of 1796, when they had forced Baco and Burnel, the two anti-slavery Commissioners of the French Republic, to re-embark with all speed. The British pro-abolitionist Secretary of State had sent John Jeremie - who had made himself notable in the West Indies with his *Four Essays on Colonial Slavery* in which he ridiculed the *Code Noire* - to Mauritius in 1832 to be the first non-Creole Procurer General. Jeremie, like Baco and Burnel, had arrived on a war ship and soldiers with fixed bayonets lined the way as he walked up the Place d'Armes to Government House. The slave-owners, white and non-white together for once, who had mustered a volunteer force, successfully opposed the appointment of Jeremie. The arrival of Jeremie had also added to the nervousness felt in Réunion about abolition since the Revolution of 1830 in Paris. The slave owners of the 'Sister Island' talked of sending an armed force to Mauritius to help their cousins drive out the 'sinister man Jeremie'. There was a plan to ambush the British garrison and turn Mauritius into an independent Ile de France. However, the Grand Port rebellion in the end never got off the ground. In typical Creole style there was a great deal of talk but there was really no will to secede from the British Empire. The slave-owners were really after the maximum indemnity payment for the emancipation of their slaves. Within the British Empire the planters had a vast market for their sugar and by 1834, when abolition came into effect in Mauritius, an alternative source of labour had already been found: the massive importation of cheap indentured Indians.

The scale of the Indian immigration after the abolition of slavery had dwarfed all previous human arrivals in the islands. Some 450,000 Indians came to Mauritius as indentured workers and most of them settled down. By 1885, when Indian immigration was stopped, 117,813 Indians had entered Réunion. Although the Seychelles, Rodrigues and the Chagos, not being suited to growing sugar, did not receive many Indians they were, as dependencies of Mauritius, affected by the transformation of the population of the principal island of the group. The ethnic composition of Mauritius was radically and permanently changed by the arrival of the Indians. Before 1830 Indians represented a small fraction of the population; thirty years later people of Indian origin made up two-thirds of the total population of the island and

this proportion has remained to the present day. The indentured Indians, unlike the slaves, came as family groups, and
thus had a better chance of salvaging elements of their
own cultures. Indians were not converted to Christianity in
any number. The Hindu and the Islamic faiths of the indentured workers have remained alive in Mauritius. But it would
be wrong to think that the new immigrants were not affected
by creolisation. The Indians replaced the slaves on the
sugar plantations and thus became part of the production
structure of Mauritius. The reproduction of the self-sufficient
agricultural village of the Asiatic mode of production in
Mauritius was out of the question.

Social mobility was not impossible in the rigid, post-slav-
ery Creole society, and from very early on the Indians
became differentiated by social class. Under British administration it was possible for Indians to buy land in Mauritius.
As early as 1825 at least one Indian was the owner of 285
slaves and was a partner with an Englishman in a large sugar
plantation.[34] The growing of sugar in Mauritius is a seasonal
activity, and in time the planters discovered that it was more
economical to employ labourers on a daily basis via a contractor, rather than keeping them tied to the plantations all
the year round. The contractor was usually an 'old immi-
grant' Indian who could speak Creole and one or more
Indian languages, and he received an agreed sum for a
number of labourers to perform a particular task where and
when required. The contractor was thus in a strategic position to draw to himself part of the surplus produced by the
labour power of his men, and with the capital thus accu-
mulated he bought land from the planters. Sugar milling has
always been more profitable than growing sugar. The
planters with mills would sometimes, in bad years, decide to
sell or lease part of their land in plots to Indians, on the
understanding that they would grow sugar and bring the
cane to their mills. The Indians, using family labour, were
able to produce sugar on marginal land that had become
uneconomical for the planters when prices fell. In the early
days, part of the wages of the men on the plantations was
in the form of rations, and these were distributed by the
Sirdars – a kind of field foreman – who kept and sold some

of the food at a profit to themselves. Occasionally, planters might give their favourite *Sirdars* small inferior plots of land for market gardening and hence extra cash. Money lending also contributed to the enrichment of some Indians. Thus, gradually, by hard work and saving, with favours from the planters, and through the exploitation of their fellow countrymen, a number of Indians amassed money and bought land. A few acquired great prosperity as large rich sugar-estate owners in their own right, while many others became 'small planters', owning anything from much less than one to several hundred acres of cane. This sizeable class of Indian sugar planters posed a challenge to the structure of the sugar industry dominated by the white Creoles. At the same time the presence of the Indian sugar planters served to mitigate the class confrontation between the white miller/planters and the Indian sugar proletariat.[35]

Just under half of the cultivated land of Mauritius is owned today by Indians. With land, the basic resource of an agricultural economy, the Indians acquired an economic base of social mobility; they could finance the education of their sons for jobs in the public administration and in the professions. The British administration provided a channel of mobility that was not under the control of the Creole hierarchy, as the sugar industry was. What was required to move up the scale in the administration was English-type education, and Indians who could afford it acquired the required qualification. Thus, unlike the ex-slaves, the indentured labourers from India in time gave rise to a middle class parallel to the Creoles, but not merging ethnically, with that earlier elite.

Among the fragments of the cultures of India that the indentured labourers succeeded in preserving there were no doubt racial values. The non-amalgamation of the Indians with the Creoles is to be explained less in terms of an innate objection of Indians to merge themselves in any alien culture and more in terms of the importance attached to race in the overall Creole society. The Indians could see that those with African phenotype were at the bottom of the Creole hierarchy. Although it was vital for the Indians to learn to speak the Creole language, it was not in their interests to identify themselves with the black Creoles. More young men than women arrived from India. However, not many marriages or long term unions with black women took place. In the unions that did occur - more with coloured than with black women -the Indian men adopted the Catholic faith, changed their names, and passed into the mainstream of Creole society. But although this process is still continuing it has affected only a small minority.[36] This integral creolisation of a minority of Indians has had a perverse effect in race relations. Indians, particularly those from north India, have 'Aryan' features which are much closer to those of the white Creoles than to those of Creoles with African phenotype, and the latter resent this queue jumping of the newcomers towards 'whiteness'. This 'unfair' advantage in the racial hierarchy reinforces the resentment towards the 'Malbar coolies'[37] that have done so much better in the class hierarchy.

Born in slavery, the Creole society of Mauritius in particular but also the societies of the other islands have retained caste-like features in their structures. Race, in particular the colour of the skin, but also other features such as the shape of the nose, the lips, the hair, have to this day great significance for Creoles. European phenotype has high positive valuation while African phenotype is negatively valued. Race is relevant, however, not because it is the 'primordial' factor that explains the social structure. The racist value system derives from the genesis of the Creole society. Legalised under slavery this system of value has been internalised and perpetuated in the Creole society structured by class and political power under colonial rule. It was not because of their European phenotype but because they controlled the sugar economy and the colonial political system that some white people were at the top of the Creole hierarchy.[38]

Unlike the Indians, the black ex-slaves have not risen in the social hierarchy through land ownership. With the arrival of the Indians, the ex-slaves became redundant for the most part. A minority, the more skilled, were able to find employment on the plantations, but most black Creoles moved to the coast and to the towns. They earned a meagre living by fishing in the lagoons with primitive equipment, and by working as dockers, drivers, and artisans. Many were more-or-less permanently unemployed and formed a *lumpenproletariat* on the margin of the sugar economy. Several went to Rodrigues, or were recruited to work on the coconut plantations in the smaller dependencies.

Even under slavery, however, the congruence between race and class was not total. From very early on some of the offspring of sexual relations between the white masters and the black female slaves were sometimes freed, but others remained slaves. A category of 'Free Coloured' emerged between the white masters and the slaves. Some in the category of Free Coloured were slave owners and soon were the equal of the whites in class terms. For instance, several of the ship-owners and captains engaged in the illegal slave trade were Free Coloured. Legally, however, the Free Coloured had an inferior status to the whites until the abolition of slavery.

Today the significance of race varies with the context, and from island to island. In the marriage market race is very relevant. But to some extent it is possible to trade race for class. A light coloured girl might marry a much darker man who is highly placed in the class hierarchy, a doctor or a successful lawyer for instance. The dark-skinned man with African features who has done well in a prestigious profession will be on the lookout for a spouse ranking higher than himself in the race hierarchy. The circumnavigation of the caste-like element of race is not easy. At the extreme end it is virtually impossible for the 'coloured' person, even for one who has a perfect European phenotype, and who ranks high in class terms, to marry into a reputed white family. At that level the criterion of discrimination is not racial appearance as such but reputed genealogy. In Mauritius nowadays, but not in Réunion and Seychelles, a distinction is made between the coloured Creoles, some of whom are in appearance indistinguishable from the white Creoles, and those who are black and have more pronounced African features. Indeed, the appellation Creole tends to be used exclusively for this section of the population in Mauritius.

Indian Ocean Area

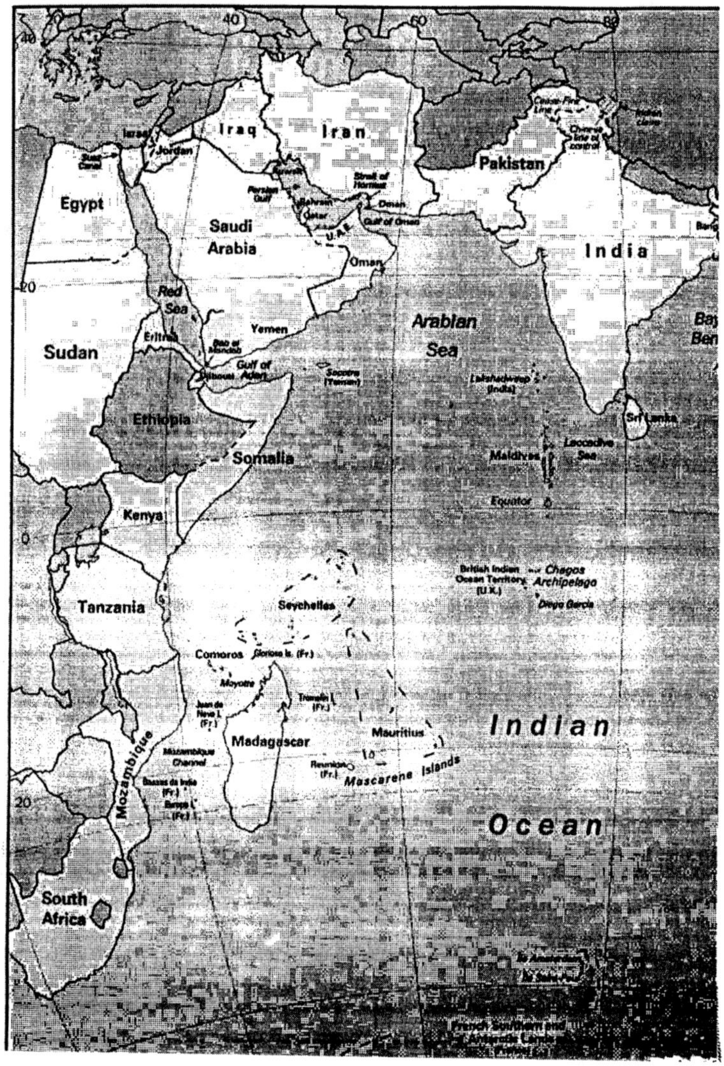

Figure 1
Map of the The Indian Ocean Region

Figure 2
"Servant and eunoch with the child of their master". Mekka, late
19th century. <u>Source</u>: C Snouk Hurgronje. *Mekka in the latter part
of the 19th century* (Leiden: E J Brill and London: Luzac, 1931),
opposite p.15.

Figure 3
"A slave making bread at El Tanem, in the Tihama, 1912".
Southeastern Saudi Arabia or Yemen.
<u>Source</u>: Andrew Wheatcroft, *Arabia and the Gulf: In original photographs 1880-1950* (London, Boston, Melbourne & Henley: Kegan Paul International, 1982). No pagination.

Figure 4

"A young boy at Kaf, 1921". Kaf is in the far north of Saudia Arabia, near the Jordanian border, the boy is clearly of African origin.

Source: Andrew Wheatcroft, *Arabia and the Gulf: In original photographs 1880-1950* (London, Boston, Melbourne & Henley: Kegan Paul International, 1982). No pagination.

Figure 5

"Zar' ceremonies. Baba Ebrahim, the Baba Zar of Bandar Abbas,
at the end of the gathering places a Koran on the head of the
woman patient". Note the drums in background. Bandar Abbas is
in southern Iran, directly opposite Oman.
Source: Z Arshi & N Kasraian, *Our Homeland Iran* (Tehran:
Sekeh Press, 1992, 5th edition), plate 130.

Figure 6
"Face of a herds woman descended from those who in the distant past were brought to this land as slaves, Baluchestan". For "distant past" we should probably read "the nineteenth century". Baluchestan is in southeastern Iran.
Source: Z Arshi & N Kasraian, *Our Homeland Iran* (Tehran: Sekeh Press, 1992, 5th edition), plate 140.

Figure 7
"Danse des Noirs". This 1861 crayon and watercolor drawing by
Hippolyte Charles Napoléon at La Réunion show two men playing
two characteristic East African instruments, a musical bow and a
reed-box rattle; note, too, the contrast between the dress of the
two men, one African, the other creole.
<u>Source</u>: *Ile de La Réunion. Regards croisés sur l'esclavage 1794-
1848* (Paris: Éditions d'Art & St Denis: CNH), p.259, plate 387.

Figure 8
"Government Palace in Mossuril, Early 19th century".
<u>Source</u>: History Department, University Eduardo Mondlane.
*History of Mozambique. Vol. I: First Sedentary Societies and
Impact of the Markets - (200/300-1886).* Maputo, DH e Tempo,
198, p.138.

Figure 9
"Mozambique Island".
Source: Collection of Portuguese Drawings, Mozambique. 11º series, picture 21, Lisbon, Rotep, 1972.

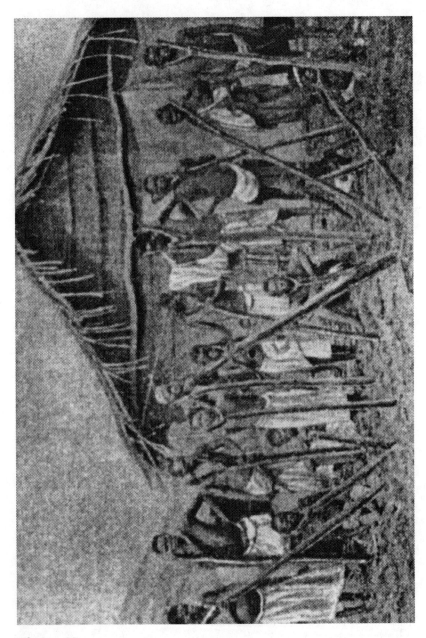

Figure 10
"Slave caravan, located by the Portuguese authorities in Mozambique, 1902".
<u>Source</u>: Historical Archives of Mozambique, Maputo.

Figure 11
"Picture depicting how the slaves travelled in the slave ships".
<u>Source</u>: Richard Howard, *Black Cargo*. London: Wayland
Publishers, 1972.

Figure 12
"Slave markets in Zanzibar, 1872".
Source: Richard Howard, *Black Cargo*. London: Wayland
Publishers, 1972.

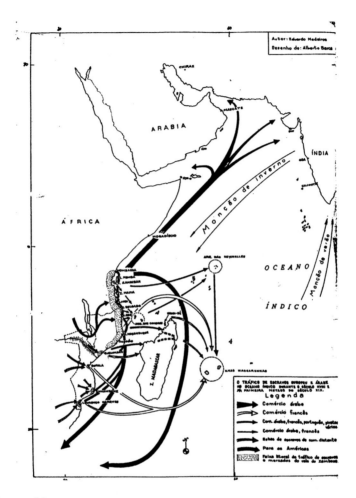

Figure 13

"The European and Arab Slave Trade Routes in the Indian Ocean during the 18th and the first half of the 19th centuries showing:
- Arab trade
- French trade
- Arab, French, Portuguese and Various Pirate Trades
- Arab and French Trade
- Commercial Slave Routes with Distant Countries
- To America
- Coastal areas of slave trade and markets of the Zambesi Valley".

Author: Eduardo Medeiros. Designed by Alberto Barca.

Figure 14
"A slave dhow outruns a British cruiser on the crossing to Madagascar".
<u>Source</u>: *Captain Colomb, Slave-Catching in the Indian Ocean.*
New edition Dawsons of Pall Mall, 1968.

Figure 15
"The Slave Trading Port of Majunga, North-West Madagascar".
<u>Source</u>: *Captain Colomb, Slave-Catching in the Indian Ocean.*
New edition Dawsons of Pall Mall, 1968.

Figure 16
"HMS Dryad of the British anti-slave trade squadron at anchor in Zanzibar, 1868".
Source: *Captain Colomb, Slave-Catching in the Indian Ocean.*
New edition Dawsons of Pall Mall, 1968.

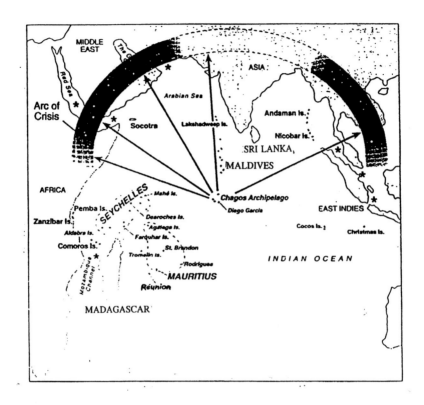

Figure 17
"The Creole islands and the Arc of Crisis".
Designed by Jean Houbert.

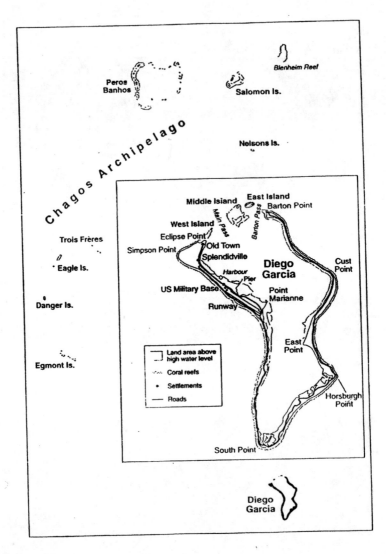

Figure 18
"Diego Garcia in the Chagos Archipelago".
Designed by Jean Houbert.

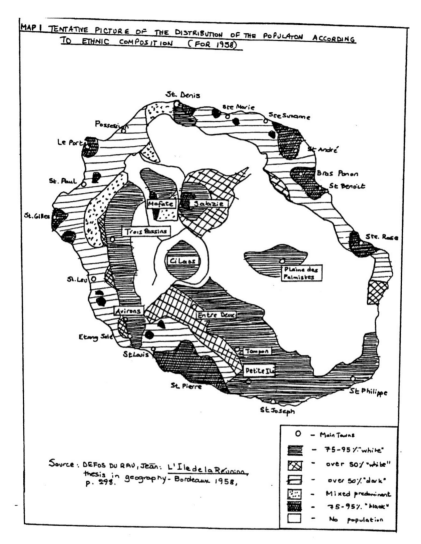

Figure 19

"Tentative Picture of the Distribution of the Population According to Ethnic Composition (for 1958)".

<u>Source</u>: Defos Du Rau, Jean. *L'Ile de la Réunion*. Thesis in Geography, Universite de Bordeaux 1958, p.298.

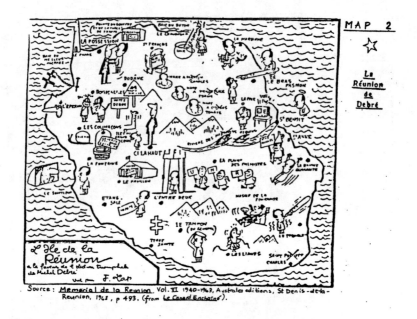

Figure 20
"La Réunion de Debré".
Source: *Mémorial de la Réunion*. Vol. VI 1940-1963, editions Australes, St Denis de la Réunion, 1958, p.463 (from *Le Canard Enchainé*)

Cartoon 1

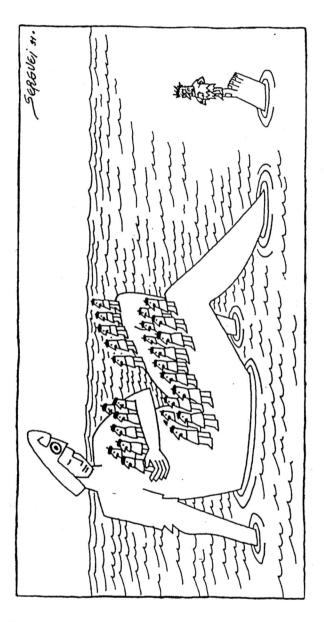

Figure 21
"Cartoon 1"
Source: Le Monde, 27.2.1991

Habitus Abiſſinorum quibus loco S. Baptiſmatis
frons nutiritur

Habyten der Abiſſynen wt paep fan ſtant welcke in plaets van
doop gebruycken brantmercken int aenſicht.   61 en 62

Figure 22

"Habshis of India". An engraving published by the late 16th century Dutch traveller John Hughen Vam Linschoten, who observes that Christians from the Land of Prester John, i.e.
Abyssinia, or Ethiopia, had their foreheads tatooed.

Figure 23
"One of the 17th century Habshi nobles". Sidi Miftah Habshi of
Bijapur. An engraving published by the German scholar Hiob
Ludolf in his *Relatio Nova hodierno Habessiniae Statu*.

Figure 24
"Sidi faqirs performing on behalf of a cult adept's fulfillment of a vow, in Gujarat, Western India".

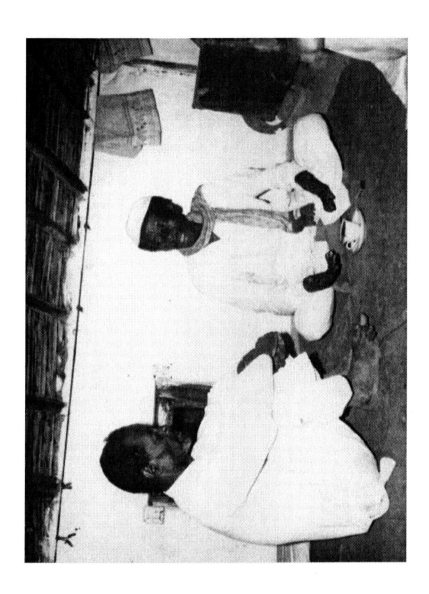

Figure 25
"Sidi men at home in Gujarat, Western India".

Figure 26
"A Sidi Family in Gujarat, Western India".

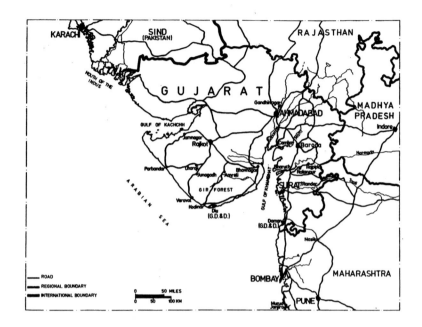

Figure 27
"Map showing Gujarat in Western India".

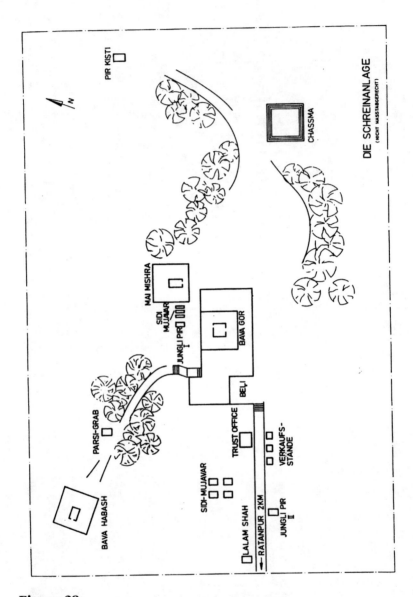

Figure 28
"The Shrines in Gujarat, Western India, showing Bava Gor, Mai
Mishra, Bava Habash, Parsi-Grab, Pir Kisti, Sidi Mujavar, Jungli
Pirs, Sidi-Mujavar, Lalam Shah, *Verkaufsstande*
and Chassma".

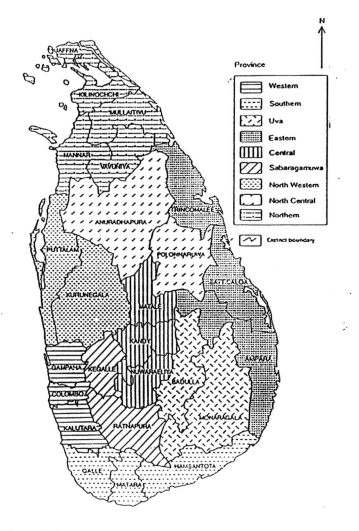

Figure 29
"A Map of Sri Lanka showing the Provinces and Cities".
Source: *Statistical Pocket Book of the Democratic Socialist Republic of Sri Lanka* (1998).
Department of Census & Statistics, Ministry of Finance & Planning, Colombo.

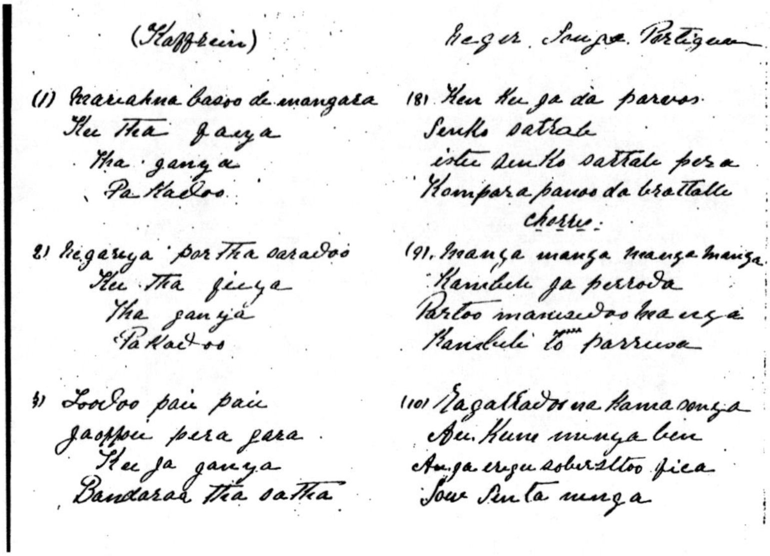

(Kaffrein)

(1) Mariahna basoo de mangara
Keu Tha ganya
Tha ganya
Pakadoo

2) Negaraya por Tha saradoo
Keu Tha ganya
Tha ganya
Pakadoo

3) Loodoo pai pai
Jaoppu pera gara
Keu Ja ganya
Bandaraa Tha satha

Neger Songs Portiguese

(8) Keu Keu ja da paroos
Senko sattale
istu senko sattale pera
Kompara panos da brattalle
chorus:

(9) Manga manga manga manga
Kandele ja perroda
Partoo manusedoo kaanga
Kandele to parrusa

(10) Nagalkadoo na kama songa
Au Kune munga ben
Anga ergu soburstoo fica
Sou Senta munga

Figure 30
"*Kaffrinha* Songs recorded in Sri Lanka Portuguese Creole".
Source: 19th century Hugh Nevill Manuscript (British Museum, London).

Figure 31
"M J Elias, a member of the Sirambiadiya *Kaffir* community, Sri
Lanka".

Decolonisation in the Changing Geopolitics of the Indian Ocean

Decolonisation can never be literally the reverse of colonisation. Least of all could this be the case in settler colonies. In the Creole islands, colonisation was integral to their whole being. Decolonisation in the islands was as much a question of the rearrangement of the internal political, economic, and ethnic balances, as a question of international status. In the latter the two distinct variants of decolonisation policies were applied: Réunion was integrated with France while Mauritius and Seychelles became sovereign states in the international system. In both variants of decolonisation the colonial power played the major role in bringing about change, in the teeth of stiff resistance from the Creole hierarchies.

In Mauritius, internal pressures for change had taken a class basis at first. A number of non-establishment Creole intellectuals had joined with a few Indian professionals to press for constitutional reforms, and for the right to strike and form trade unions. They started the Mauritius Labour Party (MLP) on a non-ethnic basis just before World War II. The birth of the MLP coincided with unrest on some of the estates, provoked by a conflict over the type of canes used by the 'small planters' and the quantity of sugar accruing to them for the canes they brought to the millers/planters. Class politics was much more of a threat to the plantocracy than ethnic politics and the colonial authorities were not dissatisfied when, with the extension of the suffrage in 1948, ethnic considerations began to dominate Mauritian politics and the leadership of the MLP passed into the hands of Indians. Their kith and kin, although largely creolised, have retained enough 'Indianness' to make it possible for them to be mobilised politically on an ethnic basis. Rich Indian planters, civil servants, and the sugar proletariat could be rallied together to provide a large electoral base for the 'moderate' Indian leaders of the MLP who were being groomed by the Colonial Office to take over at independence. The elite that had emerged from the indentured Indians owed much to British rule and was not particularly anxious for colonial rule to end. The Indians, however, opted for the formula of decolonisation that Britain favoured, as it increased their chances of obtaining state power.[39]

The Creoles thought of themselves as the first inhabitants of Mauritius, but as they had become a minority, in ethnic terms, they feared that decolonisation would mean independence under Indian rule. Consequently, although Creole 'reactionaries' and 'liberals' had been for very many years virulently divided over questions of colour and voting rights, they now closed ranks to face the 'Hindu Menace'.[40] Virtually all the Creoles, the rich white mill-owners, the middle-class-coloured civil servants and professionals, and the black unemployed were Roman Catholics. In spite of their colour/social conflicts, and the growing class gulf between them, they all in their different ways felt threatened by the Indians, and responded readily to an ethnic political appeal. In the age of decolonisation, it was out of the question for Britain to transfer political power to a minority, albeit a minority of 'natives'. Having failed in its bitter opposition to universal suffrage, the *Parti mauricien social democrate* (PMSD), backed by the Creoles, advocated a form of integration of Mauritius with Britain as an alternative to independence – following the example of Réunion, which is integrated with France.

The Creoles also gained support from other ethnic minority groups. They were joined naturally by the Chinese, shop and restaurant keepers who had emerged as middle-class Roman Catholics. In preserving fragments of the cultures of India, the Mauritians of Indian origin have retained many divisions of religion, language and caste that can be very significant in the political context. The division between Hindus and Muslims, notably, was crucial in the politics of decolonisation. Most of the Indian Muslims came to Mauritius as indentured labourers but a few came as merchants, specialising in the importation of rice and cotton cloth for the indentured labourers. Some of the merchants had taken the lead in establishing religious and cultural institutions that helped maintain a sense of communal identity among the Muslim labourers, thus keeping them apart from the Hindus. The rich Muslim merchants had special relations with the Creole hierarchy in the activities of the capital, Port Louis, which facilitated the urbanisation of the Muslim labourers. The PMSD gained much support among these urban Muslims. The Creole party also exploited with some success the caste divisions among the Hindus. The enormous resources of the sugar industry helped it to draw large numbers of Indians - particularly the young - to its rank.

The strategy of the PMSD was to press for a referendum to be held in Mauritius and appealed to all Mauritians, irrespective of their ancestral origins, to support integration.[41] The ethnic factor would have been less able to affect the outcome of a direct choice between integration and independence than an election based on ethnically-drawn constituencies. It was most improbable, however, that London would have agreed to the plans of the PMSD whatever the wishes of the inhabitants. Mauritius was a most unlikely part of the British Empire to be made part of the United Kingdom: apart from the absence of any 'kith and kin' there the Creole elite had made many of the British administrators feel alien in their own Crown Colony. The island, moreover, had problems of over-population and unemployment that the PMSD proposed to solve by emigration at a time when racism was escalating in Britain. In the economic circumstances of Mauritius at the time, however, the integration platform was more popular as the apparent prosperity of neighbouring Réunion could be attributed to it being integrated with France.

Britain was anxious to withdraw from Mauritius,[42] but characteristically 'played the Mauritians along' in order to maintain a central interest in the area.

Decolonisation was a policy of the West as well as a process reflecting the radical transformation of the configuration of power in the international system. As a policy, decolonisation was the complement of 'containment' in the Cold War. The Soviet Union, perceived as the land power poised to dominate Eurasia, had to be contained lest it expanded into the Rimland and then challenged the West at sea. The 'loss of China' and the outbreak of the bitter struggle between North and South Korea reinforced this geopolitical obsession. But the Cold War was not only about military power; it was also about internal regimes and ideology. Containment therefore was a question not just of building military pacts but of fostering the 'right' kind of political regimes. The timely transfer of sovereignty to moderate nationalist regimes in the colonies was regarded as a very effective form of containing communism in the Indian Ocean sector of the Asian Rimland. It would have been better if the newly decolonised states then joined a Western military containment pact. But even when the new states adopted non-aligned positions in the Cold War, decolonisation was still functional to containment provided that these states remained in the capitalist world market and retained regimes modelled on those of the West. These regimes would not need much prompting from the West to crack down on communists in their internal politics.

Decolonisation on land never meant that the West was abandoning power at sea. On the contrary, with the end of colonial rule in the Rimland in Asia, the geopolitical situation went full circle back to the West relying primarily on sea power. This was particularly marked in the Indian Ocean region. The Indian Ocean, unlike the Atlantic and the Pacific, is closed on its most significant northern rim by the bulk of Eurasia, opening freely only to the south. This gives considerable strategic importance to the so-called 'choke points': the narrow entry points in the northwest - the Suez-Red Sea corridor, and, in the east - the straits through the Indonesian archipelago. More significantly, during the Cold War, the repartition of land and sea meant a major geopolitical asymmetry: the Soviet Union and China could bring power to bear overland on the northern rim of the Indian Ocean without necessarily taking to the sea while the West could only intervene on land by being present at sea. With power at sea, the West could deter a possible invasion of the Middle East and South Asia by the Soviet Union or China, and provide reassurance to the newly decolonised states. Sea power also provided a fallback position if containment on land failed. With the end of the Cold War, the West has used its power at sea to intervene in the Arc of Crisis. This is a particularly unstable zone of the Third World stretching from the

Horn of Africa to Afghanistan and centred on the oil-rich Gulf. In some respects, the Arc of Crisis can be extended beyond to the narrow outlets of the Indian Ocean in the Far East. Modern sea power can be projected over very long distances. Even so, a secure Western presence in the Indian Ocean required reliable allies in the region and/or bases in territories that could be retained under the control of the West.

South Africa, Israel and Australia might have been willing to offer dependable bases in the vicinity of the choke points of the sea lanes of the Indian Ocean but were too geographically eccentric. South Africa and Israel, furthermore, were in conflict with littoral states that the West wanted to win in the ideological - if not the military - confrontation with the East. The small oceanic islands were seen as the answer to the West's need for secure bases in the Indian Ocean. Britain, the traditional hegemonic western power in the Indian Ocean, devised a scheme that could allow her to keep a substantial military presence east of Suez on a severely limited budget. The Royal Air Force envisaged the construction of a whole string of island bases that would link Africa with South-East Asia and Australia, and the UK Government favoured such a plan rather than the more costly replacement of the three ageing aircraft carriers that had been proposed by the Royal Navy. The air power of F-111s based in the islands would then be the principal means of exercising sea power in the Indian Ocean and of intervening in the Asian Rimland. The USA was involved in the scheme from the start, in part because of financial considerations. Washington had not succeeded in persuading London to commit forces in Vietnam, but with some financial help Britain would stay east of Suez. The core interest of the USA in being involved in the island scheme was, however, nuclear geostrategy. Polaris III came on stream in 1963 and was most probably deployed in the Indian Ocean at the time. With a range of 2500 km. Polaris III could reach sensitive parts of the Soviet Union from the Arabian Sea. A specially equipped surface station to communicate with Polaris was required somewhere in the islands; appropriate satellites were not available in the 1960s. and even today it is still useful to have surface facilities.

The proposed British trans-oceanic link of bases had to be scaled down and then abandoned altogether. Increasing financial constraints made it impossible to keep a military presence east of Suez, despite Prime Minister Harold Wilson's reluctance to leave America and China 'eyeball to eyeball', which meant that Britain's role would be primarily to provide the United States with secure real estate in the Indian Ocean. A whole chain of islands was not necessary for the Pentagon's military purposes, because what was required was one or two suitable locations capable of housing a sophisticated communications facility, as well as being suitable for later transformation into logistic bases for power projections into the Arc of Crisis. Most importantly, in the age of decolonisation, Washington insisted that the island(s) selected for this role should not be under the sovereignty of a newly independent and potentially unstable state or have any local inhabitants. Hence the emergence of the policy whereby Mauritius and Seychelles would gain their independence, albeit shorn of some of their 'attached' smaller islands, whose few inhabitants could then be removed, if need be, without much difficulty. Thus the Chagos islands, part of Mauritius, and three of the Seychelles islands, Aldabra, Farquhar, and Desroches, were amputated and grouped together to form a new colony: the British Indian Ocean Territory (BIOT). Since the well-located military facility that already existed in Gan, part of the Maldives, was not retained, it seems clear that the other islands were selected not only because of their locations but also because it was considered that their dismemberment and depopulation would be less problematic in the age of decolonisation.[43]

The strategy of the British delegation at the Lancaster House Conference of 1965 on the decolonisation of Mauritius was to lead the Mauritians to believe that London was willing to consider seriously the option of integration proposed by the PMSD as an alternative to independence, and would be prepared to test opinion through a referendum as requested by the Creole party.[44] The MLP felt that if it were to raise difficulties about the detachment of the

Chagos islands, or to insist on a high price for them, the British Government might lean to the side of the PMSD and grant its request for a referendum.[45] Since opinion in Mauritius showed signs of favouring integration there was a real risk, from the MLP point of view, of losing the prize of independence and political power at the last moment. This was a gamble that the Indian leaders were not prepared to take. Britain was thus able to persuade the leader of the MLP to accept decolonisation on its terms: no referendum, independence for Mauritius, but collaboration in the amputation and depopulation of the Chagos for military purposes.[46] The Creoles advocating the merging of Mauritius itself with Britain could not very well object to an operation designed to further the security of the West.[47]

The Chagos archipelago is 1900 km to the north-east of Mauritius and 1600 km from Seychelles. The Maldives, which are not Creole islands, are only 1100 km from Chagos. A Mauritian-Seychellois copra company exploited the Chagos islands under a system that had hardly changed since the days of slavery. Displaced from the sugar plantations in Mauritius by the arrival of the Indians, some ex-slaves were taken to the smaller island dependencies to work on coconut plantations. Some of these workers stayed on in the islands and in time formed the permanent population of the Chagos. To this hard core of permanent inhabitants, from time to time, depending on the market for copra, less permanent additional labourers were added. These were recruited in Mauritius and Seychelles from among the black Creoles with African features. The lease of the copra company gave it total economic power in the islands. The company controlled all the land and owned all the houses, tools and equipment. All the inhabitants, including the women, children and the old, were in principle, the employees of the company. The islanders were allowed to grow vegetables, keep pigs and chicken, and fish in the lagoons so that the cost of reproducing the labour power fell only in part on the company. The meagre wages of the *Zilois* - the inhabitants of the smaller dependencies of Mauritius are known as *Zilois* - were spent in the company's shops. In practise the manager of the company had complete political power in the islands also. The state manifested itself once or twice a year in the shape of a visiting magistrate from Mauritius on board the company's ship.

The Chagos and the other smaller dependencies (Agalega, Saint Brandon) were very marginal in the sugar plantation economy of Mauritius. Altogether these dependencies had less than 2000 inhabitants. The style of life of these islands had more in common with Seychelles - where coconut plantations were the mainstay of the economy before the recent advent of tourism - than with Mauritius.[48] The white and the coloured Creole elite in Mauritius knew very little and cared even less about the *Zilois*. The Indian politicians considered that the excision of small, distant islands and the expulsion of some poor, illiterate, black Creoles were a small price to pay for state power in decolonisation with British support. Especially as the islands were required for the purpose of enhancing the security of the West, with which Mauritius identified itself. Moreover, the British, trusted patrons of the advocates of independence in Mauritius, had promised that the Chagos islands would be returned when the security need for them disappeared.

The 1500 Zilois of the Chagos were deported to Mauritius without their consent and mainly left destitute in the slums of Port Louis. A few were left in the Seychelles.[49] In 1972 the British Government gave the Mauritian Government £650,000 to re-house the deported Zilois but the islanders did not benefit from that money. At about the same time a new and initially radical left wing political party the *Mouvement Militant Mauricien* (MMM) mobilised the Zilois to stage protest about the amputation of the Chagos from Mauritius and the deportation of the inhabitants. The MMM had rapidly gathered strength with the mass disillusion that followed independence when the MLP discarded its erstwhile ally of the decolonisation campaign, the Independent Forward Bloc (IFB), a pro-independence party which had been in the forefront of the Indian cultural revival in Mauritius, and formed a coalition with the PMSD. India, whose call for help in the 1962 war with China had been used in London and Washington to justify the need for a military base in the Indian Ocean, now led a growing campaign against the militarisation of Diego Garcia, supported by the Non-Aligned Movement and the Organisation of African Unity (OAU). Successive governments in Mauritius were under pressure from both inside and outside and requested London to reopen the Chagos file.[50]

On the question of the deported Zilois, Britain continued to maintain that they were property-less appendages of a copra enterprise that ceased to exist.[51] In fact, the British Government had bought the lease of the company, which helped to organise the 'passage' of the unfortunate islanders. Eventually, after a long campaign by the aggrieved *Zilois*, and with the MMM in the Mauritian government, the British Government agreed to give the islanders £4 million in 1982. It is not entirely clear that this 'compensation' was conditional of the *Zilois* giving up their claim to return to their islands. Today, some thirty years after their deportation, the *Zilois* who survive and their children born in Mauritius are split into two factions. One faction, *Ran nu Diégo* (give Diego back to us) Committee, still has the support of the MMM and other opposition political parties. It seems to be more interested in the claim of Mauritius to have sovereignty in the Chagos. The other faction, Social Committee of the Chagossiens, claims to be apolitical, and stresses the right of the *Zilois* to return to their islands. The United Nations has now recognised that indigenous peoples, such as the pre-Columbian Americans and the aborigines of Australia, should get redress for their losses under settler colonisation and the Chagossiens want to be accepted in that category of peoples.[52]

On the issue of sovereignty over the Chagos, Britain has turned down all requests to reopen negotiations and referred the Mauritians to the agreed terms of decolonisation, namely, that if the need for the facilities disappeared the Chagos would be returned to Mauritius. However, as an exchange of secret telegrams in November 1965 made clear 'decision about the need to retain the islands must rest entirely with the United Kingdom Government'. For good measure the Mauritian politicians who had made the deal over the Chagos were told by their British patrons that 'it would not (repeat not) be open to the Government of Mauritius to raise the matter, or press for the return of the islands on its own initiative'.[53] For internal political consumption a Minister for Foreign Affairs of Mauritius returning from London on yet another failed attempt to get the British Government to move on the Chagos question stated that: 'Diego belongs to Mauritius; there is no disagreement about that...*L'Ile est a l'ile Maurice; l'usufruct est a la Grande Bretagne'.*[54] There is little likelihood that the need for the military facilities will 'disappear' in the near future. The Cold War has ended but the base in Diego Garcia remains very useful for the interventions of the United States in the Arc of Crisis.

The development of a major military base on Diego Garcia rests on a treaty between the UK and the USA signed on 20 December 1966 making the islands of the BIOT available for military purposes for fifty years plus another twenty years extension if required. To avoid Congress, a secret annexe provided for American finance for half the cost of acquiring and depopulating the islands by cancelling a British debt owed for an R&D item on Polaris. When the scandal of the deported Zilois was uncovered Congress was the more reluctant to vote the billions of dollars needed to turn Diego Garcia into a first class military base. Nevertheless, new treaties with Britain on the 24 October 1972 and on 25 January 1976 upgraded the facilities on the island.[55]

Diego Garcia now has a long runway that handles fully loaded B 52s, dispensing with in-flight refuelling. The lagoon of the atoll has been dredged to accommodate large surface ships and submarines. The military equipment, fuel, supplies and water, sufficient for the combat requirements of a Marine brigade are loaded on 17 specially equipped cargo ships stationed there. This is part of the equipment of the Rapid Deployment Force (RDF) pre-positioned in the Indian Ocean for possible interventions in the Arc of Crisis. The enlarged fuel storage facility can cope with thirty days' requirements of a carrier taskforce. Warehouses, barracks and recreational facilities have been constructed. From Diego Garcia the USA can keep watch all over the Indian Ocean and the littoral. There are reports that nuclear weapons were stored on the island during the Cold War. The very sophisticated station can communicate with submarines at the bottom of the ocean. Diego Garcia is not an 'austere communication station', as the Pentagon in order to mollify Congress has stated, but the major naval and air base of the USA in the Indian Ocean. Diego Garcia was one of the key military facilities of the West during the Cold War and it is now indispensable for interventions in the Arc of Crisis.[57] The eight helicopters, which attempted to rescue the American hostages in Iran, were based in Diego Garcia. The base played a significant role in the Gulf War (1990-1991) and in the United States intervention in Iraq in 1996.[56]

Diego Garcia is like a very elongated horseshoe: 21 km long north to south and 9.6 km across. The atoll is almost completely enclosed, making an excellent shelter for the lagoon, which can house a whole fleet. On and off, the British had used the island as a coaling station. In the First World War a German warship called in for repairs without the islanders knowing that war had been declared.[57] In the Second World War, after the Japanese had entered the Indian Ocean and bombarded Sri Lanka, Britain stationed six Catalina sea planes in Diego Garcia to give Mauritius early warning of the presence of the enemy fleet.[58] This was the first time that the British hegemony over the Indian Ocean was challenged since the Napoleonic wars and once again Diego Garcia had the role it had played in the insular system under the French. Like the other islands of the Chagos, the copra company exploited Diego Garcia before the American base was built. Now all the other Chagos islands have been abandoned and are out of bounds to visitors, except by special permits from Britain.[59] Round the world yachtsmen occasionally visit the islands. Britain has not extended an Exclusive Economic Zone around the Chagos archipelago but in 1991 London proclaimed a 200 miles Fisheries Conservation and Management Zone (FCMZ) around the BIOT. In 1965 the British Government had promised the Mauritians that it would 'use its good offices with the United States Government to ensure that [certain] facilities in the Chagos would remain available to the Mauritian Government as far as practicable' notably 'fishing rights'. Since 1991 boats from Mauritius must be licensed to catch fish in the FCMZ of the Chagos, but they must not do so inside the lagoons.[60]

The dismemberment of one colonial entity to form another colony was not unprecedented in the Creole islands. The first was when the French insular entity was dismembered with the British conquest and Réunion returned to France in 1815. In 1903 the Crown colony of Mauritius was dismembered when the main islands of Seychelles were removed and formed into a new colony. Five years later, Coetivy was cut off and added to Seychelles that, in 1921, also got Farquhar. The difference this time, however, was that the dismemberment of Mauritius and Seychelles to create the BIOT took place in decolonisation and thus violated the United Nations resolution 1514 against the dismemberment of colonial territories. As the operation involved the deportation of the Chagos islanders without their consent, it was also a violation of Human Rights.

Unlike Mauritius, where the ethnic composition of the population was totally transformed with the arrival of the Indians, Seychelles has remained 'African'. The slave population on the eve of abolition was composed of 3924 Africans, mostly from Mozambique, 2231 Creoles of African antecedents and only 282 Malagasy.[61] The African content of the Seychelles' population was further accentuated by the British Navy landing 2532 Africans captured at sea on Arab slavers between 1861 and 1872.[62] A small number of Chinese and a few Indian merchants came in the late nineteenth century. The Indian merchants acquired landed interests and became influential in the economy but this did not transform the Creole society. Skin colour remains relevant in the social hierarchy, although much less so than in Mauritius. Before air transport and tourism metamorphosed the Seychelles, the archipelago depended on coconut plantations and fishing. The plantations were owned by a small number of white Creoles who had a paternalist attitude towards the work force of black Creoles. The practice of the white masters fathering children with their female slaves continued well after abolition right through into decolonisation. Among the black Creoles it is still fairly common for a woman to have children with several men. A black woman who has illegitimate children with an important white person is not dishonoured; on the contrary she is admired for the material advantages that this might bring. [63] It is not uncommon in Seychelles to find persons with European phenotype in the milieu of the black Creoles and sharing the same lifestyle. The white plantocracy tended to be Francophile but to be monolingual in Creole carried less of a stigma than in Mauritius. The British colonial administration had encouraged the use of Creole and English in opposition to French in Seychelles. Today the Seychelles is the only Creole island where the Creole language is one of the official languages.

Seychelles was kept under consideration in the 1960s for possible military uses until quite late in the decolonisation process and consequently was not encouraged, as Mauritius, to go for the independence solution. But as Diego Garcia was selected and developed as a major base, the Seychelles islands lost their strategic importance for the West. The Seychelles Democratic Party (SDP), led by James (Jimmy) Mancham, the pro-British party, which had advocated integration with the UK, was therefore belatedly persuaded to accept independence in 1976 in coalition with its opponent, the Seychelles People's United Party (SPUP), led by Albert Rene, that had advocated this line all along.[64] As part of the exercise of tardily preparing Seychelles for independence, the UK, with the consent of the USA, returned the three islands, Aldabra, Farquhar and Desroches, that in 1965 had been taken into BIOT at the same time as the Chagos. The international airport in Mahe, which has transformed Seychelles into a playground for rich Westerners, was originally also intended to be a military runway and was built with BIOT money, and was also handed over.[65] Tourism has moved Seychelles to the top of the league of 'African' countries for GNP per head but has also had disturbing effects, including rapidly rising land prices, and some political consequences.

The improbable regime that the UK sponsored in decolonisation lasted just a year before being overthrown in 1977 in a bloodless coup from within by the earlier champions of independence.[66] The SPUP, the party that staged the coup, was somewhat less accommodating towards the land speculators and more Francophile than the SDP, the one that had advocated integration with the UK. Unlike Mauritius, where universal suffrage meant that the real electoral prize was the Indian vote, in Seychelles it meant the support of the black Creoles. The OAU, and Tanzania in particular, played a role in the politics of independence in Seychelles. Several participants of the coup had received military training in Tanzania and Tanzanian soldiers helped the regime afterwards.[67] As long as Seychelles remained the one-party state that the coup leaders had established, it had been obsessed with real and imaginary threats of counter-coups.[68] As those who were displaced had taken refuge in Britain, the non-aligned posture adopted by Seychelles tended to be coloured by the help that the enemies of the regime may or may not have received from the UK. For a while North Korea provided the personal security of the President. Rumours that the Soviet Navy had a base in Seychelles proved unfounded. The militarisation of Diego Garcia gave the other Creole islands negative strategic significance: they had to be denied to the enemies of the West which, during the Cold War, might have posed a threat to the base in Diego Garcia. The USSR did send its 'blue water' navy to the Indian Ocean, but it would seem that this was an attempt to ward off the mortal threat posed by Polaris and not to invade the Creole islands.[69] Seychelles remained all along very dependent economically on the West. Tourism is the main industry, and investments as well as customers come from Europe. A NASA tracking station, manned by the US Navy in Mahe, had provided Seychelles with US$2.5 million a year in rent until it was closed down recently. A tuna fishing agreement with the European Union brings in $4 million a year. France cultivates the little republic, as it does also Mauritius, and was certainly influential in President Rene's decision in December 1991 that a pluralist political system should replace the one party regime.[70] A new democratic constitution was approved by referendum in 1993, followed by elections for the Presidency and the

National Assembly. Rene was reelected president and his party won the majority of seats in the National Assembly in elections that Commonwealth and French observers found to be without significant irregularities.[71]

Rodrigues had significance in the days of sail, and before sailors were able to ascertain longitudes accurately, because of its position relative to Mauritius and to India. After rounding the Cape, the ships used to sail on a parallel of latitude as far east as Rodrigues and then fall back on Mauritius. Rodrigues was also the landmark for the ships to turn north when sailing to India. Even in these early days, however, Rodrigues, did not have a maritime vocation on account of the dangerous reefs surrounding the island. Indeed, the first inhabitants had the reputation of plundering the numerous ships wrecked on the island. Rodrigues is the only Creole island of the Indian Ocean where large-scale plantations did not develop.[72] The few slaves, abandoned in Rodrigues at the time of the British conquest, reverted to a kind of subsistence peasantry, squatting on Crown land. Virtually all the land belongs to the state; the Catholic Church, which has about 50 acres, is by far the second largest landowner. Except for charging a small rent for the land, the colonial state ignored Rodrigues leaving the peasants to the care of the Catholic Church. After the defeat of France in the islands, Britain had kept Rodrigues for, unlike Réunion, the island being to windward of Mauritius could be a threat in the hands of an enemy power. The British invaders had themselves used Rodrigues as a base to capture Mauritius and Réunion. A few petty merchants from Mauritius - Chinese and Indian Muslims - exploited the peasants for the small surpluses of vegetables, chicken and dried fish. The peasants were joined later by Creole fishermen from Mauritius. The fishermen tend to be a shade lighter in colour and have less pronounced African features. There are no white Creoles in the island. The lighter skin Creoles tend to be on the coast and in the little town of Port Mathurin while the darker, more numerous, peasants are inland on the higher ground. Creole is practically the only language in Rodrigues. The poorly endowed island is over-populated with some 45,000 inhabitants and has a serious shortage of water. The ecological damage is severe and probably irreversible.

Voting for the first time,[73] Rodrigues was unanimously against independence as part of Mauritius. The Catholic islanders do not identify themselves with Mauritius, which they perceive as a country dominated by Hindus. Moreover, the Indo-Mauritian civil servants in Rodrigues can behave as 'colonialists'.[74] Resentment for the long neglect by Port Louis and the wide spread poverty compared to Mauritius fuel anti-Mauritian nationalism.[75] Yet Rodrigues remains heavily dependent on the state in Mauritius. At the time of independence, one of the two deputies elected to represent Rodrigues in the parliament in Mauritius made a plea, on the ground of self-determination, that the island should remain with the UK, but this was rapidly turned down in London.[76] Long overdue air-link with Mauritius has brought a few tourists to Rodrigues, but this cannot provide sufficient employment for the many peasants who leave the land. Unplanned emigration to Mauritius has not provided much relief to Rodrigues. The immigrants from Rodrigues live in appalling conditions in Mauritius adding to the *malaise* of the black Creoles which has recently erupted into riots.

Mauritius has done exceptionally well economically and politically since independence. Tourism and the manufacturing of a whole range of goods, from textiles to electronics, for exports to the European Union (EU) have been added to the now modernised sugar industry. Mauritius has the lion's share of the African Caribbean Pacific (ACP) quota of sugar in the EU with a high guaranteed price. More recently, offshore banking and other services for transnational capital, as well as the development of a free port have added to the success story.[77] The economic transformation has gone together with a liberal democratic political system. Elections take place regularly and defeated governments have stepped down without problems. The principal beneficiaries of economic growth have been the white Creoles while political change has favoured the Indians. The main losers are the black Creoles.

Economic growth with democracy in Mauritius can be explained in terms of a balance between economic and political power that the island inherited from its colonial history. In the colonial era, economic power was largely with the white Creole sugar plantocracy while political power rested ultimately with Britain. The white Creoles have remained dominant in the economy. More than transnational capital and expertise, it is the capital and the enterprise of the plantocracy that have diversified and developed the economy in decolonisation. Mauritian capital and enterprise have now gone beyond Mauritius and are exploiting resources in Madagascar, in Mozambique and other parts of Africa. Political power, in the postcolonial situation, was programmed to rest on the consent of the governed, albeit on a communal basis. Through the imposition of constitutional and electoral reforms, London enabled Indians to get access to political power and eventually obtain state power in decolonisation.

The cultivation of ethnic pluralism is instrumental in the political system in Mauritius. The constitution of independence explicitly divides the population into four 'communities': Hindu, Muslim, Sino-Mauritian and General Population. Thus, although Mauritius is a secular state, its political body is not made up exclusively of individual citizens. Citizens are at the same time members of the officially identified communities. The four officially identified communities do not refer to a same ethnic quality: Hindu and Muslim are religions while Sino-Mauritian is a cultural and national category. The General Population is defined negatively: 'every person who does not appear, from his way of life, to belong to one or other of those three communities shall be regarded as belonging to the General Population, which shall itself be regarded as a fourth community'.[78] All the governments of Mauritius since independence have claimed to be 'building a Mauritian nation'. This nation is not envisaged as the collectivity of all the citizens, regardless of ethnic identifications, holding certain political values in common and wanting to be together in the same state. Instead the nation is conceived in ethnic terms. The motto: 'Unity in Diversity' encapsulates the vision of the nation as a diversity of ethnic communities coexisting in the same state. Each ethnic community is encouraged to identify itself with the culture of its country of origin. A number of Cultural Centres exist to foster these cultures.

With the introduction of universal suffrage in Mauritius the electoral constituencies were drawn to reflect as far as possible the geographical distribution of the officially identified communities. This meant that to have a chance of winning elections the political parties must mobilise the electorate as communities and that the parties themselves must be primarily communal. Over 50 per cent of the electorate are Hindus.[79] A party or coalition of parties that succeeds in getting the votes of this electorate has a good chance of forming the government. The Hindus in Mauritius, however, are very heterogeneous in terms of class and of caste. Also, the minorities of Hindus whose ancestors came from South India via Madras and from the West of the Great Peninsula via Bombay see themselves as being distinct communities and do not want to be confused with the majority of Hindus that came from Northeast India via Calcutta. All these differences can be very significant in the political context. The officially identified Hindu community serves to mitigate these differences and unite the Hindus politically. Communal political support enhances the power of the Hindu government in confrontations with the Creole plantocracy. Indians in state power can provide jobs in the administration and patronage generally to communal supporters.

The General Population is not like the other communities in that it does not exclude on ethnic criteria. On the contrary its 'way of life' can be adopted by anyone who no longer wants to belong to the other ethnically defined communities. The General Population could be the basis for non-ethnic 'nation building' but this is not politically acceptable. In a nation without ethnically defined communities the electoral advantage of the 'majority community' would disappear.

In the present ethnic dispensation, the black Creoles come under the General Population community but are nevertheless supposed to identify themselves with the culture of Africa and to cultivate their 'roots' in that continent. There is an African Cultural Centre as there are French, Indian, and Chinese ones. The dilemma of the black Creoles is that they are at the bottom of the racial and social Creole hierarchy but that it is the economic muscle of the white Creoles at the top of that hierarchy that provides the effective counter power to that of the Indians who have state power. To disentangle themselves from the Creole hierarchy through 're-Africanisation' would not necessarily improve the predicament of the black Creoles and might exacerbate it.

Politically, the black Creoles are frustrated. Although they were among the first inhabitants of the island they have not inherited political power in decolonisation, which has gone to the late comers, the more numerous Indians. The Creoles have over the years produced some outstanding political leaders; but these have been white or coloured and seldom black. These leaders need the electoral support of the black Creoles at election time but are limited in what they can do in opposition or in coalitions with more powerful Indian parties. In the private sector the good jobs are given to the white Creoles or to the better qualified in terms of education and training. The black Creoles feel excluded, as they have not had the historical advantages of the coloured Creoles to produce an educated elite. The 'whitening' process associated with upward social mobility has tended to deprive the black Creoles of their elite to the benefit of the coloured Creoles.

The very economic success of Mauritius has, in relative terms, deprived the black Creoles. The economic boom has led to full employment and Mauritius, once again, imports 'contract labour' from China and Sri Lanka. Nonetheless, many black Creoles remain unemployed. Fishing in the lagoons, one of the traditional jobs of the black Creoles, has been adversely affected by the development of tourism. The mechanisation of the activities of the port and the construction of silos for the bulk shipment of sugar have greatly reduced the number of dockers, another traditional occupation of the black Creoles. Under colonial rule, the British had favoured the employment of black Creoles in the lower ranks of the police force on grounds that they were taller and reputed to be physically stronger than the Indians. After independence not only has the ethnic consideration in recruitment been reversed[80] but the black Creoles now make up the majority of the inmates of the police jails. Recently a number of black Creoles have died while in police custody.[81] Riots were triggered when a popular black reggae singer and musician was found dead in a prison cell after being arrested on a charge of smoking cannabis. Police stations were attacked in the riots that verged on a violent ethnic confrontation between black Creoles and Indians.[82]

Historically, the few Creoles with African features who became upwardly mobile in the class hierarchy ceased to identify themselves with that racial category and sought to pass into the coloured section, imitating the lifestyle of the white Creoles. There are signs that this may now be changing. Significantly, it is Catholic priests with African phenotype that have been the first to articulate the *malaise* of the black Creoles.[83] The 'whitening' process through marriage, that in other walks of life has tended to cream off potential leaders from the black Creoles, does not affect Catholic priests.

The Catholic Church in Mauritius has traditionally supported the Creole hierarchy. In return the plantocracy lavished the surplus squeezed out of the sugar proletariat on the Catholic faith. The churches, solidly built in cut stones, dominated the landscape of the island. The majority of the priests were always white or coloured Creoles. The numerous statues, inside and outside the churches, representing the Virgin Mary and the saints, had European features. During mass the black Creoles were always at the back of the churches, well away from the white Creoles in the front pews. Preaching was in French and not in the Creole language. Decolonisation, the numerical importance of the Catholics of the Third World, above all the new line adopted by the Vatican have brought changes in the Catholic Church in the Creole islands. The Pope made a point of going to Rodrigues when he visited Mauritius. Some of the priests want the Church to have a 'liberation' role.

The outspokenness of the black priests in Mauritius has coincided with the change of political regime in South Africa. After the abolition of slavery, Mauritius has had hardly any contacts with black Africa. In contrast relations with Apartheid South Africa were always maintained. Very many white Creoles and some coloured who could pass for white emigrated to South Africa. The economic links have remained after the end of Apartheid but the new South Africa might also be influencing the racial value system of the Creoles. Nelson Mandela visited Mauritius recently and on that occasion the African Cultural Centre was renamed after him.[84]

France, unlike the other maritime powers, wishes to be accepted in the Indian Ocean on the same footing as the littoral states. Britain has contrived sovereignty in the Chagos but makes no claim that these islands are part of its national identity. In fact by reiterating that the Chagos will be returned to Mauritius when no longer needed for military purposes, Britain excludes such an interpretation of its position. The French argue that France is different in that it is not an external power with a military presence in the Indian Ocean but that it belongs to the Creole islands. France maintains substantial military forces on land and sea in the region but it was not involved at all in the British-American military redeployment in the Indian Ocean.[85] Réunion is the territorial and human expression of France's claim to be a nation-state of the Indian Ocean.

There is a long tradition in France of envisaging the ultimate purpose of colonisation as the creation of a Greater France through the gradual integration of the colonies into the metropolitan state. Decolonisation would then be more a question of equality of citizenship and individual self-determination within the Republic than of national self-determination for the colony leading to sovereignty in the international system. Réunion, one of the Creole islands created by France in the middle of the Indian Ocean, was particularly well suited for the policy of decolonisation through integration in the Republic. At the end of the Second World War the French Communist Party, then at the peak of its strength, saw the integration of Réunion with France as the most effective way of demolishing the power of the plantocracy in the island.[86] But this assumed that the Communists would remain part of the government in a France closer to Moscow than to Washington. The Cold War in Europe and the hot war in Vietnam isolated the

Communists in opposition in France. The *départementalisation* of Réunion was not reversed, however, under the Fourth Republic (1946-1958), and with the return of De Gaulle to power in May 1958 a systematic sustained effort was made really to transform the island into an integral part of France.

The massive transfer of the institutions of an advanced industrial society to an island in the Indian Ocean has effectively demolished the old Creole structure in Réunion, as much if not more than independence has done in Mauritius. In all the domains that are in the prerogative of the state, *départementalisation* has thoroughly decolonised Réunion. The island is a *Région* as well as a *Département* of the French Republic. Both *Région* and *Département* have their own local assembly. The islanders vote in all elections just as other citizens of the French Republic and send five Deputies to the National Assembly in Paris as well as two Senators. The political parties are branches of metropolitan ones or closely allied to them. The Communist Party has remained stronger in Réunion than in metropolitan France, but decentralisation of local government went some way towards the Communists' *autonomie* programme and they are now as *départemantalistes* as the parties of the right. Except for a tiny and electorally insignificant grouping - the *Mouvement pour l'indépendence de la Réunion* (MIR) - there are now no advocates of independence. At one point Libya attempted to get the OAU to support independence for the island, but the numerous clients of France in Africa ensured that this initiative was rapidly squashed.

It is against the law in France to classify people according to ethnic origins; but as a generalisation it can be said that in Réunion today one-third of the population has Indian antecedents, one third European, and one third African or Malagasy antecedents. Unlike in Mauritius, the Indians of Réunion have, by and large, been completely integrated into the mainstream of Creole society. Except for a small minority of Indian Muslim merchants - known as *Zarabes* - the Indians have adopted Christianity while preserving some of the practices of Hinduism. The Indians tend to work in the sugar plantations in the lowland parts of the

island. The white Creoles are divided into two distinct categories: the few very rich *Grand Blanc*, who are still associated with ownership of sugar estates, and the more
numerous *Petit Blanc*. The latter are the descendants of the
first Europeans and children of unions between Europeans
and Malagasy/Africans of the *habitation* stage of creolisation.
Many of the small whites, from very early on, left the plantations and became a kind of subsistence peasantry high up
in the more mountainous parts of the island. These small
whites remained as poor as the black Creoles. The small
whites of the mountains are interesting linguistically for they
have preserved the way of speaking of the *habitations* and
were largely illiterate until *départementalisation* tried to rein-
tegrate them. The existence of a largish group of white but
poor Creoles in Réunion contributed, to some extent, to dis-
sociate skin colour from social class. *Départementalisation*
has brought a new class of civil servants from metropolitan
France. The presence of these powerful white persons,
operating in public life with the universalist values of the
secular French state, erodes the traditional Creole society.[87]

The material achievements of the state in Réunion are
outstanding: the airport, the network of modern highways,
the public buildings, the supply of electricity and of water,
the hospitals, the schools, the university, are as good if not
better than in metropolitan France. The success is the more
remarkable in that the physical geography of the island is
somewhat forbidding. There are limits, however, to what the
state can do in transforming a tropical island in the middle
of the Indian Ocean, with a plantation economy originally
based on slavery, into an integral part of an advanced
industrial society. Indeed, the very success of the state has
perverse effects. Unemployment is very high. *Départementalisation* has modernised the sugar industry but mechanisation and centralisation have meant a reduction in the
number of people earning a living in this sector of the economy that has fallen steadily with improvements in production. The primary sector as a whole provides employment to
less than 15 per cent of the active population. Sugar had to
be further mechanised as government forced up wages by
initially paying workers five times more than the private

sector. The massive investments in the infrastructure provided jobs in construction for a period but have not led to development of manufacturing industries. In spite of all the incentives from the government, including subsidies, tax holidays, the superb infrastructure, cheap electricity, 'assured political stability'; no new industry of any importance has been tempted to settle in Réunion. The high salaries of the civil servants create demands for the kind of luxury French goods that are cheaper to produce in France and export to Réunion than to produce in the island. Réunion, as a part of France, is within the common custom barrier of the EU. The island cannot protect itself adequately - assuming that it would want to - from competition of goods produced in Europe. The biggest handicap of Réunion in trying to emulate Mauritius and produce goods for export is the high cost of its relatively unskilled labour. For although there is a large surplus of labour in the island, French legislation and wages paid by the government keep its price very high by the standard of the region. Wages in Réunion are aligned with those paid in France. The lowest wage that an employed person gets by law in Réunion for one hour's work is more than a factory worker's earnings in an eight-hour working-day in Mauritius. When the numerous obligations which firms have towards their employees under French legislation are taken into account as well, it is not surprising that the multinationals, beginning with the French based ones, do not set up shop in Réunion but go to Mauritius.

Départementalisation has given Réunion a much higher standard of living than that which prevails in the other Creole islands. Yet total dependence on metropolitan France, unemployment, and living on state assistance engendered frustrations which provided the Communists with the continued basis of their strength in the island while they were declining in popularity in metropolitan France. The frustrations have not affected all equally: the small whites (the urban ones not those of the mountains) have done better than the *Cafres*[88] living in Debre's[89] high rise flats in the outskirts of Saint-Denis. It was among these unemployed black Creoles that the ban on a popular radio station in 1991 triggered riots, which resulted in much looting and burning of supermarkets, those symbols of the affluent European consumer society that has been transplanted to Réunion.[90]

Paradoxically Réunion's failure to develop in spite of - indeed because of - the efforts of the state suits the interests of the neighbouring islands. The generosity of the French state towards its *département* gives the Réunionais - some more so than others - the standard of living and the purchasing power of the citizens of an advanced industrial society. This rich market is open under the EU-ACP agreement to the competitive goods based on cheap labour in Mauritius, contributing to its capitalist development. The French from Europe and Réunion top the list of the tourists visiting Mauritius and the Seychelles. Economic interests thus reinforce historical and cultural considerations in the acceptance by other islands of the status of Réunion. Brussels, taking its cue from Paris, supports with millions of Euros the Indian Ocean Commission (IOC) that brings Réunion together with the other islands of the region that are members of the African, Caribbean, Pacific countries linked to the EU, the ACPs.[91] When the islands recognise Réunion as a part of France they recognise France as a littoral state of the Indian Ocean. The international legitimacy of the status of Réunion is thus strengthened together with France's presence in the Indian Ocean as part of its ambition for an independent role in global politics.[92]

Because of Réunion and also as a result of its role in the genesis of all the Creole islands, France does much for them. France provides soft loans and grants for economic development. French experts and *coopérants* are seen in the remotest villages and islands. The first dentist of Rodrigues was a French *coopérant*. The islands are full members of the numerous Paris-financed French speaking international organisations. France finances schools and institutes and provides scholarships to Réunion and other French universities. France finances Indian Ocean Island games and football tournaments. Radio and television programmes beamed to Réunion by satellite are very popular in Mauritius. Plays and artists, subsidised by the state on visits to Réunion, take in the other islands on their tours. Air France helps to train the crews and service the planes of Air Mauritius.

The Creole islands are wooed and not coerced, aided and not exploited by France. The 'dependence' of these micro-states is not perceived by most of the inhabitants as being all in one direction, because France depends on them, at least to some extent, for her international acceptance as a member state in the region. Diego Garcia is not primarily concerned with the external security of the Creole islands, which in any case can only be threatened by their own patrons: the maritime powers of the West. The presence of France in the region, however, adds to the sense of security of the Creoles in the internal politics of Mauritius. Paris helped to bring about the post-independence political coalition between the PMSD and the MLP and reconciled the Creole hierarchy to decolonisation. The proximity of France in Réunion alleviates anxieties in Creole circles over the 'Indianisation' of Mauritius.

Conclusions

The discovery of the sea gave Europe a global reach early on in modernity. Thalasocratic hegemony was translated into European colonial rule over most of the land surface of the planet. European settler colonisation was categorically different from non-settler colonisation. The former radically and irreversibly transformed the planet. The indigenous populations of the New World of the Americas and of other similar lands were eliminated or displaced and replaced by European settlers and by slaves mainly from Africa. The goals of the Europeans, in their first phase of expansion in the Indian Ocean, were trade monopolies in Asia and hegemony over the ocean rather than colonisation. The exception was the uninhabited oceanic islands to the east of Madagascar where European settlers and Malagasy/African slaves created a little New World of Creoles.

Creolisation was a very original variant of settler colonisation. The African and the Malagasy slaves, who formed the bulk of the inhabitants, lost their cultures and were acculturated in the Creole societies that emerged in the oceanic islands under European colonial rule. The islands fulfilled

commercial and military logistical functions under the
French who organised an insular system centred on
Mauritius aimed at regaining control in India. The insular
system lost its *raison d'être* when Britain replaced France in
all the islands except Réunion. The Creoles turned to the
land and plantations, particularly of sugar, which became the
main stay of the islands. The well-entrenched structure of
the Creole plantation societies was not fundamentally transformed by the abolition of slavery. The racial value system
had been internalised and Creoles with African phenotype
remained at the bottom of the social hierarchies of the
islands. Abolition, however, led to the massive arrival of
Indians that radically and permanently changed the ethnic
composition of the population of Mauritius and, to a lesser
extent, that of Réunion. In Mauritius the ex-slaves became in
effect redundant, subsisting on the margin of the sugar plantation society and in Rodrigues or the 'lesser dependencies'.

The islands were creolised in the context of the geopolitics of European colonisation. The New Thirty Year War
(1914-1945) put an end to the Europe-centred international
system and gave birth to the global system of the Cold War.
The global system polarised on two gigantic states: the USA
and the USSR, which dwarfed the European colonial
powers. The two superpowers, for different reasons, were
not prepared to support the European colonial empires. All
the European colonial powers were the allies of the United
States in the Cold War and were dependent on Washington
not only for security in Europe but also for economic aid
under the Marshal Plan. The USA, itself an erstwhile settler
colony, was well placed therefore to exercise its considerable influence on the European states to get them to move
out of their colonies. Were the European powers to refuse or
to delay too long in transferring power to the moderate
nationalists in the colonies there were the risks of their being
displaced by more radical elements who would then turn to
the USSR. Decolonisation, however, did not signify that the
West was abandoning power at sea. On the contrary with
the withdrawal from the colonies in Asia and Africa, power
at sea became more - and not less - important for the West.

In the Indian Ocean in particular with decolonisation on

land in Asia and Africa the geopolitical situation turned full circle back to the West relying principally on the sea. Unlike the Atlantic and the Pacific, the Indian Ocean is virtually landlocked on its most significant northern side by the bulk of Eurasia, opening freely only to the south. This meant a basic asymmetry in the Cold War: while the USSR and China could bring power to bear overland on the countries on the rim of the ocean, without necessarily taking to the sea, the West could only intervene by having a presence in the Indian Ocean. Power at sea enabled the West to give reassurance to its friends in the newly decolonised states in Asia and Africa and provided a fallback position in case 'containment' failed on land.

The Creole islands regained considerable geopolitical significance with decolonisation in Asia and Africa. With the modern technology of weapons, however, it was not necessary for the strategic purposes of the West to retain all the islands. An oceanic base for the projection of the military might of the superpower of the West was found in the Chagos through the latest dismemberment of the little New World in the Indian Ocean. Communalism in the politics of decolonisation in Mauritius led it to collaborate fully in its dismemberment and the depopulation of the Chagos to serve the geopolitical interests of the West in the Indian Ocean. The Cold War is now over but the military base on Diego Garcia remains all-important for the West. The function of the base is now to facilitate the interventions of the USA in the so-called Arc of Crisis. This is centred on the oil-rich Gulf, and the West remains dependent on the oil of the Middle East. The West will use force if necessary to maintain the flow of oil. Future interventions will preferably be UN-authorised, as was the 1991 initiative designed to end Iraq's occupation of Kuwait. On that notable occasion, the giant bombers of the USA flew their sorties from the island base on Diego Garcia, and they did so again in 1996, with British support but without UN authorisation.

Decolonisation means a change of international political status: from colony to independence or integration within the parent state on the basis of equality. Decolonisation also might or might not imply change in the internal political structure of the colony. Internal change, if any, depends on which group in the colony inherits political power in decolonisation. Decolonisation, however, can seldom be literally the reverse of colonisation. Least of all can this be the case in the decolonisation of a settler colony. In successful settler colonies decolonisation meant transfer of power to the settlers, never to the natives. In the Creole islands decolonisation was accompanied by universal suffrage and this gave political power to the representatives of the majority of the citizens. In Mauritius, the majority of the citizens was translated into the 'majority community', that is the Hindu Community. The Indians, however, were not 'successful settlers' in Mauritius in the same sense as the Europeans were successful settlers in Australia or America. The Indians had arrived in Mauritius in a position of economic and political weakness. They were more the colonised than the colonisers in the Creole society under colonial rule. In a decolonised Mauritius, the Indians have political power but this is balanced by economic power, which remains largely with the white Creoles. In a democratic political system qualified by ethnic communalism, the black Creoles of Mauritius have neither the economic clout nor the numerical strength and political organisation to effectively challenge the Indians in state power. The principal condition for the decolonisation of Mauritius whereby the Indians inherited state power was the integral 'decreolisation' of the Chagos: that is the physical removal of its black Creole population. Rodrigues, with its population of largely black Creoles, remains poor and dependent on the state in Mauritius. The betterment of life for the Creoles of Rodrigues cannot be at the top of the priorities of the state of Mauritius as long as ethnic communalism remains the determinant consideration in politics.

Unlike Rodrigues, Seychelles got its own state in decolonisation. The Creoles with African phenotype are in the majority in Seychelles and with universal suffrage they are the determinant factor in state power. Seychelles is the only state in the Indian Ocean where the Creoles have state power. Will Seychelles become a non-racial society and yet remain a Creole society? By way of contrast, decolonisation through integration in the French Republic decreolises Réunion to the extent that in becoming integrally French the Réunionais are becoming less Creoles.

Notes and References

1. Edward Brathwaite, *The Development of Creole Society in Jamaica 1770-1820* (London, 1971), pp. xiv-xv. According to Robert Chaudenson, the etymon of Creole is *creolo* ('yes') in the maritime dialect of 17th Century French. Robert Chaudenson, *Des Iles, Des Hommes, Des Langues* (Paris, 1992), p. 6

2. *The Times Atlas of the World, Comprehensive Edition* (London, 1994), however, puts the islands on the map of the Indian Ocean. See p. 26. Mauritius as well as Seychelles are members of the Organisation of African Unity (OAU).

3. Richard Hall, *Empires of the Monsoon, a history of the Indian Ocean and its invaders*, (London, 1996). K. N. Chaudhuri, *Trade and Civilisation in the Indian Ocean from the rise of Islam to the Seventeenth Century*, (Cambridge, 1985). The first part of Kenneth McPherson, *The Indian Ocean, A History of People and the Sea*, (Delhi, 1998).

4. For the historical background of the Creole islands in the context of the history of the Indian Ocean, see Auguste Toussaint, *Histoire des Iles Mascareignes* (Paris, 1972) and Auguste Toussaint, *History of the Indian Ocean* (London, 1966). For the human geography and a great deal of other information about the islands, see the four volumes of Jean-Francois Dupon, *Contraintes insulaires et fait colonial aux Mascareignes et aux Seychelles* (Paris, 1976). R. Barnes, 'New Light on a 400 year old mystery, being an investigation of the Shipwreck reported by Van Warwijck at Mauritius in September 1598', as yet unpublished paper presented at an International Conference in Mauritius in 1998. This paper discards the thesis that Arab, Greek or Phoenician navigators might have visited Mauritius before the arrival of modern Europeans.

5. On settler colonies, see A. Lemon and N. Pollock, Eds. *Studies in Overseas Settlement and Population* (London, 1980). On Russian settler colonisation, see Jean Houbert 'Russia in the Geopolitics of Settler Colonization and Decolonization' in *The Round Table*, Vol. 344, pp. 549-561 (1997).

6. J. C. Parry, *Europe and the Wider World 1415-1715* (London, 1979) and J, C Parry, *The Discovery of the sea*, (Berkeley, Cal., 1981).

7. Carlo Cipolla, *Guns and Sails in the early phase of European expansion 1400-1700* (London, 1962).

8. Two recent outstanding books on the exceptional role of Europe in the globalisation of modernity are E. L. Jones, *The European Miracle, Environment, Economics and Geopolitics in the History of Europe and Asia*, (Cambridge, 1985) and David Landes, *The Wealth and Poverty of Nations*, (London, 1999). On the struggle between Europeans over Asia, see David Gillard, *The Struggle for Asia 1828-1914* (London, 1977). A.T. Mahan, *The Problem of Asia*

and its effects upon International Politics (Boston, 1900).

9. Marx and Engels, *On Colonialism. Reprints of articles from the New York Daily Tribune* (London, 1976). For a criticism, based on Marx's arguments, of the Leninist view of the 'unprogressive' nature of colonialism, see Bill Warren *Imperialism: Pioneer of Capitalism* (London, 1980). V. G. Kirnan, *Imperialism and its Contradictions*, (London, 1995) has a similar position to that of Warren.

10. Reverend Thomas Atkins in Tasmania in 1836 wrote: ' that savage tribes disappear before the progress of civilised races (was) a universal law in the Divine government' cited in Kiernan, op. cit. p. 111.

11. G. V. Scammell, *The First Imperial Age, European overseas expansion 1400-1715*, (London, 1992) p. 107. Landes suggests that slavery in tropical countries was caused by the prevalence of diseases. Specifically in tropical Africa, slavery was connected to sleeping sickness. Op. cit. pp. 7 and 9.

12. Eric R. Wolf, *Europe and the People Without History* (London, 1990) pp. 195-231. Eugene D. Genovese *The World the Slaveholders Made, two essays in interpretation* (Middletown, Connecticut, 1988).

13. S. Arasaratnam, 'Slave Trade in the Indian Ocean in the Seventeenth Century' in K.S. Mathew Ed. *Mariners, Merchants and Oceans* (New Delhi, 1995) pp 194-208.

14. C. R. Boxer, *The Portuguese Seaborne Empire 1415-1825*, London, 1965).

15. J.M. Filliot, *La Traite des Esclaves vers les Mascareignes au XVIIIe Siecle* (Paris, 1974).

16. On the Dutch occupation of Mauritius, see Albert Pitot, *T'Eyland Mauritius, esquisses historiques* (Port Louis, 1905). P. Moree, *Discovering the undiscovered country: Dutch Mauritius 1585-1710*, (Amsterdam, 1998). Also a collection of papers presented at an International Conference in Mauritius in 1998: *'Globalisation and the SouthWest Indian* Ocean', sponsored by the Dutch government, to commemorate the four hundredth anniversary of the first Dutch landing in Mauritius in 1598, is shortly to be published in book form by the University of Leiden. On Réunion, see A. Scherer, *Histoire de la Réunion*, (Paris, 1966); Auguste Toussaint, *Histoire des Mascareignes* op. cit., and the first part of Filliot op. cit. in particular pp. 21-32.

17. Filliot, op. cit. pp. 21-22.

18. Jean-Michel Racault, 'Pastorale ou "Degeneration": l'image des populations Créoles des Mascareignes a travers les recits de voyages dans la seconde moitie du XVIIIs Siécle' in Claude Wanquet et Benoit Julien, Eds. *Révolution Francaise et Océan Indien* (Paris, 1996) pp.71-82.

19. Historical background in Gerald Graham, *The Politics of Naval Supremacy* (Cambridge, 1965) and by the same author: *Great Britain in the Indian Ocean* (Oxford, 1967). C. Northgate-Parkinson, *War in the Eastern Seas*, (London, 1954) a well-researched book on the Franco-British duel in the Indian Ocean.

20. On the British capture of the islands, see The *London Gazette Extraordinary* (London, 13 February 1811); Raymond D'Unienville,

Letters of Sir John Abercromby, September 1810- April 1811, (Port Louis, 1969); James Prior, *Voyage in the Indian Seas in the Nisus Frigate 1810-1811,* (London, 1820): the author was a British naval officer who took part in the landing in Mauritius. The last French Governor of the Mascareignes, was a young General that Napoleon sent to the islands as part of his plan to defeat Britain by conquering the British Empire in India. As it turned out the General had to be content with reinvigorating slavery in the islands before surrendering them. See H. Prentout, *L'Isle de France sous Decaen.* (Paris, 1901).

21. Deryck Scarr, *Slaving and Slavery in the Indian Ocean,* (London, 1998) p.46. The Nisus, already mentioned, was the British ship that brought the news of the fall of Mauritius to Seychelles and wanted to claim the islands as a prize of war.

22. Filliot, op. cit. p. 54.

23. Gwyn Campbell, 'Madagascar and the Slave Trade in the South West Indian Ocean', unpublished paper presented at an International Conference in Mauritius in 1998, Globalisation *and the South West Indian Ocean.* The author argues that Indonesians were involved in the shipment of slaves from the east coast of Africa to Madagascar as early as the tenth century.

24. A Spanish coin that was in general use in the islands in the eighteenth century.

25. 'Capitalism does not entirely rule out the possibility of the existence of slavery at isolated points within the bourgeois production system. But this is only possible because it does not exist at other points of the system and appears as an anomaly in opposition to the bourgeois system itself.' Marx, quoted by M.C. Howard and J.C King (eds.), *The Economics of Marx* (London, 1976), p. 87.

26. Philip Baker, *Kreol: A Description of Mauritian Creole* (London, 1972). Robert Chaudenson, op. cit.

27. These were the places where the first French settlers resided together with their slaves in Réunion. Housing was very elementary with hardly any furniture. Slavery, at that stage, was mostly of the domestic kind.

28. Before the French language was standardised, Northern France spoke the *langue d'oil* while Southern France spoke the *langue d'oc.* Oil and Oc were early variants of *Oui,* modern French 'yes'.

29. Newly arrived slaves, not Creoles, not born in the islands.

30. Robert Chaudenson, *Les Créoles* (Paris, 1995).

31. Newly arrived slaves did their best to remove the marks on their skin that proclaimed him or her to be non-Creole. Scarr, op. cit. p. 157.

32. For the thesis that slavery enabled Britain to take off into the Industrial Revolution and that abolition in the British Empire was principally motivated by economic interests, see Eric Williams, *Capitalism and Slavery* (Chapel Hill, N.C. 1944). For the role of sugar in the development of capitalism, see Sidney W. Mintz, *Sweetness and Power, the Place of Sugar in Modern History,* (London, 1986).

33. For the contrast between the free worker and the slave, see Marx, *Capital,* (London, 1990), vol. I, pp. 1031- 1034.

34. This Indian, Annasamy, might have been a front man for Farquhar. He denied any Farquhar connection, but it is difficult to see where else he could have got the capital so rapidly, for he arrived as a clerk with the British forces in 1810. Scarr, op. cit. p. 173.

35. On the development of the sugar industry in Mauritius, see Roland Lamusse, The *Economic Development of the Mauritius Sugar Industry* (B.Litt. dissertation, University of Oxford, 1958). British scientists and co-operation/conflict with the Creole plantocracy, in William K. Storey, *Science and Power in Colonial Mauritius,* (Rochester, NY, 1997). For the plots of sugar-land sold to Indians, see H. C. Brookfield, 'Problems of Monoculture and Diversification in a Sugar Island: Mauritius' in *Economic Geography,* (Worcester, Mass. 1959) 35, pp. 25-40.

36. A good analysis by a Social Anthropologist: Burton Benedict, *Indians in a Plural Society,* (London, 1961).

37. 'Malbar' is a pejorative Creole expression for Indian. The first Indians to come to Mauritius under French rule were from the Malabar Coast.

38. Burton Benedict 'Stratification in Plural Societies', *American Anthropologist,* vol. 64, no. 6, (1962).

39. The leader of the MLP, Sir Seewoosagur Ramgoolam, who became the first Prime Minister of Mauritius, is on record as saying that although he himself had been prepared to advocate the integration of Mauritius with the UK, 'we are told [by the UK Government] there is not the slightest chance of this country being integrated with Great Britain...Great Britain has no time for us. It is painful for me to stand in this House and say so, because I am a loyal citizen of the British Empire. I owe my fidelity and loyalty to this great Empire...' *Mauritius Legislative Council Debates,* 13 June 1967, cols. 791-2.

40. The PMSD was originally known as *Parti Mauricien* but *social démocrate* was later added, mainly to impress the British Labour Government. The *Parti Mauricien* had the reputation of being anti-Hindu, and the MLP used to embarrass the PMSD by reminding them of the time when 'Malbar nous pas oulé' (we do not want Indians) had been their slogan. *Mauritius Legislative Assembly Debates,* 23 March 1965.

41. Hindu mon frère' (Hindu my brother) became the slogan of the PMSD on island platforms, if not in the intimacy of Creole clubs and drawing rooms.

42. *The Manchester Guardian* (London, 1 February 1965)

43. For the British chain-of-islands scheme, see Phillip Darby, *British Defence Policy East of Suez* (London, 1973); John Darwin, Britain *and Decolonisation* (London, 1983); and Clive Ponting, *Breach of Promise: Labour in Power, 1964-1970* (London, 1989). For the debate in the British Parliament over Labour's East-of-Suez policy, see *Hansard* (London) Vol. 756, 1967-1968, 5th series, cols. 1577-1618, 1787-1911, and 1955-2011. For American involvement, see reports in *The Washington Post,* 9th. May 1965, The *Guardian* (London), 2nd. October 1975, and *The International Herald Tribune* (Paris), 26 January 1976.

44. *The Times,* 6 and 22 October 1965.

45. *The Guardian,* 6 and 8 October 1965.

46. Anthony Greenwood, the British Secretary of State for the Colonies, in turning down the holding of a referendum as requested by the PMSD stated that, 'the main effect of the referendum would be to prolong the current uncertainty and political controversy in a way which could only harden and deepen communal divisions and rivalries...'See *Mauritius Constitutional Conference, 1965, Report by the Chairman Mr A. Greenwood* (London, 1965) Cmnd. 2797,p. 77. and also *The Times*, 25 September, 1965.

47. 'Le PMSD n'est pas contre le principe de céder les Chagos pour la defence de l'Occident.' *Le Mauricien*, 13 November 1965.

48. For a good description of a typical coconut plantation island in the Seychelles, see Bernard Koechlin, 'Les Hommes et les Cocotiers de Coetivy' in B. Koechlin, ed. *Les Seychelles et l'Océan Indien* (Paris, 1984) pp. 81-134.

49. The 'passage' out of the people of the Chagos resembled that experienced by their slave ancestors. A small steamer, the *Nordvaer,* with room for only ten passengers, carried up to one hundred *Zilois* at a time, in the holds, on top of the last cargoes of copra. On the way to Mauritius the ship called in Seychelles to unload some of the copra and the then British colonial government in Mahe had the *Zilois* put in a jail for the days that the ship was in port. A British author has written a novel based on the plight of *Zilois* some of whom were driven to suicide. See, Peter Benson, *A lesser dependency*, (London, 1989).

50. *Le Mauricien* 13 June and 8 July 1980; L'Express (Mauritius) 17 July 1980.

51. The British Government stated: 'the people were... Mauritians and Seychellois contract labourers...none owned property...the company undertook the arrangements for the evacuation...all went willingly.' *London Press Service,* 10 September 1975. An ex-Governor of Mauritius, Robert Scott, has written a book that provides a wealth of information about the Chagos. This book was available to the British Government at the time when the decision was taken to deport the *Zilois* and makes nonsense of the claim that the Chagos had no permanent inhabitants. See, Robert Scott, *Limuria: the lesser dependencies of Mauritius,* (London, 1961).

52. *Weekend* (Mauritius) 6 December 1998. The present British Labour Government has been reviewing the status of the remaining British overseas territories and has concluded that: 'There are both legal and pragmatic difficulties in permitting ilois to return to live on the outer islands of BIOT...[and that] the only viable prospect for the remaining ilois was better integration into mauritian life...' Report of Baroness Symons Committee as quoted in *Weekend,* 25 October 1998.

53. The opposition, led by the MMM, won a landslide victory in a general election in 1982 and during its short period in office – before the coalition broke down largely because of communalist discord – investigated the circumstances surrounding the excision of the Chagos. The secret documents, treaties, press reports, and testimony of the politicians involved have been published in Mauritius as: Mauritius Legislative Assembly, *Report of the Select Committee on the Excision of the Chagos Archipelago* (Port Louis, 1983). Further

details are now available in recently declassified documents held in the Public Record Office, Kew, and used by Henri Marimootoo in a series of articles published in the Mauritian newspaper *Weekend* between May and July 1997. These documents do not appear to alter substantially the interpretation presented in this paper.

54. A short while before the same person had commented as follows: 'Diego is legally British. There is no getting away from it. This is a fact that cannot be denied. No amount of red ink can make it become blue. In any case, I am not in a hurry to see the Americans go.' *Le Mauricien*, 27 June 1980; and 10 July 1980.

55. The US informed Britain in January 1980 that it was spending another $170 million on the base straightaway, with more to come. *Le Monde*, 12 January 1980.

56. There is a growing literature on the military base in Diego Garcia; see, in particular, Joel Larus, ' Diego Garcia: the military and legal limitations of America's pivotal base in the Indian Ocean' in W.L. Dowdy and R. Trodd, eds. *The Indian Ocean: perspectives on a strategic arena* (Durham, N.C., 1985) pp. 435-451. ' Diego Garcia: Pivot of US Strategy', chapter 5 of Manoranjan Bezboruah, *US Strategy in the Indian Ocean: The International Response,* (London, 1977) pp 57-91. Gary Sick ' The Evolution of US Strategy Toward the Indian Ocean and Persian Gulf Regions' in Alvin Z Rubinstein, ed. *The Great Game* (New York, 1983) pp. 49-80. Frank Broeze ' Geostrategy and Navyports in the Indian Ocean since 1970' in *Marine Policy* Vol. 21 No. 4 pp. 345-362 (1997). Helen Mazeran *Geopolitique de l'Ocean Indien* (Paris, 1994).

57. *The last Corsair, the story of the Emden,* (London, 1984) pp. 107-110.

58. Bede Clifford, *Proconsul,* (London, 1964) p.268. Sir Bede Clifford was the British Governor of Mauritius during the Second World War. Among his duties then was to be host to Reza Shah, who had been exiled to the island, and planning the invasion of Madagascar to dislodge the French loyal to Marshal Petain.

59. Simon Winchester in 1984 was allowed to anchor for a few hours in Diego Garcia and has related what he saw in a book. Simon Winchester, *Outposts*, (London, 1985).

60. *WeekEnd*, 8 March 1992.

61. Scarr op. cit. p. 199.

62. Scarr op. cit. p. 200. The 92 islands of Seychelles are spread over an immense stretch of over 500,000 square miles of the Indian Ocean. But altogether there are only 171 square miles of dry land. The islands fall into two distinct categories: 32 granite islands, which are permanently occupied, and 60 coral islands, very few of which are inhabited all the year round. In contrast to Mauritius and Réunion, which are of volcanic origin, and relatively new, the granite islands of Seychelles are composed of some of the most ancient rocks on the planet. They are the remains of the original Gondwana continent, and are unique as granitic oceanic islands. Over 88 percent of the present population (some 66,000) of Seychelles are in Mahe, the main island (56 square miles), which also has the only town, Victoria.

63. Marion and Burton Benedict, *Men, Women and Money in the Seychelles,* (Berkley, Cal. 1982) in particular pp200-219.

64. On doing his about-turn on the issue of independence Mancham wrote a letter to *The Times* in which he said how sad he was to see the Union Jack go down over the Seychelles; Callaghan told Mancham how very touched he had been by the letter and that he would never forget. But when 'Jimmy' was toppled Jim, wisely, did. *Seychelles Bulletin*, 28 January 1976. For a very pro-Mancham survey, see C. Lee, *Seychelles, Political Castaways*, (London, 1976). Political background leading to independence in J.M. Ostheimer, 'Politics in the Islands of Love', in The *Journal of Commonwealth and Comparative Politics*, Vol. 13, No. 2, pp. 174-192 (1975). And M. Denuziere, 'Les Seychelles au plus pres du bonheur' in *Le Monde*, 25 and 26 May 1976.

65. The airport had cost £10 million; the US financed half the cost of setting up the BIOT, including that of the airport. *Seychelles Bulletin,* 19 March 76, and *The Times,* 20 March 1976.

66. Jean Houbert, 'Report on the Seychelles' in *Race and Class*, (1978).

67. *The People*, (Mahe) 27 March 1974; *The Nation*, (Mahe) 16 April, 15 June 1979.

68. There was a real attempt at a counter coup by white mercenaries led by Mike Hoare from South Africa. The attempt was foiled when the mercenaries disguised as tourists were discovered at the airport. The mercenaries then hijacked an Air India plane and got away. See, The *Indian Ocean Newsletter,* (ION), (Paris), 8 May, 29 May, 21 August 1982. Also President Rene speeches in *The Nation,* 15 October 1979, 2 November and 21 December 1979. Mike Hoare has given his version in which he implicates the government of South Africa, M. Hoare, *The Seychelles Affair* (London, 1987).

69. *Le Monde*, 25 and 28 May 1976, *The Guardian*, 20 June 1981, *The Times*, 9 November 1987. Also J. Moine, 'Les Seychelles, beaucoup de bruit autour d'un si petit pays' in *L'Afrique et L'Asie Moderne*, Vol. 119, pp. 2-23, (Paris, 1978). For the USSR naval presence, see Geoffrey Jukes, 'The Indian Ocean in Soviet Naval Policy' in *Adelphi Papers*, No. 87, (London, May 1972).

70. Visit of Mitterand to Mauritius as reported by Radio France Internationale, 11-16 June 1990, *Le Monde*, 6 and 20 June 1990, and *Weekend*, 10 and 17 June 1990.

71. *Le Monde*, 28 July 1992 and *Financial Times,* 28 July 1992.Also La *Lettre de l'Océan Indien*, (Paris, 1 August 1992). For a criticism of the one party regime by a French author who was very close to some of the ministers at the time, see Pierre Soubirou, *La Poudriere des Seychelles* (Paris, 1992)

72. On Rodrigues the indispensable reference works are: A. North-Coombes, *The island of Rodrigues*, (Port Louis, 1971). J-F Dupon, op. cit. and by the same author, *Recueil de documents pour servir ?_ l'histoire de Rodrigues*, (Port Louis, 1969). The government of Mauritius publishes annually *Report on Rodrigues*. The island is 600 km to the east of Mauritius and with its 105 square km is by far its largest 'dependency'.

73. The Colonial Office when planning the decolonisation of Mauritius had at first intended that Rodrigues should not have the right to vote. This would have further reduced the electoral strength of the Creoles. The Secretary of State for the Colonies answering questions

in the Commons said: ' It was never the intention that the island of Rodrigues and the other dependencies of Mauritius should be included in the electoral districts...' See, *Report on Mauritius,* (Port Louis, 1967), p. 5. Also S.A. De Smith, 'Mauritius: Constitutionalism in a Plural Society' in *Modern Law Review,* Vol. 31, No. 6, pp. 601-622, (November 1968). The author was the constitutional advisor to the Colonial Office for the independence of Mauritius. To this day the two remaining 'smaller dependencies', Agalega, which has a permanent population, and Saint Brandon, which has not, do not have the vote. The inhabitants are black Creoles.

74. See Mauritius *Legislative Assembly Debates,* 21 December 1967 cols. 1752-1756 for an exchange between a deputy of Rodrigues and Ramgoolam.

75. The GNP per head in Rodrigues is less than one eighth that of Mauritius. In 1962, on a population then of 18, 335 there were 11, 236 illiterates and only 786 had a primary school certificate. Even the few who did learn to read and write soon forgot how to in an island without books, without newspapers. The state has done something for Rodrigues but the island remains the poorest district of Mauritius. *Weekend,* 27 September 1998.

76. *Mauritius Legislative Assembly Debates,* No. 22, (1968) Appendix 2, pp. 47-48, and also *The Times,* 3 January 1968.

77. See, Edward and Bridget Dommen, *Mauritius, an island of success, a retrospective study 1960-1993,* (Oxford, 1999).

78. Louis Favoreu, *La Constitution de la Republique de Maurice en versions Anglaise et Francaise,* (Port Louis, 1993) p.250.

79. The census of 1962 is used to determine the size of the communities. These were: Hindus 51.8 % of the total, Muslims 16.5 %, Chinese 3.2 %, and General Population 28.5 %.

80. The employment of Creoles in the Public Sector generally has fallen from 89.7 % in 1901 to 70% in 1946, to 15.5% in 1985, to 11.4% in 1992. *Weekend,* 27 September 1998.

81. *Weekend,* 4 March 1999.

82. Several days of riots in the towns and in the countryside left at least four dead and damages estimated at £ 20 million. *Weekend.* 18, 21, 23, 24 and 25 February 1999. Also *Le Monde,* 25 and 26 February 1999.

83. *Weekend,* 30 August and 6 September 1998.

84. *Weekend,* 20 September 1998.

85. France has a *Force d'Action Rapide,* (FAR), a smaller version of the American Rapid Deployment Force, that can be deployed in the Indian Ocean very rapidly by air. Facilities exist in Djibouti that can be used if necessary as half way point to Réunion. Réunion is itself the home of the FAZOI, (the headquarter of French forces in the South of the Indian Ocean). Units of the French Navy are regularly deployed around the islands. *Le Monde,* 24 May 1979,25 November 1983. Admiral H. Labrousse, 'Perspectives géopolitiques et stratégiques' a paper presented at an International Conference in Aix- en Provence on the theme 'L'Europe et l'Océan Indien' (Aix-en-Provence, 1981).

86. On the early stage of *departementalisation* in Réunion, from a pro-Communist viewpoint, see M. Robert, *La Réunion, Combats pour*

l'Autonomie, (Paris, 1976).

87. *Le Monde* has published a number of special supplement on Réunion – for example, 'La Réunion à bout de bras' 5-8 April 1968; 'Les Petites Frances d'outre mer', January 1975; 'La Réunion sous le vent du changement', 13 March 1982; and ' Une semaine avec la France du grand large' 11-15 September 1984. See also, *L'Année Politique*, (Paris), yearly since 1947, and *Annuaire des pays de l'Océan Indien* (Aix-en-Provence) which has provided first-class analyses of developments in the Creole islands since 1974, as well as regular bibliographies, chronologies, and other documentations. *La Lettre de l'Océan Indien*, (Paris) is a very informative weekly. This also comes out in English as *The Indian Ocean Newsletter*.

88. This is the term in Réunion for black Creoles with African features. From the Arabic Kaffir, a term used by the Arabs for black Africans who had not been converted to Islam, peoples without the faith, heathens.

89. Michel Debré was one of the 'grave diggers' of the Fourth Republic and the 'brain' behind De Gaulle's return to power in 1958. He wrote the Constitution of the Fifth Republic and was its first Prime Minister, then Minister for Foreign Affairs and Minister of Defence. Elected First Deputy for Réunion in a by-election in 1963, Debré was continually re-elected with large majorities over the communist opposition. Debré did more than anyone to focus the attention of France's ruling elite on the problems of Réunion. Debré, an outspoken nationalist, was an *enragé of départmentalisation* for Réunion. The re-housing of the poor of the island in cyclone-proof block of flats in the outskirts of Saint-Denis was one of Debré project. Debré has written numerous articles and a book making a strong plea for a vigorous French policy in the Indian Ocean. See Michel Debré, *Une Politique pour la Réunion* (Paris, 1974) and among the articles especially Michel Debré, 'Océan Indien, présence de la France gage de la paix et de l'espérance' in the special number of *La Pensée Nationale*, (Paris, 1975).

90. *Le Monde*, 27 February, 6, 19, and 21-22 March 1991, and *L'Express* (Paris) 15 March, 5 and 12 April 1991.

91. IOC, *La Commission de l'Océan Indien*, (Port Louis, 1991) The *Annuaire des pays de l'Océan Indien 1982-83*, is devoted entirely to co-operation between the islands. See also Emile Martinez, *Le département francais de la Réunion et la coopération internationale dans l'Océan Indien*, (Paris, 1988).

92. For further reading on Réunion the doctorate thesis of Helen Hinjens, *Réunion, France and the EEC: the State in North-South Relations*, (Aberdeen, 1987) is highly thought of in academic circles here and in France.

THE ETHIOPIAN DIASPORA TO INDIA: THE ROLE OF HABSHIS AND SIDIS FROM MEDIEVAL TIMES TO THE END OF THE EIGHTEENTH CENTURY

Richard Pankhurst

Commercial contacts between Ethiopia and India, which were much facilitated over the centuries by the Trade Winds blowing between Africa and Asia, date back to early times. The scope and extent of such relations are indicated in the *Periplus of the Erythraean Sea*, a Graeco-Egyptian commercial manual written around the 1st century AD. This work shows that the Aksumite port of Adulis, on the Red Sea coast of Africa, traded extensively with various parts of Western India, which supplied Ethiopia with both textiles and spices. Aksumite exports consisted mainly of ivory and rhinoceros horn, but, the Roman writer Pliny says, also included slaves. The latter were also shipped, according to the *Periplus*, from Opone, later known as Ras Hafun, a promontory on the Indian Ocean coast of Africa, ninety miles south of Cape Guardafui.[1]

Aksumite trade with the East was an on-going affair in ancient times, as evident from an early sixth century Graeco-Egyptian text, the *Christian Topography* of Kosmas Indikopleustes. It states that the Aksumites were at that time trading with India and Taprobane, i.e Ceylon, as well as Arrabia and Persia.[2]

The coming of Ethiopian, and other East African, slaves to India a millennium or so later is abundantly documented in Indian, and in particular Gujarat, records. These refer to such slaves mainly by three more or less alternative names: Habshis, Sidis, and Kaffirs.

The term Habshi was a corruption of Habash, the Arabic name for Abyssinia. This name is believed to have derived from Habashat, the name of a Semitic people located in northern Tegray in present-day Ethiopia, and a neighboring stretch of Eritrea. They are believed by many to have migrated in ancient times from Yaman.[3]

The word Habshi, as its derivation implies, doubtless at first applied primarily to Abyssinians (or, in modern parlance, Ethiopians), but was later used more widely for any Africans. However, most slaves taken from Africa to India would, for geographical reasons, have originated on the eastern side of the continent. For much of the time covered in this paper they would probably have included a substantial, if not a predominant, proportion of Abyssinians.

The term Sidi by contrast was a corruption of the Arabic Saiyid, or "master".[4] The word, as Edwardes notes, had "an honourable import" when first assumed, but, in common parlance, had become "rather an appellation of reproach than distinction".[5] This is confirmed by the Frenchman François Pyrard of Laval, who, reporting on a visit to the Maldives in 1607, observed that "the greatest insult that can be passed upon a man is to call him a cisdy", i.e. Sidi.[6]

The term Kaffir was derived from the Arabic Kafir, originally an Infidel, or Unbeliever in Islam. The word tended to be used in India for any non-Muslim, and was in many, though not all, cases applied to African immigrants and their descendants.[7]

Ethiopian and other African slaves taken to India (or indeed Arabia, their first port of call) were for the most part converted to Islam. This change of religion sometimes occurred even on the boats transporting the captives across the sea. After conversion they almost invariably abandoned their pre-Muslim names, in favour of Islamic ones. This was unfortunate from the historical point of view, for it destroyed the possibility of identifying the slaves' places of origin from their personal or family names.

Slaves in Islamic India, on the other hand, benefited from their conversion, in that it facilitated their integration into

Indian Muslim society. Unlike Negro slaves in the New World, slaves in Muslim India were largely free from racial discrimination. They differed from slaves in America and the West Indies, moreover, in that they were not subjected to plantation labour. Many slaves in India entered the personal service of rulers and other politically important personalities, in not a few instances as palace guards. This enabled them, like such functionaries in many lands, to exercise immense power, not only as king-makers, but, after successful *coups d'etat*, as kings themselves.

From the Early 13th to the Late 15th Century

The first Ethiopian slaves arriving in the Indian sub-continent may have come early in the Christian era. This would appear probable, in view of the antiquity of the Horn of Africa's slave exports, and the extensive trade between Ethiopia and India indicated in the *Periplus of the Erythraean Sea*.

Documentation on African slaves in India is, however, scarcely available for over a millennium, until the early 13th century.

The North and West: Delhi, Gujarat, the Gulf of Cambay, and Malabar

The first Hapshi of whom there is a historical record was probably Jamal al-Din Yaqut, a royal courtier in the kingdom of Delhi, in the north of the sub-continent. A handsome and most likable individual, he won the favour of the then reigning sovereign Queen Radiyya (1236-1240). This incurred him much jealousy at court, on which account he was eventually murdered by his rivals.[8]

Habshis, it is evident from 14th century reports, were then also prominent in several other parts of India. The largest concentrations of slaves was apparently found in the north-west, facing Africa: in Gujarat, and, immediately to the east, around the Gulf of Cambay. Both areas had long been in close commercial contact, across the Arabian and Red Seas, with Ethiopia and the Horn of Africa.

Evidence of an Ethiopian slave presence in the sub-continent is provided by the famous Moroccan traveller Ibn Battuta. Describing the situation between 1333 and 1342, he recalls that on embarking on a ship at Qandahar, or Gandhar on the west coast of India, he found on board "fifty Abyssinian men-at-arms", and adds, with admiration: "these latter are the guarantors of safety on the Indian Ocean; let there be but one of them on a ship and it will be avoided by the Indian pirates and idolaters".[9] Half a century later, in 1375-6, Gujarat was reported as paying a tribute of 400 slaves, described as "children of Hindu chiefs and Abyssinians".[10]

A sizable number of Habshis were also found much further south, at Calicut, which also faced the African continent, and traded with Ethiopia. Ibn Battuta tells of a shipowner's agent at the port, who, when going ashore, was "preceded by archers and Abyssinians with javelins, swords, drums, trumpets and bugles".[11]

Habshis were likewise in evidence further south again, at Colombo, in Ceylon, where Ibn Battuta reports that Jalasti, "the wazir and ruler of the sea", had "about five hundred Abyssinians".[12]

The North: Alapur and Jaunpur

Habshis were also reported in the interior of northern India. Ibn Battuta recalls that at Alapur, north of Delhi, the governor was "the Abyssinian Badr..., a man whose bravery passed into a proverb". He was "continually making raids on the infidels alone and single-handed, killing and taking captive, so that his fame spread far and wide and the infidels went in fear of them". Gossip had it that he had retained some non-Indian ways: according to Ibn Battuta he used to eat "a whole sheep at a meal", and, "following the custom of the Abyssinians", would, after consuming it, drink a pound and a half of ghee, or clarified butter.[13]

Later in the century a slave called Malik Sarwar,

described as a Habshi, was appointed further north as governor of Jaunpur. He was succeeded by his son Mubarak Shah, who struck coins in his own name, and was succeeded in turn by his brother Ibrahim Shah. The latter reigned for almost forty years, and is remembered as a patron of literature and the arts.[14]

The North-East: Bengal

Numerous Habshis and other foreign slaves were likewise politically very prominent in 15th century Bengal, a region in north-east India which also enjoyed extensive trade with Ethiopia and other parts of Africa. The then Bengali ruler, Sultan Rukn al-Din (1450-1474), reportedly had no less than 8,000 African slaves, some of whom rose to positions of considerable importance.[15] Such slaves were particularly influential during the ensuing reign of Jalal al-Din Fath Shah (1481-1487). This caused the modern Indian historian Sir Jadu-Nath Sarkar, a stern critic of the Habshis, to remark:

"The Abyssinians... presented a serious problem... they had captured most of the high positions and now swarmed in the palace and in the city. Power made them arrogant and like the Turks in the employ of the later Abbaside Caliphs, they behaved with the citizens with increasing violence. The more defiant of them, according to Firishta, were consequently punished 'with the scourge of justice'".[16]

The Habshis were in fact so powerful in Bengal that a group of them, including the chief eunuch, conspired to overthrow Jalal al-Din Fath. Taking advantage of the absence on campaign of the loyal Habshi commander-in-chief, Amir al-Umara Malik Andil, the Habshi commander of the palace guards, Sultan Shahzada, assassinated Jalal al-Din. "From protectors of the dynasty", one historian wrote, "the Abyssinians became masters of the kingdom".[17]

Shahzada duly assumed the throne, in 1486, and adopted the name of Barbak Shah.[18] He was, however, soon afterwards killed by the Habshi Amir al-Umara who in his turn made himself king, with the name Sayf al-Din Firuz (1487-1490). A kind man, he is said to have confounded his treasury officials by the largesse of his gifts to the poor. His reign was, however, short, for he was replaced only three years later by an infant king. Real power, however, fell into the hands of another Habshi, Habash Khan, who was later killed by yet another Habshi, Sidi Badr "the madman", who had the young king put to death. Badr then seized the throne, under the name of Shams al-Din Muzaffar Shah, and instituted a reign of terror. His cruelty, however, provoked strong opposition against him, and by extension against Habshi domination. His army, which included no less than 5,000 well-armed Habshis, was besieged for three months, at the end of which he died.[19]

The Habshis, who had thus shown themselves so formidable in the bloody struggles of the time, were then banished from Bengal. Many sought refuge further north, in Delhi and Jaunpur, after which they drifted to the Deccan and Gujarat, where many of their number had earlier lived.[20] The memory of their immense power in Bengal was nevertheless so strong that the early 16th century Portuguese traveller Tomé Pires observed, with truth, that for three-quarters of a century it had "always been Abyssinians - those who are very near the king" - who had reigned.[21]

The South: The Deccan

The Deccan, in south-western India, was another area in which the Habshis gained prominence, and, as elsewhere, became involved in many conflicts of the day. At the beginning of the 15th century the local Bahmani ruler, Sultan Firuz (1397-1422), had many Habshi slaves as his personal attendants, as well as in his bodyguard, and *harem*. He incurred the enmity, however, of his brother Ahmad, who subverted the Habshi bodyguard, by one of whom Firuz was assassinated. Ahmad, though brought to power by the Habshis, feared their growing strength, and placed his trust instead in Persians, Turks and other foreigners of the Shiah faith. The Habshis and local Deccanis, both of whom were Sunni, thus both lost favour.[22]

Ahmad, unlike the rulers of Bengal, did not, however, banish the Habshis, who therefore continued to be both prominent, and powerful. During the subsequent reign of Ala-ud-Din Ahmad (1436-1458), they stood for example on the left of the throne, though the other foreigners were assigned the more prestigious position on the right. This did not, however, prevent Habshis from continuing to play a major role in political affairs, as when Ala-ud-Din's son and successor, Humayan "the tyrant", was stabbed to death by a Habshi maid-servant, in 1461.[23]

Several other notable Habshis feature in the Deccan annals of the time. One, named Khudavand Khan, served as governor of Mahur, while another, a eunuch called Dastur Dinar, ruled Gulbarga. Habshis thus governed two out of the four Bahmani provinces. A third Habshi, Mahmud, was keeper of seals, while a fourth, Jauhur, is on record as executing one of the principal nobles, who had been accused, perhaps falsely, of disloyalty to the ruler. [24]

Ethiopian and other African slaves were at this time probably arriving in India in considerable numbers. The *Gazetteer of the Bombay Presidency,* a generally reliable compilation, states that around "the middle of the 15th century... the fashion arose of bringing to western India large numbers of Abyssinian and other East Africans", i.e. Habshis or Sidis. Turning to the political role of these immigrants, the *Gazetteer* concludes: "Though most Habshis came to India as slaves, their faithfulness, courage, and energy often raised them to positions of high trust in the Bahmani court".[25]

The influence of Habshis in the Deccan at this time was also emphasised by a British historian of the Mogul Empire, Robert Orme. He observes that the slaves "gained ascendance" over a king of Bijapur, and were "exalted by him to highest employments in the state... they gathered all of their own country they could procure either by purchase or invitation, and even the Coffrees [kafirs, or blacks] of other parts of Africa". On the skill with which the Sidis involved themselves decisively in the political life of their country of adoption, he adds: "The natural courage of these people, not unmixed with ferocity, and always foremost in battle, awed the envy of their rivals, however indignant from the pride of their ancient descent, although the Siddees had likewise taken their religion".

The first marriages, of the Habshis, Orme continues, "were with natives of India", but later ones were largely "among their own families, which preserving their nationality, in time formed a numerous community, distinct in figure, colour, and character from all the other races of Mahomedans; which nevertheless could not have subsisted, if the body of the people amongst whom they had intruded, had not been, as themselves, Mahomedans. Later, during the reigns of Nizam (1461-1463) and Mahomed III (1463-1482) the Habshis regained influence, and in the latter reign in particular they shared in the offices of state".[26]

During the subsequent reign of Mahmud Shah (1482-1518), another Habshi, Dilavar Khan, became finance minister, but was later ousted by Malik Hassan, a Muslimised Hindoo, who then made himself dictator. Dilaver Khan tried to assist Mahmud against the latter, but, failing, was obliged to flee the country. The unfortunate king later appealed for help to the Habshi Dastur Dinar to free him of the usurper, but Dastur, despite strenuous efforts, proved unable to do so.[27]

The kingdom of Deccan, torn apart by continuous strife, was by then beginning to decline. In 1490 Ahmadnagar, Bijapur and Berar declared their independence of Bihar, where a Turkish minister, Qasim Barid ul-Mamilik, usurped power. Almost immediately afterwards the Habshi Dilavar Khan returned from exile to assist Mahmud, but was defeated and killed. Qasim Barid-ul-Mamalik then consolidated his position, and in 1495 demoted Dastur Dinar, who was then governor of western Telingana, and appointed him governor of Gulbarga. The Habshi leader resisted this demotion, but was defeated. He was, however, subsequently reinstated in Gulbarga, but as a result of further strife was later driven from the city, and eventually killed, in 1504.[28]

The conflict in Bijapur between the factions nevertheless continued. A stern decree was issued in 1510 prohibiting Deccanis, Habshis, or even their children, from holding office.[29] This law was, however, later reversed by Ibrahim Adil Shah (1534-1558), who restored the Sunnis to power, in

1537. He then divided offices of state between the Habshis and Deccanis, and thus brought an end to Shiah paramountcy.[30]

Several other Habshis were nevertheless prominent during the ensuing period of strife. They included Khudavand Khan's two sons, Shaza Khan and Ghalib Khan, and Dastur Dinar's son Jahangir Khan.[31]

The importance of the Habshis of this time is further evident from the fact that a hill outside the capital city of Bidar, where once they had their stronghold - and where many of them were buried - is to this day known as Habshi Kot.[32]

The West Coast

Habshis at this time were also prominent at several points along India's western coast. They were particularly powerful at the island fort of Janjira, and in the nearby creek of Danda-Rajpuri, where they were almost invariably referred to as Sidis.[33]

There are different accounts as to how the Sidis established themselves at Janjira. According to a history of Ahmadnagar, one of the kings of that state, Malik Ahmad (1490-1508), entrusted the island to his Abyssinian slave Yaqut, and established the Sidis as the latter's captains.

Another story holds that the Habshis made their appearance when one of their number, Perira Khan, and a group of other "Abyssinians" in the service of Malik Ahmad disguised themselves in 1489, as merchants. They obtained permission from Ram Patil, the chief of the island, to land 300 large boxes supposedly containing wine and silk. Ram Patil gave them leave, after which they regaled the garrison with wine. When the men had drunk to excess, the Habshis opened their boxes, in which armed soldiers were hidden. Taking advantage of their opponents' surprise, they then easily captured the fort.[34]

Other versions of the story suggest that the Habshis gained control of Janjira somewhat later, possibly in the early 16th century. There is, however, no denying that they remained in effective charge of the island, as we shall see, for the next two hundred years.[35]

Further north, at Daman, on the coast of Ahmadnagar facing Africa, the governor at the time of the Portuguese occupation in 1530 was a Habshi chief called Sayf al-Mulk Miftah, who had a force of 4,000 fellow Habshis.[36] To the south meanwhile, at Goa, Habshis were also prominent. In 1493, the Bahmani admiral Sidi Yaqut is said to have been sent with a fleet of 20 vessels against the Gujarat fort of Mahim near Bombay, and succeeded in capturing it.[37] Habshis were likewise to the fore at Calicut, the population of which, according to the modern Indian historian K.M. Panikkar, continued to include many people from Abyssinia.[38]

Cambay

Cambay, to the north-west of the sub-continent, at this time still also had a considerable Habshi population. Some made their way into the interior, including Mandu, whose sultan, Shah Khalji (1469-1500) reportedly had "five hundred Abyssinian slave girls dressed in male attire". Known as the Habiwash band, they were armed with swords and shields.[39] A decade or so later, the Portuguese traveller Tomé Pires recalled that the Cambay rulers had "many" warriors, among them Abyssinians, with whose assistance they were "constantly fighting with the neighbouring kingdoms".[40] The importance of such Habshis as fighters is likewise recognised by the Bombay *Gazetteer*: it claims that they were "among the most skillful and daring soldiers and sailors in Western India".[41]

The Habshis of Cambay were, however, not only soldiers, but also included many people engaged in the agate trade. One of their traditions, cited in the Bombay *Gazetteer*, holds that early in the 16th century "an Abyssinian merchant came to Gujarat, and established an agate factory at Nandod in Rajpila". The merchant reportedly died at Nandod, and was buried near the tomb of Baba or Bawa Ghor by the river Narboda.

Another tradition asserts that the shrine was actually

raised in honour of the merchant. It is said that "while wandering from place to place as a religious beggar, he did business in precious stones, and, becoming skilled in agate, set up a factory at Nimodra", where he "prospered and died rich".[42] The British ethnographer R.E. Enthoven, who refers to him as "an Abyssinian saint and great merchant", states that he came to be venerated by the Sidis, "many" of whom were "imported to work in these mines".[43] According to the modern Indian scholar D.K. Bhattacharya, the supposed Abyssinian trader was the only such holy man "revered generally by all the Sidi".[44]

The 16th Century: The Rise of Imam Ahmad Ibn Ibrahim, or Grañ, and its Aftermath

The advent of fire-arms in the Red Sea and Gulf of Aden region led, in the late 15th and early 16th centuries, to major changes in the balance of power in the Horn of Africa. One of the most important of these developments was the rise of the Muslim state of Adal, in the east of what is now Ethiopia, bordering Gulf of Aden. This was followed, in the late 15th and early 16th century, by some twenty-four years of instability, in which Imam Mahfuz, the Muslim ruler of the Gulf of Aden port of Zaila, carried out annual slave-raiding expeditions from Adal into the Ethiopian interior. Such raiding resulted in a considerable expansion in the slave trade, and in particular to the export of numerous Ethiopian slaves to Arabia, India and elsewhere.[45]

The importance of this slave trade, the source at this time of most of India's Habshis, was noted by the Portuguese traveller Francisco Alvares, who travelled widely in Ethiopia in the early 1520s. He observes that slaves from Damot, in the south-west of the Ethiopian empire, were especially "much esteemed by the Moors", i.e. Muslims. He adds that "all the country of Arabia, Persia, India, Egypt, and Greece", was "full" of such slaves, who reportedly made "very good Moors and great warriors".[46]

Slave-raiding was subsequently intensified by Mahfuz's more famous son-in-law Imam Ahmad ibn Ibrahim, better known in Ethiopia as Imam Ahmad Grañ, or the Left-handed. A charismatic leader of Adal, and a man of no small military ability, he rose to prominence immediately after Alvares's departure. In 1527 he began a series of expeditions which took him much further into the Ethiopian interior than Mahfuz had ever gone. In the course of these military operations Ahmad captured innumerable slaves, and thereby gave an immense new fillip to the slave trade. This resulted in a vast, but incalculable, increase in the number of Ethiopian, or Habshi, slaves arriving in the Indian sub-continent, and in particular Gujarat.

The prominence acquired in India by persons of Ethiopian, or other African, origin in the aftermath of Imam Ahmad's campaigns is confirmed by foreign travellers of the time. Towards the middle of the 16th century the Portuguese mariner Joam de Castro for example declared that Ethiopian slaves, serving in India as soldiers, were "strong and valiant to such a degree that there was a proverb throughout India that good soldiers or *ascaris*, or servants, must be Abyssinian". Such men, he adds, were "so well regarded in Bengal, Cambaia, Ballagate and other places [in India] that all those who command the armies or have a rank there are taken from among this race".[47]

The Habshi presence in India was also discussed in the last quarter of the century by the Dutch traveller John Huyghen Van Linschoten. Referring to slaves from the country of Prester John, i.e. the Christian empire of Ethiopia, he states, in an old English translation, that there were "divers men" there who sent slaves and free-men into India who served as "Sailors in the Portugalles ships".[48] He also observes:

"There are many Arabians and Abexiins in India... the Abexiins some are Mahometans, some Christians after their manner, for they are of Prester John's land... There are many of them in India that are slaves and captives, both men and women which are brought (thither) out of Aethiopia, and sold like other Oriental Nations... the Abexiins that are Christians have their faces 4 burnt markes in the manner of a Crosse, one over their nose in the middle of the forehead, betweene (both their) eyes, on each of their cheekes one, betweene their eies, and their eares, and one under their neather lip, (down) to the chin".[49]

Linschoten, who published "pictures of the Arabians and Abexijns with their wives, as they goe in India", also reports a significant foreign slave presence in Goa. Its population at this time, he states, included, "many Persians, Arabians, and Abexijns, some (of them) Christians and some (of them) Moores".[50]

Gujarat

The relationship between Imam Ahmad ibn Ibrahim's expeditions and the influx of Habshi slaves was evident to the contemporary Gujarat scholar Abdallah Muhammad ibn Omar al-Makki, al-Asafi, Ulugh Khan, generally known as Haji ad-Dabir. He mentions the impact of the fighting in Abyssinia in his Arabic *History of Gujarat*, completed around 1605. His observations are significant because he was particularly well aware of things Habshi. He was in fact successively in the service of two Gujarat Habshi noblemen: first Muhammad Yaqut Ulugh Khan, from 1559 to 1573, and later Abdul Kerim Sayfud Muhammad Fulad Khan, in 1599-1600.[51]

Haji ad-Dabir considered Imam Ahmad's fighting so central to the experience of north-west India that he included in his *History of Gujarat* long excerpts from the chronicle of the Imam's Yamani scribe Shihab ad-Din Ahmad ibn al-Qader, also known as Arab-Faqih.[52]

In his Gujarat *History* Haji ad-Dabir thus quotes from the Yamani writer's account of the Adal ruler's many victories over the Christian Ethiopians. He reports that many of the latter, taken prisoner at the battle of Dir, or Ad Dayar, and elsewhere, were sent to Amir Salman of Zabid, in the Yaman, and were handed over to him at the Yamani offshore island of Kamaran. Amir Salman, it is said, selected the most promising Abyssinians, who are referred to as Rumikhanis, and put the rest to death. Those spared were obliged to embrace Islam, but were otherwise treated kindly and, significantly, received a training in arms as well as letters.[53]

Amir Salman was murdered, in 1529, after which his slaves from Abyssinia were inherited by his nephew Mustafa ibn Bahram. The latter received orders in 1531 from his father in Constantinople to proceed at once to India to help the Gujarat sultan Bahadur (1526-1537) in his conflict with the Portuguese. Mustafa immediately set out, taking with him the newly captured slaves, by then irrevocably converted to Islam.[54]

The significance of the arrival of such large numbers of Abyssinians in Gujarat was emphasised by Haji ad- Dabir. He claims that they were as good as Arabs in everything except descent, but were often disliked by ordinary Indians, who were sometimes incited to murder them.[55] There were later, he adds, no less than 5,000 Habshis at Ahmadabad, and 1,500 in Baroda, in 1561-2. When the Mogul Emperor Akbar (1556-1605) subsequently entered Gujarat in 1572 there were likewise 700 Habshi horseman on the scene.[56]

The importance of this influx of slaves from war-torn Ethiopia was not lost on the British historian of India, Denison Ross. Recalling the bitter fighting on the Horn of Africa, the resultant extensive capture of slaves, and their subsequent political importance on the sub-continent, he observes: "the Habshis who rose to such prominence in Gujarat in the 16th century were for the most part the prisoners or sons of the prisoners captured during the Muhammadan invasion of Ethiopia". It was "in this manner", he adds, "that these Abyssinians came to Gujarat", and "the manner in which many of them rose to prominence and independence forms one of the most interesting features of this story".[57]

Elaborating on the above theme, he declares that in the disorders in India which began with the accession of Mahmud III (1537-1554), the Abyssinian slaves, i.e. those captured in Imam Ahmad's wars, "found a scope for rising to favour and prominence", though "their rivalry with the local nobility, and with the leaders of other foreign mercenaries, brought about a state of dissension which enabled

Akbar to conquer Gujarat almost without a blow ".[58]

The above-mentioned wave of Habshi immigration, though crucially important was, it should be emphasised, only one phase in an on-going, and largely involuntary, movement of population from East Africa to Western India. Discussing migration to Gujarat, Ross observes that "from the end of the 13th century to the end of the 17th... soldiers, traders, and slaves kept flocking into Gujarat by land and sea". Immigrants, he adds, included Abyssinians and Arabs, as well as persons of many other races. Emphasising the cultural significance in particular of the Habshis, he concludes: "A close study of the history of Gujarat in the 15th and 16th century has led me to the conclusion that European historians, following in the wake of Muhammedan chroniclers, who no doubt had their prejudices, have failed to attach sufficient importance to the part played by the Habshis in the history of that country".[59]

* * *

Most of the Habshis who arrived in Gujarat in the aftermath of Imam Ahmad's expeditions in Ethiopia and the Horn of Africa lived a life of near anonymity, and scarcely feature in records of the time. A number of their leaders, however, attained prominence, and deserve mention.

Three notable Habshis were accorded the honorific title of Ulugh Khan.

The first Habshi to hold this title was Mandal Dilawar Khan, who attracted the attention of Sultan Mahmud III, and was appointed captain of the latter's bodyguard in 1553, but died in battle in the same year.

The second Habshi Ulugh Khan was Sultan Mahmud's vizier Yaqut Sibit Khan Habshi, also known as Yaqut Begi Sultani, who, on the death of Mandel Dilawar Khan, succeeded to his title and military commands. He commanded a Habshi force under Imad-ul-Mulk Arslan, and obtained the latter's rank when Imad became chief minister to Sultan Ahmad II (1554-1562). On the death of Yaqut, in 1558, he was buried at Sarkhej, beside Bilal Jhujhar, another famous Habshi of the day. The latter, like other Habshis of that

name, was probably named after the Prophet's first *muezzin*
Bilal, the son of an Abyssinian slave woman in Arabia.
Muhammad had spoken of him with appreciation as "the
first fruit of Abyssinia".[60]

The third Habshi bearing the title of Ulugh Khan was
Yaqut's son Muhammad, also known as Shams ud-Dawlah
Muhammad al-Habshi, who served as vizier to his father
from 1543-4 to 1557-8. Also called Khayrat Khan, he also
held the title of al-Majlis al-Ashraf al-Ali, and is remembered,
as we have seen, as one of the patrons of the Gujarat historian Haji ad-Dabir. Muhammad Ulugh Khan appointed as
his vizier yet another Habshi, Bilal Falah Khan, and, according to the Indian historian M.S. Commissariat, "secured the
same devotion as his father had enjoyed from the Habshi
troops in Gujarat and was thus able to take an active part in
the confused politics of the time". He sided sometimes
with Itimad Khan and sometimes with Imad-ul-Mulk Arslan,
but after Akbar's conquest of Gujarat ended his days in captivity, and was buried at Sarkhej beside the graves of his
father Yaqut and his son Ahmad.[61]

The prestigious title of Jhujhar Khan, as Commissariat
notes, was likewise successively held, by "two Abyssinian
commanders" of Gujarat. The first was Bilal Habshi, who
was appointed in 1538-9, and was governor of Burhanpur
under Mubarak Shah of Khandesh (1537-1566). He was subsequently killed in battle before the great commercial town
of Surat in 1558-9, and was buried at Sarkhej. His son, Aziz
Khan, and grandson, Amin Khan, both acquired some
prominence in Gujarat.

The second Habshi with the title of Jhujhar Khan was
Bilal Habshi's son Marjan Sultani Habshi, who held the fiefs
of Bahmanul and Munda. The adopted brother of Yaqut
Ulugh Khan, he died in 1573, when he was executed by
being trampled on by an elephant.[62]

Other prominent Habshis of this time included Said
Safar Salami, who, after Bahadur's death in 1537, became
governor of Surat with the title of Khudavand Khan; Bilal
Falah Khani Habshi, vizier to Muhammad Ulugh Khan,
who subsequently became an independent chieftain with
the title of Khayrat Khan and died in 1563-4; and Fulad

Khan Sandal, who ruled the town of Jamud, until his death in 1569-70.[63]

Yet another important Habshi of Gujarat was Shaik Said al-Habshi Sultani. Originally a slave of Rumi Khan, he later entered the service of Sultan Mahmud III. On the latter's death in 1554 he joined the great Habshi captain Jhujhar Khan, and, after a long and distinguished military career, received valuable fiefdoms from the latter, who reportedly regarded him as a brother. Shaik Said managed his land efficiently, and acquired great wealth. He collected a fine library, and had over a hundred slaves, probably mainly or entirely Habshis, as well as numerous horses and camels. Until Emperor Akbar's conquest of Ahmadabad, he dined daily in the company of many nobles and divines, and maintained a public kitchen, which distributed food daily to nearly a thousand destitute persons. He died in 1576;[64] and is perhaps best remembered as the builder of a famous mosque, known by his name, in Ahmadabad.[65]

Akbar's conquest of Gujarat had major consequences for the Habshis, as well as for others, in the territory. Most of the nobles, among them two Habshis, Muhammad Ulugh Khan and Marjan Jhujhar Khan, were obliged to submit. The latter, who had uttered abusive words against Akbar, was punished, as we have seen, by being thrown under an elephant and crushed to death. His son Walil Khan was on the other hand given a command in the Akbar's Gujarat army. Another Habshi, Abdul Kerim Sayfud Muhammad Fulad Khan, the son of the afore-mentioned Fulad Khan, was the ruler of Songir under the kings of Khandesh. He subsequently transferred his allegiance to Akbar, who responded by reaffirming his possession of Songir. He later became, as we have seen, Haji ad-Dabir's second patron.[66]

Bijapur

Habshis in this period after Imam Ahmad's campaigns continued to be prominent further south of the sub-continent, in Bijapur, where their power was bitterly, and almost continuously, contested by other military factions.

Ibrahim Adil Shah's old policy of dividing power

between the Habshis and Deccanis, both of them Sunnis, was reversed by his son Ali (1558-1580). He once more dismissed the Habshis and other Sunnis, in favour of the Shiates. Later, however, during the reign of Ibrahim Adil Shah II (1580-1627), a Deccani nobleman seized the dowager queen Chand Bibi, and made himself master of the realm. Three Habshi nobles, Ikhlas Khan, Hamid Khan and Dilavar Khan - the second Habshi of that name - nevertheless soon afterwards drove him from the capital. Ikhlas, who is clearly depicted in a contemporary picture as being of African descent, or at least a man of dark colour,[67] became regent for a short time. He was, however, shortly afterwards dismissed by Chand Bibi, but later resumed his dictatorship which was, however, soon challenged by the other foreigners.

The more northerly Kingdom of Ahmadnagar, taking advantage of these serious dissensions, attacked Bijapur in 1567. The Habshis, realising that they could not defend their city alone, thereupon tended their resignation to Chand Bibi. This, in the view of the British historian Wolseley Haig, provided "the only example of self-denying patriotism to be found in this strife of factions". The Shiah foreigners then rallied to the defence of the city, and the Ahmadnagar army was forced to withdraw, whereupon the struggle at Bijapur was, however, renewed. Ikhlas Khan attacked his fellow Habshi Dilavar Khan, but was defeated by the latter, who became the supreme ruler from 1582 to 1591. In the latter year he was defeated in a battle with the Ahmadnagar army, as a result of which his power in Bijapur collapsed. He thereupon fled to Ahmadnagar where he found service with Burhan II, who had by then seized control there. The ruler of Bijapur complained at this employment of the former Habshi dictator, but Burhan replied by declaring war. He was, however, unsuccessful, and was obliged to make peace. The Deccanis then rebelled against him, and found a ready leader in Dilavar's old rival the Habshi Ikhlas Khan who failed, however, to capture Ahmadnagar.[68]

Burhan was succeeded by Ibrahim Nizam Shah (1595-1596), whose mother had been a Habshi. His chief minister, a Deccani, allowed Ikhlas Khan to return to Ahmadnagar.

Ikhlas then persuaded the king, against his minister's advice, to declare war on Bijapur. Ibrahim was killed, a further struggle for succession ensued. Ikhlas Khan proposed the accession of one prince, while two other Habshis, Ahang Khan and Habashi Khan, supported another.

The above struggles, in which the Habshis, as so often, thus played major roles, immediately preceded the conflict between Ahmadnagar and the Mogul empire which led to the latter's decisive victory in 1597.[69]

Sailors

Numerous Habshis were meanwhile employed as sailors in Indian waters. The Dutchman Linschoten recalls that besides Arabs there were also "Abexiins" serving as sailors around India, where they were replacing the Portuguese, who considered such work incompatible with their prestige. "These Abexiins and Arabians, such as are free", he declares, "doe serve in all India for Saylers and sea faring men, with such merchants as saile from Goa to China, Japan, Bengala, Mallaca, Ormus, and all the Oriental coast... These Abexiins and Arabians serve for small money, and being hyred are very lowlie (and subiect), so that often times they are (beaten and) smitten, not as slaves, but like dogs, which they bear very patientlie, not (once) speaking a word".[70]

Some Habshis sailed even further east. They travelled indeed as far as Siam, where the Portuguese mariner Ferdinand Pinto told of "Turks, Abyssins and Moors" engaged in fighting in 1548.[71]

The 17th and 18th Centuries

Indian trade with the Red Sea, Gulf of Aden and Eastern coast of Africa continued to flourish in the 17th century, and was accompanied by many further shipments of slaves. The number arriving in India seems, however, to have been significantly less than at the time of Imam Ahmad, with the result that Habshis on the whole began to play a diminishing role in Indian political affairs.

Travellers to India in the 17th century, however, still report a significant Habshi presence. The Englishman Edward Terry noted for example early in the century that there were "many Abissines" in "Indostan".[72] His compatriot the historian W.H. Moreland, writing of the time of the death of Emperor Akbar in 1605, agrees that "Abyssinians were in much demand", and "sometimes" rose to "very responsible positions".[73]

The demand for Habshi slaves was likewise subsequently reported by the early 17th century British envoy Thomas Roe. He recalls that he was requested by the Mogul Emperor Jahanger (1605-1627) "to buy three Abassines (for fortie Rupias a man) whom they suppose all Christians", but he refused, declaring, "I could not buy men as slaves".[74]

Later in the 17th century another Englishman, William Crooke, stated that Habshis, or "Syddies" as he called them, were raised to some of "the Chief Employments" in the land, with the result that "Frizled Woolly-paled Blacks" rose to "great Preferments".[75]

Habshis were still in demand in the 18th century, at the close of which J.H. Grose, a British traveller, declared that the "Moors", i.e. Indian Muslims, were "fond of having Abyssinia slaves, known in Indian by the name of Habshee Coifrees", i.e. Kafirs, or Africans. Such slaves, he believed, came mainly from the Ethiopian region via the Red Sea and Arabian ports. The slaves' principal place of origin, he thought, was the southern Ethiopian province of Enarya, bordering upon what was "commonly called Negroeland, in the heart of Africa". It was from Ethiopia, he claims, that such slaves were "selected, and a great traffic made of them, all over the Mogolistan and Persia". As for the character of these slaves, he observes that they were "highly valued for their courage, fidelity, and shrewdness; in which they so far excel, as often to rise to posts of great trust and honor, and are made governors of palaces; when they take the title of Siddees", i.e. Sidis.[76]

Though there was still a considerable demand for Habshi slaves, as Grose suggests, most, by the 18th century, were probably descendants of immigrants imported into Ethiopia earlier rather than immigrants themselves.

Malik Ambar, and Other Prominent Habshis

The best known Habshi of the early 17th century was probably Malik Ambar (1549-1626), an "Abyssinian" slave purchased in Baghdad, who became chief minister in the shrunken kingdom of Ahmadnagar. He won renown in 1601 by defeating the Mogul forces in south-west Berar, and subsequently established Murtaza Nizam Shah (1603-1630) as the nominal ruler of the land. He also reorganised the tax system, and improved the training of the soldiers.[77] The Mogul court chronicler, Mutamid Khan, wrote: "This Ambar was a slave, but an able man. In warfare, in command, in sound judgment, and in administration he had no rival or equal".[78]

On the death of Malik Ambar his son, Fath Khan, submitted to the Moguls, but soon afterwards joined Murtaza Nizam Shah in attacking them. The latter, however, subsequently appointed another Habshi, Hamid Khan, to the post of minister, and fell completely under his influence and that of the latter's wife. She became the recognised means of communication between the monarch and his subjects, and on occasion even assumed control of the army. In 1626 she overcame the army of Bijapur, which, however, in the following year decisively defeated her husband.[79]

Meanwhile another Habshi, Yaqut Khudavand Khan, led a group of fellow Habshis over to the Mogul Emperor Jahanger in protest against the influence of Hamid Khan and his wife. The defectors, however, soon deserted the Emperor, whose forces then hunted them down. The Habshis fought bravely, and reportedly "gathered together like ants and locusts", but were defeated. Hamid Khan's grandsons, realising the futility of the struggle, later made their submission to the Jahanger, who in return granted them fiefs in the Deccan.[80]

Hamid's defeat had fatal consequences. Malik Ambar's

son Fath Khan, uncertain of his influence over Murtaza, killed him, and replaced him by the latter's son Husayn Nizam Shah III (1630-1633). Randola Khan, a prominent Habshi general in Bijapur, then persuaded Fath Khan to join in the struggle against the Moguls, but the two Habshis were eventually defeated. Fath Khan nevertheless received honourable treatment from the victors, and was allowed to live in Lahore with an ample pension.[81]

Several other Habshis held important positions later in the century. They included Atish Habshi (d. 1651), sometime governor of Bihar and later of the Deccan;[82] Habsh Khan Sidi Miftah Habshi, who was honoured by Emperor Aurangzeb, and attracted the interest of the German scholar Hiob Ludolf, who reproduces his portrait in his *Relatio nova de Hodierno Habessinae Statu*; Habsh Khan's son Ahmad Khan;[83] Dilavar Khan (d. 1702-3), another sometime governor of the Deccan, who was in turn succeeded as its ruler by another Habshi;[84] and Malik Marjan, Ibrahim Adil's governor of Bidar.[85] Mention may also be made of an unidentified Habshi of Breampur, who, according to the Frenchman Pierre du Jarric, was "a very brave captain", and one of the principal guardians of the fortress of Asirgath.[86]

Hyderabad

There was at least one prominent Habshi in 18th century Hyderabad, in the interior of central India. He was Rahut Jung, also known as Sidi Asud Ula (died 1796), an infantry commander, described by the historian J. Clunes as "a native of Abyssinia".[87]

The Indian West Coast, and Janjira

Though the influence of the Habshis in the sub-continent was as a whole declining, they continued to hold power at the island of Janjira, on the west coast, where they were almost invariably referred to as Sidis. They were also prominent in the Nizam Shahi fleet of Ahmadnagar. In the early 17th century, during the reign of Malik Ambar for example, two Habshis, Habash Khan and Sidi Ambar, served as admirals of this fleet, while a third, Sidi Bulbul, was in command of Rairi.[88]

The Sidis played a notable role in the struggle between Emperor Aurengzeb and the Maratha leader Shivaji (1674-1680). No less than "three of the principal provinces" of Bijapur, according to Orme, were then governed by Sidis. One of them was the admiral of the Bijapur fleet, and had under his jurisdiction a "considerable" stretch of coast both north and south of Janjira.[89] Shivaji took the offensive in 1659 when he attacked Janjira, but failed to capture it. He nevertheless succeeded in seizing the nearby fort of Danda-Raipuri.

Several mutually irreconcilable accounts of this struggle are extant. One author, Muhammad Hashim Khan, claims that Fath Khan, the then ruler of Janjira, had "three Abyssinian slaves, Sidi Sambal, Sidi Yaqut, and Sidi Khariyat, each of whom had ten Abyssinian slaves, which he had trained and drilled". They were so well organised that "the management of the island and many domestic concerns" fell into their hands. Learning that Fath Khan intended to surrender the island to the Muslim leader Shivaji, they reportedly plotted together to forestall the betrayal. They succeeded in taking Fath Khan prisoner, and made Sambal ruler in his stead, after which they appealed to Aurengzeb's imperial armies for help.[90]

Conflict between Shivaji and the Habshis, according to this account, later "grew more violent". The Maratha leader collected forty or fifty warships to use against the Habshis, after which "there were frequent naval fights between the opposing forces, in which the Abyssinians were often victorious". Sidi Sambal was then given the title of commander of nine hundred, and, before his death, appointed Sidi Yaqut his successor, and "enjoined all the other Abyssinians to pay him a loyal and cheerful obedience". Yaqut, it is said, was distinguished for his "courage, benignity and dignity", and "strove more than ever to collect ships of war, to strengthen the fortress and to ward off naval attacks. Armed and ready night and day, he frequently captured ships of the enemy, and cut off the heads of many Marathas". He and

Sidi Khariyat later launched a surprise attack, with scaling ladders, on Danda Rajpuri, in the course of which its powder magazine caught fire, and the Habshis made themselves masters of the area.[91]

Another, rather different, version of the story, cited by Orme, and elaborated upon in the Bombay *Gazetteer*, claims that the Sidis on the mainland, faced with Shivaji's growing strength, escaped to Janjira. Several Sidis were then "in high military command" there. One of them, Sidi Joreh, an admiral of the Bijapur fleet, was sent on an expedition against Shivaji, but, failing in his mission, was suspected of treachery and put to death. His successor, Sidi Sambal, and a group of other Sidis then opened negotiations with Emperor Aurengzeb's generals in Gujarat and the Deccan. The Sidis offered them their services, and the support of Janjira fort and the entire Bijapur fleet. They nevertheless reserved the right to rule at Janjira, and to recapture whatever former Sidi property in Bijapur they could.

Aurengzeb, according to this account, accepted the Sidi proposals, and Sambal was duly appointed a Mogul admiral. He was raised to the dignity of a commander of nine hundred, and given "a large stipend on the revenues" of the town of Surat, whence he afterwards received continuous support against Sevaji.[92]

The Sidis, we are told, were at this time rich, and reportedly gained as much from their trade as from a stipend from Aurengzeb. Their administrative organisation, which was in some ways unusual, is described by Orme, who observes:

"Reverence to the higher family, and to the Mogul's choice, had given the pre-eminence of command to Siddee Sambole; but the other captains preserved the distinct command over their own crews and dependents, and an aristocratical council determined the general welfare of this singular republic; in which the lowest orders from their skill and utility, maintained some influence, and proud of their importance, merited, by the alacrity of their service, in so much that they excelled all the navigators of India, and even rated themselves equal to Europeans; and indeed the onset of their sword was formidable in boarding, and on shore".[93]

A similar picture is drawn by the 18th century British

writer R.O. Cambridge. He asserts that the Sidis beside possessing "many vessels of force", "carried on a considerable trade".[94]

Sidi Sambal's appointment as admiral resulted, according to Orme in Sidi Kassim becoming commander of Janjira, and Sidi Khariyat ruler of Danda-Rajpuri. Kassim subsequently succeeded Sambal as admiral in 1677, after which he expanded his fleet, and captured many Maratha ships, while Sidi Khariyat became governor of Janjira, and held this position until his death in 1696.[95]

Though some details of the above events are obscure, and differently reported, there can be no denying that the Sidis were in "constant war with the Marathas", between 1673 and 1707, as the Bombay *Gazetteer* states. "Sometimes laying waste large tracts of Maratha territory," they were "at other times stripped of their own lands", and only "with difficulty" held on to their island of Janjira". [96]

The Habshi admirals of the Mogul empire, it should be noted, enjoyed an influence far beyond Janjira. The Indian seas, as Cambridge noted in the mid-18th century, had long been "infested to an intolerable degrees by pirates", and it was for this reason that "the Mogul appointed the Siddee, who was chief of a colony of Coffrees to be his admiral". The Mogul rulers, who were "equally moved by zeal for the Mahometan religion, and concern for the interests of commerce", were then every year sending a large vessel to the Red Sea. In return for its protection by the Sidis of Janjira, the Mogul authorities granted the latter's admiral a revenue called *tanka*, valued at three *lak*, or 300,000 rupees, annually. This sum was raised partly from the revenues of Surat, and partly on rents from adjacent lands.[97]

After advent of the British in Bombay, the Sidis of Janjira appealed to them for help against Shivaji, in 1672. The British, however, refused, and instead adopted a policy of strict neutrality. For the next seven years the Sidis nevertheless made their way to Bombay, where, with or without leave, they passed the monsoon. Their object was to use the port, as Rawlinson explained, as a base for operations along the coast against the Marathas.[98]

Half a century or so later, in 1733, the British concluded an offensive and defensive alliance with the Sidis.[99] The death of the Sidi leader Yaqut in the following year, was followed, however, by a dispute over the succession. This weakened afterwards the power of the Sidis, after which the Peshwa seized many of their forts.[100]

The power of the Sidis was by then fast declining. Their ships, as the Bombay *Gazetteer* notes, proved "no match for the Maratha fleets", and were therefore unable to protect the shipping of Surat.[101]

Sidi Massut, who had been denied some of his revenue from Surat, nevertheless sailed there with fleet in 1759, and remained there throughout the monsoon period. During this time the Sidis "not only retained the government of the castle", as Cambridge asserts, but also "greatly encroached on that of the town": they appropriated no less than one-third of its revenues.[102]

The British shortly afterwards, in 1761, gave the Sidis their support, and forced the Marathas to restore part of the Sidis' former land in Kontan. A new dispute over the Sidi succession nevertheless occurred in 1784, whereupon the Marathas attempted once again, though unsuccessfully, to capture Janjira.[103]

The Sidis thus held their own at Janjira throughout the seventeenth and eighteenth centuries. They had been engaged, as Clunes noted in 1828, "in constant wars, by sea and land", until only 15 or 20 years previously, and their principality, "though circumscribed in its limits", still maintained its independence.[104]

The Deccan

The continued prevalence of Habshis, further south, in the Deccan, was noted in the early 17th century by the British traveller William Fitch. He recalls that one of the generals of the king of the area was an "Abashad", i.e. Abyssinian, or Habshi, who had with him "some ten thousand of his owne coste (caste), all brave soldiers".[105]

Two generations later another Englishman, William Crooke, told, in racist terms, of a Portuguese at Barvi in the

Deccan, who had "a bloody Leash of Coiferies", i.e. Kafirs. Crooke also refers to a certain Khawas Khan, an Itoby Caphir", i.e. Ethiopian Kafir, who had been "made a free Denizen and Naturalised". He was allegedly "so terrible" to Shivaji's followers that they declared that these Habshis, with their swords, were able to "cut down Man and Horse" alike.[106]

Elaborating on the position of Habshi slaves in the Deccan, Crooke observes that the "Coiferies", on their first arrival as slaves, became "endeared to their Master" who accorded them the "first places of Honour and Trust". His only Proviso was that they should be "faithfully obliged to their Lord", in which their newly acquired Muslim faith "rarely failed them". Self-interest moreover taught them to be "true to him that raised them", for only those who were not raised "at the Will of their Master, are tied to their Good Behaviour".[107]

Western Coastal Areas

Habshis were also to the fore in several other areas along the western coast of India.

In the Bombay area, the southern part of Kalyan province was controlled in 1648, according to James Duff, by an "Abyssinian" called Jaghi. He had the responsibility of maintaining a naval force, for the protection of trade, as well as of pilgrims travelling to Mecca. His appointment was not hereditary, but "conferred on the most deserving Abyssinian of the fleet", who was styled wazir. Many of his crews were reportedly Abyssinians, who had created "a small African colony" in the Konkan area.[108] The same was apparently true at the two fortified rocks of Henara and Canara, at the mouth of Bombay harbour. Both, Grose noted in 1722, had until recently been in Sidi hands. [109]

Goa in the 17th century, according to Crooke, likewise had a sizable population of "Cofferies", though these, according to François Pyrard of Laval, by then came largely from Mozambique, rather than from Abyssinia. This is largely confirmed by Crooke, who observes that "most" of these slaves then originated in Mozambique and Mombasa (rather than, we may comment, in Abyssinia, as formerly). The Portuguese, he adds, ran a school, where they were "taught to sound on Trumpets", and produce "Loud Musick".[110]

Further north, in Kathiawar, the port and small territory of Jafarabad were handed over to one of the Habshis, Sidi Hilol, then admiral of the Mogul fleet, in 1731. Sidi claims to the area were later confirmed by the British in 1759, after which Sidi control of the area continued for many years.[111]

Sailors and Pirates

Habshi sailors, of often uncertain origin, meanwhile continued to be active in Indian waters. Indian boats from the islands of the East, according to the mid-17th century Dutchman Gautier Schouten, were "full of Blacks", armed with spears, swords, shields, and muskets. One such sailor, the 17th century Englishman Peter Mundy reports, was his interpreter, Antonio, a "Capher Eathiopian Abissin, or Curled head", who had defected from the Portuguese to join the Chinese.[112]

Slaves from Africa, as Mundy suggests, travelled widely. They were reported as far away as Bassein, in Burma, where the Portuguese, according to Crooke, liked to display their wealth by the number of their slaves as well as by the number of their umbrellas. Such slaves were at times apparently unruly, for Crooke claims that it was "dangerous to walk late for fear of falling into the Hands of those Pilfering Abusive Rascals".[113]

There was also at this time a sizable number of Sidi pirates operating along the Western Indian coast. They were described by Clunes as "terrible", and "more dreaded, than all others, on the pirate coast". Their presence is confirmed by the *Bombay Gazetteer*, as far as the Thane, north of Bombay is concerned.[114]

The Decline of the Slave Trade

The Ethiopian slave trade, which apparently reached its peak after the fighting and slave raiding at the time of Imam Ahmad ibn Ibrahim, in the first half of the 16th century, thereafter significantly declined.

Later evidence nevertheless suggests that slave exports from Ethiopia and the Horn of Africa in the first two-thirds of the 19th century was by no means inconsiderable. Such exports (which were destined for Arabia and other areas as well as India) were then running at close on ten thousand a year, i.e. almost a hundred thousand per decade, or nearly a million per century . The average annual break-down of slaves was as follows:[115]

From Tajura and Zayla: 6,000 slaves

From Massawa: 1,750 slaves

From Beilul: 1,500 slaves

Total: 9,250 slaves

Such figures indicate that though the number of slaves entering the Indian sub-continent probably fell substantially in the 18th century, the slave trade had by no means fully dried up. This would in turn suggest, as far as the Indian sub-continent is concerned, that there was probably still a not insignificant influx of slaves from Ethiopia and the Horn of Africa, and that they would have at least partially replenished the ranks of the long-established Habshi population.

Habshis, or their descendants, continued in fact to be reported in various parts of the sub-continent, and the comprehensive investigation of their descendants, by social scientists, and linguists, no less than by historians, should prove rewarding.

Notes

1   R. Pankhurst, *An Introduction to the Economic History of Ethiopia* (London, 1961), pp. 16-24.

2   J.W. McCrindle, *The Christian Topography of Cosmas Indicopleustes* (London, 1929), pp. 365-6, 368, 372.

3   On the Habashat see C. Conti Rossini, "Sugli Habas at", *Rendiconti della Reale Accademia dei Lincei* (1906), XV, 39-50; J.S. Trimingham, *Islam in Ethiopia* (London, 1952), pp. 32-3; E. Ullendorff, *The*

Ethiopians. An Introduction to Country and People (London, 1973), pp. 48-9.

4   H.Yule and A.C. Burnell, *Hobson-Jobson* (London, 1886), p, 806: *Gazetteer of the Bombay Presidency*, XI, 433.

5   J.C.G. Duff, *A History of the Marattas* (London, 1921), I, 111.

6   A. Gray, *The Voyage of François Pyrard of Laval to the East Indies, the Maldives, the Moluccas and Brazil* (London, 1888), I, 173,

7   Yule and Burnell, *Hobson-Jobson*, pp. 140-2

8   J. Briggs, *History of Mohomedan Power in India till the Year A.D. 1612, translated from the Original Persian of Mohomed Kasim Ferishita* (London, 1829), I, 220; E. Thomas, *Chronicles of the Parthan Kings* (London, 1871), p. 106; S. Lane-Poole, *Medieval India under Mohomedan Rule* (A.D. 412-1764) (London, 1903), pp. 75-6; *The Cambridge History, of India,* edited by Sir Wolseley Haig (Cambridge, 1928), III, 60; R.C. Mujumdar, H.C. Raychaudhuri and K. Datta, An *Advanced History of India* (London, 1956), p. 286.

9   H.A.R. Gibb, *Ibn Battuta, Travels in Africa and Asia, 1324-1354* (Cambridge, 1962) , pp. 229-30.

10   K.K. Basu, *The Tarikh-i-Mubarak Shadi* (Calcutta, 1932), p.139: Lane-Poole, *Medieval India* , p. 147.

11   Gibb, *Ibn Battuta*, p. 236.

12   Gibb, *Ibn Battuta*, p. 260.

13   Gibb, *Ibn Battuta*, p. 224.

14   J. Burton-Page, "Habshi", *Encyclopedia of Islam"*, p.14.

15   Majumdar and others, *Advanced History*, p. 345; *Cambridge History*,III, 268.

16   Jadu-Nath Sarkar, *The History of Bengal, II The Muslim Period 1200-1757* (Ramma, Dacca, 1948), p. 137.

17   Sarkar, *History of Bengal*, II. 139.

18   Majumdar and others, *Advanced History*, pp. 345-6; J.C. Powell-Price, A *History of India* (London, 1955), p. 208.

19   Sarkar, *History of Bengal*, II, 139; Majumdar and others, *Advanced History*, p . 346; C. Stewart, *The History of Bengal* (London, 1913), pp. 102-3, 106-7, 208; Lane-Poole, *Medieval India*, p. 154; Powell-Price, *History*, pp. 189, 202; *Cambridge History,* III, 269-70.

20   Stewart, *History of Bengal*, p. 111; *Cambridge History*, III, 271.

21   A. Cortesào, *The Summa Oriental of Tomé Pires* (London, 1944), p.80.

22   Powell-Price, *History of India*, pp. 195, 197.

23   *Cambridge History*, III, 412.

24   *Cambridge History*, III, 412-14, 417-20; Cortesào, *Summa Oriental*, p. 51.

25   *Gazetteer of the Bombay Presidency*, XI , 433.

26   R. Orme, *Historical Fragments of the Mogul Empire* (London, 1782), p. 80.

27   *Cambridge History,* III, 422-5. See also G. Yazdani, *Bidar: its History and Monuments* (Oxford, 1947), p. 11.

28   *Cambridge History*, III, 428-31.

29   *Cambridge History*, III, 434.

30   *Cambridge History*, III, 439-40.

31   *Cambridge History*, III, 458

32   Yazdani, *Bidar*, pp. 180-4, and plate CXIX.

33 Duff, *History of the Marattas*, I, 111.
34 *Gazetteer of the Bombay Presidency*, I, part II, 34, XI, 434-5; J. Clunes, *Appendix to the History of Western India* (Bombay, 1828), p. 24; Duff, *History of the Marattas*, I, 110.
35 Burton Page, "Habshi", p. 15.
36 Burton Page, "Habshi", p. 16,
37 *Gazetteer of the Bombay Presidency*, XI, 434.
38 Pannikar, *Malabar and the Portuguese*, p. 11.
39 R. Skelton, "The Ni'mat nama: a Landmark in Malwa Painting", *Marg* (1959),XX, no. 3, p. 34.
40 Cortesão, *Summa Oriental*, p. 34.
41 *Gazetteer of the Bombay Presidency*, XI, 434.
42 *Gazetteer of the Bombay Presidency*, VI, 206. See also J, Copeland, "Account of the Cornelian Mines of the Neighbourhood of Baroach", *Transactions of the Literary Society of Bombay* (1819), I, 289.
43 R.E. Enthoven, *The Tribes and Castes of Bombay* (Bombay, 1922), III, 332. See also *Gazetteer of the Bombay Presidency*, IX, part II, p. 12; M.S. Commissariat, *A History of Gujarat* (London, 1938), I, 269-70.
44 D.K. Blattacharya, "Indians of African Origin", *Cahiers d'Etudes Africaines* (1970), X, 580.
45 C.F. Beckingham and G.W.B. Huntingford, *The Prester John of the Indies* (Cambridge, 1961). II, 410-15.
46 Beckingham and Huntingford, *Prester John*, II, 445.
47 A. Kammerer, *Le routier de Dom Joam de Castro* (Paris, 1936), , p. 80
48 P.A. Tiele, *The Voyage of John Huyghen Van Linschoten to the Indies* (London, 1855), I, 34.
49 Tiele, *Voyage*, I, 264-5.
50 Tiele, *Voyage*, I, 222, 276-7.
51 Commissariat, *History of Gujarat*, I, 471; E. Denison Ross, *An Arabic History of Gujarat* (London, 1910-28), I, vii.
52 Denison Ross, *Arabic History*, I, 584-9, 503-8.
53 Denison Ross, *Arabic History*, II, xxxiii.
54 Denison Ross, *Arabic History*, II, xxxiv; Commissariat, *History of Gujarat*, I, 470.
55 Denison Ross, *Arabic History*, II, *Arabic History*, 407; Commissariat, *A History of Gujarat*, I, 470.
56 Denison Ross, *Arabic History*, I, 447, 455, II, xxxvii; Commissariat, History of Gujarat, I, 470.
57 Denison Ross, *Arabic History*, II, xxxiii-iv; Commissariat, *History of Gujarat*. I, 470.
58 Denison Ross, *Arabic History*, II, xxxiii-iv; Commissariat, *History of Gujarat*. I, 470.
59 Denison Ross, *Arabic History*, II, xxii, xxxviii.
60 W. Muir, *The Life of Mahomet* (London, 1878), p. 64.
61 Denison Ross, *Arabic History*, I, xiv; Commissariat, *A History of Gujarat*, I, 471, 495.
62 Denison Ross, *Arabic History*, I, xiv-xv; Commissariat, *History of Gujarat*, I, 471, 4956.
63 Denison Ross, *Arabic History*, I, ii, xv.
64 Commissariat, *History of Gujarat*, I, 502-3.
65 Commissariat, *History of Gujarat*, I, 502-3; *Gazetteer of the Bombay Presidency*, I, part II, p. 34; *Cambridge History*, III, 616.

66 Denison Ross, *Arabic History*, I, ii, xv; M.S. Commissariat, *History of Gujarat*, I, 495-6; H. Beveridge, *The Akhbarnama of Abul-l-Fasl* (Calcutta, 1903-10), III, 46, 76,

67 British Library, Ad. MS. Orient 5,234, folio 34. See also Orient 22,282, folios 16, 20.

68 *Cambridge History*, III, 458-61.

69 *Cambridge History*, III, 464-6.

70 Tiele, *Voyage*, I, 265-7. See also *Gazetteer of the Bombay Presidency*, I, part II, p. 62.

71 *The Voyage and Adventures of Ferdinand Mendez Pinto* (London, 1663), p. 179.

72 W. Foster, *Early Travels in India 1583-1619* (London, 1921), p. 307.

73 W.H. Moreland, *India at the Death of Akbar* (London, 1820), p. 26.

74 W. Foster, *The Embassy of Sir Thomas Roe to the Court of the Great Mogul 1615-1619* (London, 1889). On slaves at Goa, see also Gray, *Voyage*, II, 65.

75 W. Crooke, *A New Account of East Indies and Persia being Nine Years' Travels 1672-1681* (London, 1915), I, 62, II, 5, 53.

76 J.H. Grose, *A Voyage to the East Indies* (London, 1772), I, 148-9.

77 J.N. Chaudhuri, *Malik Ambar* (Calcutta, n.d.); *Cambridge History*, III,159, IV, 148. For contemporary paintings of Malik Ambar see A.K. Coomaraswami, *Catalogue of the Indian Collection of the Museum of Fine Arts, Boston* (Boston, 1930), VI Mogul paitings, p. 49, plates XXXVII and XXXVIII; I.S. Stchoukine, *Le peinture indienne* (Paris, 1929, plate 29; K. Khandalavala, "Identification of the Portraits of Malik Ambar", *Lalit Kala* (1956), nos. 1-2.

78 *Cambridge History*, IV, 180, 203-4. See also Powell-Price, pp. 291-3; Majumdar and others, *Advanced History*, p. 446,

79 *Cambridge History* IV, 189, 263-4.

80 Sansamu-d-Daula Nawas Khan, *The Masiru-e-Umara* (London, 1911-1914), I, 990.

81 *Cambridge History*, IV, 192-3, 264-5; Samsamu-d-Daula Nawas Khan, *The Masiru-e-Umara*, I, 532, II, 626.

82 Samsamu-d-Daula Nawas Khan, *The Masiru-e-Umara*, I, 305.

83 Samsamu-d-Daula Nawas Khan, *The Masiru-e-Umara*, II, 33.

84 Samsamu-d-Daula Nawas Khan, *The Masiru-e-Umara*, II, 994.

85 Yazdani, *Bidar*, pp. 14, 49.

86 Pierre du Jarric, *Akbar and the Jesuits* (London, 1926), pp. 102-6.

87 Clunes, *Appendix*, p. 38.

88 Duff, *History of the Marattas*, I, 110; *Gazetteer of the Bombay Presidency*, I, part II, p. 34.

89 Orme, *Historical Fragments*, p. 80.

90 H.M. Eliott, *The History of India as Told by her Own Historians* (London, 1877). VII, 289-90; *Gazetteer of the Bombay Presidency*, XI, 437-8.

91 Elliot, *History*, VII, 290-1. See also Clunes, *Appendix*, p. 24; *Cambridge History*, V, 101.

92 Orme, *Historical Fragments*, pp. 9-11, 80; *Gazetteer of the Bombay Presidency*, II, 89, IX, 3, XI, 433-4, 436-7, XIII, part II, p. 227; B.V. Gokhale, "Bombay and the Shivaji," *Journal of the Royal Asiatic Society* (1958), XXXIII, 72.

93 Orme, *Historical Fragments*, pp. 80-1.

94   R.O. Cambridge, *An Account of the War in India* (London, 1761),
      p. 216.
95   Orme, *Historical Fragments*, pp. 32-4, 39, 43, 78; *Gazetteer of the
      Bombay Presidency*, XI, 437; Gokhale, "Bombay and the Shivaji",
      72.
96   *Gazetter of the Bombay Presidency*, I, part 1, pp. 71-2, II, 117, XI,
      437.
97   Cambridge, *Account of the War*, p. 216-17.
98   Orme, *Historical Fragments*, pp. 42-3, 62, 108-9, 152; Crooke, *New
      Account*, I, 195, 201, II, 18, 57, 63, III, 163; J. Ovington, *A Voyage
      to Surat in the Year 1689* (London, 1929), p. 10; *Gazetteer of the
      Bombay Presidency*, I, part I, pp. 71-2, II, 117, XI, 437
99   *Gazetteer of the Bombay Presidency*, XI, 444. See also D.R. Banaji,
      Bombay and the Sidis (London, 1932).
100   Duff, *History of the Marattas*, I, 231-2; *Gazetteer of the Bombay
      Presidency*, XII, 498.
101   *Gazetteer of the Bombay Presidency*, II, 117, XI, 443-4.
102   Cambridge, *Account of the War*, p. 217.
103   *Gazetteer of the Bombay Presidency*, II, 250; *Cambridge History*, V,
      369.
104   Clunes, *Appendix*, p. 24,
105   Foster, *Early Travels*, p. 138.
106   Crooke, *New Account*, I, 352, II, 5, 53.
107   Crooke, *New Account*, II, 52.
108   Duff, *History of the Marattas*, p. 110.
109   Grose, *Voyage*, I, 58.
110   Crooke, *New Account*, II, 16, 23; Gray, *Voyage*, II, 223.
111   *Gazetteer of the Bombay Presidency*, VIII, 161, XI, 447; Clunes,
      Appendix, p. 52.
112   G. Schouten, *Voyage de Gautier Schouten aux indes orientales
      commencé l'an 1658 et fini 1665* (Rouen, 1725), I, 108; R.C.
      Temple, *The Travels of Peter Mundy, in Europe and Asia 1608-
      1667* (London, 1919), III, part 1, p. 192, part II, pp. 241, 260, 312,
      511.
113   Crooke, *New Account*, I, 62.
114   Clunes, *Appendix*, p, 24; *Gazetteer of the Bombay Presidency*, XIII,
      488.
115   R. Pankhurst, "The Ethiopian Slave Trade in the Nineteenth and
      Early Twentieth Century: A Statistical Inquiry", *Journal of Semitic
      Studies* (1964), IX, no. 1, pp. 220-8.

SLAVE, SOLDIER, TRADER, FAQIR : FRAGMENTS OF AFRICAN HISTORIES IN WESTERN INDIA (GUJARAT)

Helene Basu

The western coast of India is dotted with settlements of people of East-African origins situated at the fringes of local South Asian societies. The largest group of African Diaspora (c. 40- 50,000) lives in the Northwest of the sub-continent, in the district of Sindh - close to the Makran coast - in modern Pakistan. Much smaller communities are encountered at present in Gujarat (6 – 7000), in Bombay (ca. 400) and further South in the Indian state of Karnataka. [1] Wherever they live, they call themselves 'Sidi' . The name has been subjected to a wide range of spellings, probably corresponding to local pronunciations, such as Siddhi, Sheedi or Siddi. Another appellation for Africans usually found in connection with Muslim history in South Asia is 'Habshi', a term derived from 'Habash', the Arabic name for 'Ethiopia' or 'Abyssiniya'. There is, however, no simple correspondence between the denotations and the denoted subjects. During fieldwork in the late eighties I found the Sidi in Gujarat resenting being called 'Habshi' because they associated social discrimination with the term, whereas Sheedi in Sindh (Pakistan) used 'Habshi' as a general term encompassing different social sections of Africans in the local context of competing political identities.[2]

Most of the historical literature concerned with the African presence in India follows one of two contradictory assumptions: either Africans are said to have remained completely separated and isolated from the host societies or they are seen in a process of assimilation which ultimately would erase their 'African-ness'.[3] However, neither of these two options seems to adequately describe the social situation as perceived by the Sidi themselves. Wherever the Sidi are settled, they seem to have acquired the local language, local forms of social classification and/or religious practices while at the same time retaining a social image of their community as being African and therefore doing things differently from their neighbours. The evocation of social difference, however, is not a unique feature of African Diaspora conditions but is part and parcel of the social order in South Asia, where everybody belongs to a social category in the sense of 'kind, type, genus' which is translatable as caste (*jati*). Neither Africans nor Muslims (nor any other religious community) seem exempt from this rule – however abridged and modified.[4] In Gujarat, Muslims use the term *jamat* for denoting their caste. Moreover, the facts of caste also resist an easy merging or assimilation of Africans (or any other outsiders) with the local population because caste as it historically evolved implies notional endogamy. The Sidi follow an endogamous marriage rule in terms of hair – a wife should look like an African and possess "curly hair". Even though intermarriages have occurred between African men and local women, their accounts show that as soon as there was a group of African men, a nucleus of a patrilineal caste was formed which tended to reproduce itself through marriages with close relatives in the following generations.[5] What is meant here by speaking of caste in relation to descendants of African slaves relates to the process in which the Sidi have created a ritual system that links them collectively to the wider society in Gujarat. In this paper I shall first discuss some aspects of the historical workings of the east African slave-trade and its connection with Gujarat and Gujarati merchants. The second section attempts to historically contextualise the often quoted information on prominent Habshi military leaders of medieval India. After looking at the African Diaspora in a global and a political elite context, I shall delineate local constructions of Sidi identity in Gujarat that are embedded in a cult of African saints.

African Slaves and
the Indian Ocean Trade

In the Arabic-Persian Dictionary of Steingass the following definitions of 'Habashi' and 'Sidi' are given:
"*Habashi*" (A): of, or belonging to Abyssinia or Ethiopia;
Abyssinian, Ethopian; Negro, Black Slave".: "*Saidi*" (A):
lordly; an apellation of Africans; a Negro".[6] It is not entirely
clear, however, how the two contradictory semantic images
of 'lordly' and 'negro' have evolved. In the Muslim world
'negro' was associated with the opposite of a lord, with a
'slave'.

Abdulaziz Lodhi also notes the co-existence of the two
appellations. He thinks that "these ethnonyms partly tell us
that they were in the employ of Sayyds, the Muslim rulers of
India, and partly that they came from Ethiopia".[7] Yet, this
explanation raises a number of problems. Firstly, the Muslim
rulers of India were not Sayyid – which is primarily a religious category - but represented different ethnic backgrounds at different periods of time.[8] Secondly, the Sidi were
not necessarily in the service of Sayyids, not even Muslims,
but served those who acted as masters and paid the price:
Hindu or Muslim kings, chiefs and merchants, or Parsis.
Thirdly, far from being confined to Ethiopia, the trade in
black slaves shifted its recruitment areas and its trading centres along with historical changes in the balance of power
along the Indian Ocean.[9]

Richard Pankhurst, one of the first scholars to address the
question of what had become of the objects of the slave-
trade in the respective countries they had been taken to,
noted that "Habshi" was used in India as a "generic term" for
slaves coming from the Horn of Africa "or even from the
whole of East Africa".[10] Echoing this view, Burton-Page
wrote the following in the *Encyclopedia of Islam*:

"Habshi – term used in India for those African communities whose ancestors came from the Horn of Africa,
although some doubtless sprang from the neighbouring
Muslim countries. The majority, at least in the earlier periods,
may well have been Abyssinian, but certainly the name was

applied indiscriminately to all Africans, and in the days of
the Portuguese slave-trade with India many of such 'Habshis'
were in fact of the Nilotic and Bantu races".[11]

Thus, while in the Indian context the appellation 'Habshi'
was deconnected from any actual, knowable and meaningful ethnic content, in the Ethiopian context it apparently
retained at least some ethnic or regional reference.
According to Mordechai Abir, slaves classified as "Shangalla"
or "Sidi" included Oromo and others who did not leave
Ethiopia, whereas those termed 'Habshi' –"red Ethiopians" -
did.[12] This might also point to the use of 'Habshi' as reflecting primarily the view of outsiders, of the "Other", i.e. the
Arab slave trader.

As Pankhurst noted, slaves were amongst the most
important "raw materials" from East-Africa which Arab
traders exchanged for the cotton of Gujarat.[13] The area
called Gujarat neighbouring Maharashtra and stretching
westward to Saurashtra and Kutch has always been known
as a land of traders. Since the 2nd century, trading connections between Western India and East Africa have been
reported.[14] After the rise of Muslim power, Gujarat's large
and small ports – Surat, Bharuch, Cambay in the east,
Mundra and Mandvi in the west (Kutch) – were increasingly
engaged in overseas trading relationships with similar ports
along the countries bordering the shores of the Indian
Ocean. Das Gupta points to the cordial relationships, in the
centuries before the Portuguese assumed supremacy over
Indian Ocean trading networks, between Arab and Indian
traders, which "emphasised the cooperation between Indians
and Arabs in the Western Indian Ocean, a peaceful sharing
of profit".[15] This "peaceful sharing of profit" also seemed to
have extended to the slave-trade. From the eighth century
onwards, Arab traders settled along the western coast of
India,[16] some centuries later Gujarati merchants established
permanent trading posts in the Arab city states along the
Swahili coast. From the 14th century onwards, Arab and
Portuguese sources make repeated mention of the slave-
trade carried on by traders in Kilwa and the selling of
black slaves to India and other places in Asia.[17] When Ibn
Batuta visited Kilwa in the fourteenth century, he noted fre-

quent slave raids undertaken by the sultan who also presented slaves as gifts to religious institutions.[18] Across the ocean, Gujaratis "virtually monopolised overseas trade in East Africa, collecting gold and ivory and slaves in exchange for their cloths (...)".[19] The merchant town of Cambay was then the major port of the Sultanate of Delhi and one of the major ports – as was Mundra in Kutch some centuries later – through which African slaves reached Indian soil. In 14th century Cambay, a regular market (*nakka*) was held for selling of slaves.

The lively interaction between people from diverse social and cultural backgrounds involved in overseas trade exchange not only entailed the violence of slavery but also resulted in a great heterogeneity of local populations all along the countries bordering the Indian Ocean. Arab traders settled in India, Gujarati merchants settled in East Africa. Once in India, many Sidi were employed by traders as domestics and thus remained in the heterogeneous urban milieu of Gujarat. This milieu consisted of Hindus and Muslims, of Turks, Jains, Parsis and, finally, of numerous other local castes involved in small-scale, and grain trade. According to Pearson:

"The great merchants at the ports of Gujarat were either Hindu, Jains, or Muslims originating from outside Gujarat but now resident there. (...) Most of these foreign Muslims were resident in Gujarat, with their own houses there, and so were in fact subjects of Gujarat, whatever their country of birth, which could be Turkey, Egypt, Arabia or Persia. Some, however, were only itinerant, being domiciled in such places as Alexandria, Damascus, (...) and Afghanistan".[20] Precolonial Gujarat under Muslim domination was, therefore, at least in its coastal urban centres, rather cosmopolitan.

Although the Indian Ocean slave-trade never gained the scope of its Atlantic counterpart, slaves were sold under Portuguese and later British supremacy until the late 19th century. Yet, as Beachey notes, the Portuguese did not particularly favour the trade in slaves to India although they also made use of slave labour.[21] In the mid-16th century, after the Portuguese had conquered Goa, they maintained a regiment at Diu, a port on the shore of the peninsula of

Saurashtra, consisting of "600 Africans as soldiers".[22] In the 18th century, Muscat became a flourishing centre of the slave-trade carrying mainly to the demands of Arab societies along the coast of the Persian Gulf.[23] From Muscat and later Zanzibar an estimated number of ten thousand slaves stemming from all over the hinterlands of East Africa were annually dispersed to the Middle Eastern world.[24] Some of them always reached Western India as well, a port either in Sind, Kutch or in South Gujarat. When the British began to explore Sind they found that "in Balutchistan, no family of any consideration was without male and female slaves, and the greater number of Sidis, or negroes, came from Muscat".[25]

In the nineteenth century the British campaigned against the Arab dominated slave trade, which had again shifted its centre, this time to Zanzibar. Gujarati merchants who had settled on the Swahili coast, as Arab traders proved to be adverse to the abolishment of slavery. Almost 6,000 slaves were known to be in the possession of Indians.[26] Amongst the slave-owners were Bhatia too, a Hindu trading caste originating from Kutch (Mundra) with extended ties to East Africa. In Kutch of today, they belong to the wealthiest communities and "*deshi* people" ("the locals") remember them as the main agents of the slave trade in this region making a fortune in its course. However, in the late sixties of the nineteenth century the slave-trade was formally abolished. The British tried to enforce their policy by controlling Arab and Gujarati ships for the transport of slaves. Within three years (1866-1869), British patrol boats captured "129 slave vessels and 380 slaves were freed".[27] In order to deal with freed slaves taken from captured slave *dhows*, an "African Asylum" was first established some hundred miles from Bombay by Christian missionaries which was later taken over by the Bombay government. Between the 1860s and 70s about 200 African slaves were received in the Missionary Society.[28]

This brief glance at the history of the Indian Ocean slave trade shows that the category 'Habshi' cannot be taken as a referent of any particular ethnic identity nor even a regional origin but rather serves as a general denotation for people from Africa. Moreover, it seems that rarely were large groups of slaves with a common cultural background brought to India. Rather, individuals from all over East Africa were gathered in Zanzibar and then dispersed to different places in the Middle East and India. Thus, the relatively small number of African slaves reaching Gujarat till the end of the nineteenth century were mostly uprooted individuals without social, cultural or linguistic ties with each other. In spite of this, as I shall demonstrate later, in Gujarat Africans were absorbed neither by the heterogeneous urban populations nor by the locals but developed their own community with a distinct self-identity based on their African origins.

African Slaves, Islamic Notions of Slavery and Muslim Power

While African slaves continued to be sold to India till the late 19th century, their roles varied in different historical contexts. The status of 'slave' did not prevent them from accumulating wealth and power, and the most famous and often quoted instances of African presence in Indian history relate to Habshis in high government and military positions. This was the result of a complex interaction between Islamic notions of slavery, the history of conquest and Muslim state building in South Asia and, finally, the prevailing conditions in the Indian society itself which did not rely on slavery but had other means of organising labour.

In contrast to the European system of slavery prevalent in the Americas in which slave labour was mainly used in production and plantation work, an important dimension of the Islamic system – especially in the early centuries – consisted in the use of slaves as soldiers and military personnel.[29] It is here that one finds, as Daniel Pipes has shown, the distinguishing feature of Islamic slavery; no other civilisation developed such a highly specialised system of military slavery: "For a full millenium, from the early 9th century until the early 19th century, Muslims regularly and deliberately employed slaves as soldiers. This occurred through nearly the whole of Islamdom, from Central Africa to Central Asia, from Spain to Bengal, and perhaps beyond. Few dynasties within this long time-span and broad area had no military slaves".[30] It is in this context that the repeated occurrences of Habshis acquiring state power in medieval Bengal or in the Deccan should be understood.

The military dimension of Islamic slavery resulted in a continuous and high demand for slaves. Africans were not the only ones to be enslaved, rather, slaves were captured wherever Muslims went on conquering raids and sold from many marginal areas of the Islamic world. The distinguishing mark Islamic law set up between people who could be enslaved and those who could not was the question of belief. The main principle of Islamic notions of slavery rested with "*kufr*", non-belief.[31] Accordingly, only non-believers, i.e. non-Muslims could be captured and sold as slaves. In this sense, then, slavery appeared as a transitional state which marked the transformation from a "barbarian" to a "civilisational" social existence. In Islamic scriptures, the slave is the equivalent of the wild, unruly beast that is tamed and humanised by its believing owner. Thus, when a slave was converted to Islam the success of the taming process was proved which simultaneously enabled the owner to acquire religious merit in accordance with the Quran by liberating his former slave.[32] Theoretically, then, ethnic affiliation did not matter in Islamic law for determining unfree status in contrast to free status.[33] As Levtzion pointed out, however, at least since the 15th century, the Islamic ideology of slavery was increasingly contradicted by the practice of slave capturing in parts of Africa where Islamisation had already penetrated deeply into the population.[34] Like their Christian counterparts in later centuries, Muslim writers turned to the so-called "Hamitic hypothesis" in order to justify the continued enslavement of African believers. The "Hamitic hypothesis" refers to the biblical myth of Noah cursing his son Ham for having emasculated him.[35] The descendants of Ham should be of black skin and remain forever the servants of non-blacks. In Willis' words this meant that "the link between Ham and the darker humankind is fully forged – blackness becomes a simile for the servile condition".[36]

Still, in spite of these attempts to justify the capture of believers as slaves in Africa, within the Islamic system of slavery in India, at least, African slaves apparently were not treated differently from other enslaved subjects. Moreover, the status of military slaves did not prevent them from maintaining aristocratic positions within Muslim states. Daniel Pipes delineated the role of military slaves in the process of Muslim state building in newly conquered areas at the time of the caliphate. First of all, an army of slave soldiers, trained at a young age by Muslim soldiers, had the advantage of being subservient to and dependent upon the sovereign power; even though slaves might be freed later, the existing ties could be transformed into patron-client relationships in order to ensure continued loyalty to the ruler even though the soldiers fought in distant places.[37] According to Pipes, this is the typical cycle through which slave-soldiers first conquered an area and built a government, with which the former conquering soldiers then became identical. At this stage they would demand concessions and privileges from the sovereign power. The latter would ultimately lose control over conquered possessions in distant lands. This process is historically well documented for the establishment of the early Muslim governments of the Delhi Sultanate which was founded by Turkish slave soldiers.[38] Eventually, such a state would declare its independence from the paramount power and at the same time use slave-soldiers in order to consolidate its power *vis-à-vis* the conquered nobility. The same cyclic process is observable in Indian history with its waxing and waning of Muslim empires alternating with intermediate phases of autonomous regional sultanates. It was during such intermittent times of uncertainty of succession that Habshi slave-soldiers rose to state power. The most well-known examples are from Bengal (Abyssinian rule from 1481-1487) and the Deccan. However, Africans were not the only slaves involved in the process of Muslim state-building in India. For example, Sultan Firuz Tuqluqh possessed 180,000 slaves which included many other foreigners as well as native Indians. At the time when Gujarat was a province of the Sultanate of Delhi in the fourteenth century, it is recorded that the sultan demanded 400 "Abyssinian and Hindu slaves" as a tribute from the governor.[39]

When looking at the system of Islamic slavery in general it comes as no surprise that the history of Muslim rule in India testifies from its beginning in the thirteenth century to the presence of Habshis or African slaves in India.[40] This also shows that slavery in medieval India had less to do with needs of labour than with the organisation of Muslim states. It is in this context that Habshi slaves occasionally surfaced not only as military leaders (as the famous Malik Ambar in seventeenth century Deccan) but also – albeit for short periods of times - as rulers. Much has been written about the medieval Habshi of Hydarabad and the Deccan as well as on the famous Sidi of Janjira who controlled parts of the Konkan coast from the small fortified town in the 17th and 18th centuries.[41] However, in order to understand the phenomenon that African slaves could at times assume regional state power in India, it is also necessary to look at the relationship between the nobility and the army in medieval Muslim states.

Pearson, in a study of merchants in sixteenth century Gujarat, pointed out that the relationship between the sultan and his nobles was fragile and shaped by factionalism and rivalries for power.[42] The nobility included the relatives of the sultan, slaves, foreigners and natives who tended to build factions that were at least partly based upon ethnic affiliation. In the 1550s there were Turkish, Afghan, Habshi, Persian and Mughal groups of nobles distinguished by reference to the respective place of origin.[43] The most prominent Habshi noble of that time was Shaykh Sa'id al-Habshi who patronised the building of the 'Sidi Sa'id' mosque in Ahmadabad. The army reflected the divisions of the nobility which was partly a result of the rule that nobles had to raise troops for the sultan. Thus, in 1560 the Gujarat cavalry consisted of 12,000 men who were divided into "eight racial groups, each under its own leader".[44] One of these "racial groups" consisted of troops of African soldiers under Habshi leaders. During the reign of Sultan Bahadur (1526-1537) a contingent of 5,000 Habshi soldiers was stationed in Ahmadabad; the fort of Daman was defended by a Habshi leader with 4,000 African soldiers against Portuguese attacks.[45] In order to enlarge the troop and compensate losses, Habshi nobles were also amongst the purchasers of incoming slaves.

Indian history provides many instances of fighting Habshi – not only by land but also by sea. In the latter context a connection between Habshi and the Mughal power was established in the second half of the 17th century. The fame of the 'Sidi of Janjira' stemmed from their successful resistance against all attempts by greater powers to conquer their fort at the Konkan coast upon which their military superiority at sea was based. Not many rulers maintained strong fleets at sea.[46] While till the mid-17th century the Sidi were allied with Bijapur in the Deccan as the latters' sea power, during the second half of the 17th century they were turned into allies of the Moghul power in Delhi. Under Aurangzib, the Sidi of Janjira were joined with the Mughal marine and their commander was made admiral of the Moghul fleet in Surat:

"His duty was to hold the fleet which his Habshi clan had built up at Janjira, someway below Bombay, at the service of the imperial government and every year collect a salary from the customs of Surat. (...) the shipping of the Sidis was much in evidence at Surat and their agent (...) who lived at the port was among its most important citizens".[47]

The Sidi fleet, which was renowned for its strength in battle at sea, served the Mughals against the rising Mahratta powers, and could not even be conquered by the British. However, while the Sidi were battling against British warships, the emperor Aurangzieb entered into a treaty with the British East India Company giving them concessions which eventually turned the Sidi fleet into allies of the British. When the British in the course of time failed to pay their dues from the Surat customs, the Sidi turned to piracy and began to attack merchant ships along the coasts of Konkan and Gujarat. Das Gupta characterised the Sidi in the middle of the 18th century rather unflatteringly: "This African clan was at the time literally being pushed into the sea (...). There was no central leadership in the clan, not much discipline, but only a blind instinct for survival and power enough to make things unpleasant for the Gujarati merchant who no longer had a protector".[48] Tensions between the British and the Sidi continued until 1759 when the British took over the admirals' post from them. As a compensation the Sidi received the town of Jaffrabad at the coast of Saurashtra as a *jagir* (rights to revenue). During colonial rule three former Sidi *jagirs* were given the status of a "Princely State": Janjira at the Konkan coast, Sachin near Surat and Jaffrabad on the coast of Saurashtra.[49]

It would be wrong to assume that with the vanishing of the Habshi nobility the African Diaspora in Gujarat would also have disappeared. Rather, the Habshi nobles one encounters during a *tour de force* through Indian history appear as but a fraction of African slaves in India. They neither represent the African Diaspora in South Asia nor are they identical with them. Their existence points instead to the fragmented history of Africans in India, the diverse routes and historical circumstances Africans coming from different backgrounds took or were forced to take at different times in history. There can thus be no historical continuity expected between those Sidi living in present-day Gujarat and those who acted in former times. Still, a kind of symbolic continuity is created by the Sidi themselves through the medium of religion, as I shall demonstrate below.

The next section, introduces the Sidi of the present-day who are probably the offspring of slaves serving as domestics who reached Gujarat until the end of the 19th century. In the living memory of the Sidis I met in the eighties there were still many people who had come direct from Africa. They were remembered for their peculiar ways of speaking Hindustani and their knowledge of Swahili. Some people knew that one of their parents had come as a slave. The first Englishman who met the Sidi in the first half of the 19th century was Richard Burton.[50] Apparently, during his time, people were still closer to their African origin than Sidi today. Burton was able to collect a list of names of tribes from Sidi in Sindh which served Freeman-Grenville more than a hundred years later as the foundation of an attempt to reconstruct the tribal and regional origin of the Sidi in east Africa on a linguistic basis.[51] My approach will be different, though, as I intend to demonstrate how rituals created ties between Sidi, i.e. black people identified as "African", that knit them into a caste.

Bava Gor - Inventor of a Craft and Sidi Saint

Turning from elite politics to the local level, one encounters traces of African presence in Gujarat in the writings of colonial and post-colonial government employees and ethnographers in two different contexts: a) in connection with a craft, i.e. agate mining, and the carnelian mines in Ratanpur, a village in a small former "Princely State" in south Gujarat not ruled by Muslims but by a Rajput king; b) in connection with syncretic religious practices and a regional cult of *faqirs*. In both contexts, a saintly person called Bava Gor figures prominently.

Cambay was not only an important port within the network of the slave-trade but it also linked the hinterland of Gujarat with places overseas. An important local strand consisted in the mining of agate beads in Ratanpur and the craft of beadmaking in Cambay. The first European reference to beads exported from Cambay stems from the 16th century traveller Ludivica di Varthema. During the reign of the Mughal emperor Akbar, an agate called *babaghori* was used as a measurement for coins. These stones were made in a village called Limodra which was in the immediate vicinity of Ratanpur. According to Francis "(...) in Ratanpur ("Village of Gems") (...) stones are dug with primitive tools (...). The stones are made into beads in the (...) city of Cambay, the chief beadcutting center of Gujarat (...)".[52] When Francis came to Ratanpur in the late eighties of this century, it seemed a peculiar village to him. Half of its population identified themselves as Bhil, the other as Sidi or "African Muslims". While the former were involved in mining, the latter were *faqirs*. The mines, consisting of shafts dug into the ground of about ten meters, are found at a hill topped by a shrine (*dargah*) named after a saint called Bava Gor who, on the one hand, is said to have invented the craft of agate bead making, and on the other hand, is identified as the *kulpir* (lineage saint) of the Sidi in whose name they carry out "the work of *faqirs*" (*faqir nu kam*). While the Bhils dug low tunnels into the ground in the dry winter months,[53] the Sidi were not involved in the craft but served the shrine ritually and acted as professional musicians.

There are basically two different kinds of legends referring to Bava Gor which relate either to the craft of beadmaking or to a fight against a "demoness". On all accounts, Bava Gor is referred to as an Abyssinian, a Habshi or Sidi. Moreover, he is never depicted as a single person but always related to saintly "brothers" and "sisters", the most important of whom are a brother, Bava Habash, and a sister, Mai Mishra.[54] The first account is current mainly among Hindu bead workers in Cambay involved in the finishing of agate adornments. In their version, Bava Gor is the inventor of the bead craft but also a kind of ascetic, a religious beggar or itinerant *faqir* who was illuminated while meditating. When Bava Gor practised austerities over the fire at the spot where his tomb is now situated, he noticed the effects of heat upon the stones.[55] Afterwards, he developed the craft of bead cutting, he taught it to the people of Limodra (a neighbouring village) and started the agate business. His brother, Bava Sabun, was a trader who travelled to Africa and Arabia selling the finished beads. Bava Sabun is buried in Cambay where his tomb is also venerated as a *dargah* (shrine).[56] In the second type of legend, Bava Gor was a Habshi military leader who led his relatives, the Sidi, from Mecca to India on a holy mission.

When British government officials discovered the carnelian mines while travelling through the hinterland of British possessions in the early 19th century, they found the *dargah* (shrine) of Bava Gor to be the only representation of Muslim power in an area otherwise under the authority of a Hindu king. The majority of the population were tribal Bhils. In 1819 Lieutenant Copland described Bava Gor as the "tutelar saint of the country (...) to whom adoration is paid more as a deity than as a saint (...)" and "under whose protection are the carnelian mines, (...) to whom the miners recommend themselves before descending into the pit

(...)".[57] The first author mentioning the Sidi was Lieutenant Fulljames who wrote in 1832: "... on the summit of (a hill) there is a peer's tomb. The only people residing there are a few Sidees or negroes (...)".[58]

Due to the lack of reliable historical sources, it is impossible to reconstruct the history of the relationship between Bava Gor, the agate craft, the Bhils and the Sidi. When I did fieldwork in the same village in the late eighties, however, the connection between the agate business in Cambay and the shrine of Bava Gor was still recognised. Once a year, the owners of bead factories in Cambay took their workers on a pilgrimage to Ratanpur and sponsored a charitable meal for the Sidi residents there (about 100) which was cooked by the former. For beadmakers in Cambay, the Sidi are the "children" of the patron saint of the carnelian mines and thus the worthy receivers of offerings addressed to him. Moreover, the Habshi saint Bava Gor is not only venerated by people involved in beadmaking but represents the focus of a regional cult in which the Sidi act as religious specialists mediating the favours of this and many other related saints all classified as black, Sidi, saints.[59]

In colonial writings on the local conditions in Sindh and Gujarat in the nineteenth century, the Sidi are never mentioned without some reference either to Bava Gor or another Sidi saint, or to begging, singing, dancing. Richard Burton was the first to observe Sidi dances. When he travelled in Sindh in the first half of the nineteenth century, he saw the Sidi dancing at a "well known place of pilgrimage near Kurrachee, called Magar-Pir" which has remained till the present an important local Sidi centre.[60] His description highlights music and dance: "... music and dancing (...) are usually combined, and present a most grotesque appearance. The males and females are either mixed together, or placed in two bodies opposite each other. The dance is a monotonous one at first (...). At last, excited by the furious music of the kettle-drums, with the singing and the peculiar cry uttered by the females, the slaves, who are seldom found in a state of complete sobriety, become almost dementet".[61] In the Gazetteer of 1899 the Sidi were described as "the only

Gujarat Musulmans who are much given to dancing and singing. (...) Their chief object of worship is Baba Ghor, an Abyssinian saint and great merchant, whose tomb stands on a hill just above the (...) cornelian mines (*sic*) (...). (...) men and women together dance and sing in circles to the sound of the drum (...) and a rough rattle (...). They call the (...) rattle the instrument of (...) Mother Mishra, and their big drum that of a leading male saint. In begging they go about in bands of ten to fifteen, playing the drum and singing in praise of Baba Ghor (*sic*)".[62]

In these colonial accounts elements of the cult of the Sidi are evoked which I have described in its present form in detail elsewhere (Basu 1993; 1994; 1995; 1996; 1998). What appeared as a combination of insanity and begging to colonial observers are signs of ritual descent to the Sidi. This comes out clearly in statements made by Sidi leaders from Ratanpur in a court case in the early eighties, when they defended their position as customary owners of the *dargah* of Bava Gor against the claims of other Muslim followers attempting to wrest control over the management of the shrine from them. In an application to the Charity Comissioner the following statement was made:[63]

> "Bavagor Auliya, who was from Macca Sharif, had come to this area with his brother, Bava Habash, and his sister, Mai Mishra, who were all Sidis. We applicants and those persons whose names we have given are all members of the Sidi *jamat* (caste). Our people are situated in Ratanpur, Ahmadabad, Surat, Bombay, Hydarabad and in Saurashtra, Junagadh, Jamnagar, Rajkot, Bhavnagar and other places. Wherever our people reside, there are Bavag Hor Dadas Takiyas, i.e. places like *dharamshala* (resthouses) have been built. We, i.e. all the people of the Sidi community are actually the descendants of Bava Gor and Bava Habash. So, still our profession is to say *jikro* (*dhikr*)[64] in Swahili, to worship the *dargah* (*dargah nu puja*), to make journeys as *faqirs* to nearby places, to pray to Dada in the form of *damal* dancing. We celebrate the traditional '*urs* on Bava Gor *dargah*, we do different forms of worship and at the same time, we are given free food at different *dargahs* at

their respective '*urs* celebrations[65]. We are given presents and also a lot of respect. We also do the rituals of worshipping Bava Gor. We sing prayers in Swahili and thus prey to Dada. The day-to-day needs of most of the people of the Sidi community are met by the different gifts given at the *dargah*.

The shrine is under the ownership of the Sidi caste. We were given villages from the state of Rajpipla. People had been given agricultural fields as gifts(...). In the arrangements made then (...) all the appointments were made according to the customs handed down from generations and this right to ownership of the shrine has also been handed down (...).

On seeing the situation historically (...) and socially, the entire management of the trust should be placed in the hands of the Sidi community. According to Muslim religion, Muslims do not do any other form of worship except their own and pray to no one except Allah. We, the people of Sidi community are different. From years together we have been bound to this *dargah* and in this way our customs can be compared to those practiced by some Hindu *sadhu jamats* (orders). And because of that it is not proper to allow any outside Muslim to manage the trust. They do not perform the traditional worship of the *dargah* and they do not know our rituals. Apart from Muslims, others such as Hindus, Christians and Parsis also come to this *dargah* to fulfil their vows, to find release, to wear the *bedio* of truth and falsehood, to listen to *jikro* and Quawwali and to go through all the rituals other Muslims do not know. If proper guidance is not given to the travellers, they are injured ".

Another application addressed to the Charity Commissioner reads as follows:

"I, the applicant, am a member of the Sidi jamat and live in Ratanpur. I do farming and sing Quawwali and other devotional songs at the *dargah* as part of my business. In our Sidi community about 900 years ago a great saint by the name of Bava Gor Dada was there. This *dargah* is situated on a hill named Bava Gor near the village Ratanpur. Since the times of our ancestors we have always been doing various rituals and have

always served the *dargah* faithfully. (...) Till today we consider
Bava Gor a *kuldevta* (lineage god) and show our respect by
doing *pujavidhi* (rituals).
The entire Bava Gor *dargah* is a very sacred place (*samadhi*)
and as all the saints coming there have a liking for Ghazals and
Quawwalis and this music is very dear to the saints. In the same
way, to make Bava Gor Dada happy and to obtain his blessings
I have been coming to the *dargah* on every Thursday, since I
was a child of 10-12 years and sing Ghazals and Quaawalis. On
every Thursday, the Hindu and Muslim travellers come to the
dargah to fulfil their desires and feel happy by hearing these
Ghazals and Quawwalis".

In these statements several striking propositions are
made which seem typical for the Sidi who tend to bring the
foundations of all neat distinctions, assignments and cate-
gorical boundaries to collapse. What was (and is) at stake for
the Sidi at this *dargah* is the question of "right rituals"
looked at from the perspective of Islamisation. Since the seventies, the shrine of Bava Gor began to attract an increasing
number of visitors from all over the region, most of them,
however, urban Muslims from the large cities of Surat and
Broach. While, on the one hand, the Sidi welcomed the
increasing popularity of their shrine, on the other, this
brought more and more Muslims who favoured a substitution
of Sidi dancing (*damal*) and other Sidi rituals by readings of
the *fatiha* and Quranic prayers. So, while the first statement
begins by clothing Bava Gor in the guise of a respectable Sufi
saint (*auliya*) and linking him further with the place most
sacred to Muslims – and thus with the Prophet – it ends by
emphasising the profound differences between Sidi and
Muslims who are identified with Islamic forms of worship
seen in contradiction to their own rituals. In order to
strengthen their argument, the Sidi point to the practical syncretism which has been so characteristic of the cult of Bava
Gor in general; implicitly they evoke an African heritage
(Swahili songs, *damal*) but since this makes no sense within
the context of modern bureaucracy geared to religious
endowments administered by the Charity Commissioner in

Gujarat, they rather argue for similarities with Hindu *sadhus*. This is no pure invention, though, since the cult of the Bava Gor does include many Hindu elements as, for example, the worship of a ritual fire which is of central importance to Shaiva ascetics. At the shrine of Bava Gor, the fire at which Bava Gor is supposed to have meditated for twelve years is continuously kept burning.

The statement most clearly reflects the situation the Sidi face locally: they are in-between, neither Muslim nor Hindu, but yet are forced to identify themselves as belonging either here or there. This is also reflected by the vocabulary used by the Sidi applicants; especially the second statement is full of a mixture of Muslim and Hindu terminology such as "*samadhi*" for *dargah* or *Pujaviddhi*, for shrine rituals. Far from getting "extinguished" or "assimilated into the local Muslim communities" as Khalidi thought "it (..) safe to predict",[66] in Gujarat the Sidi continue to keep to their own ways and rituals by defending the "lineage saint" Bava Gor against Muslim encroachments and Islamic patronising.

Ritual Constructions of a Sidi Caste (jamat)

Nothing in the evidence presented here seems to suggest a simple "either/or" answer to the question of what happened to African slaves in Gujarat. Neither did the Sidi of the present appear "to have remained in isolation",[67] nor did they become indistinguishable from other Muslims. Louis Dumont once remarked that foreigners were absorbed into Indian society in two ways: either as conquerors and rulers or as impure Untouchables.[68] Like the first, this view does not really present a satisfying explanation of the situation of present-day Sidi. Although some Africans had come in the retinue of conquering Muslim armies and even occupied state power occasionally, the Sidi of today are not associated with them and do not derive their status within the wider society by reference to noble slave descent. Considered in terms of normal middle class and high caste standards, the Sidi are low and do not require to be treated respectfully;

yet, they are not normally seen as impure and untouchable. For example, when I did fieldwork, the applicant of the second statement and Quawwali singer regularly participated in calendar festivals performed at a nearby Hindu temple dedicated to the god Hanuman by singing *bhajans* (devotional songs). Even though some Hindus might consider them impure and equivalent Untouchables, the interactions the Sidi maintain with people from other social backgrounds are not related to ideas of purity or impurity but to ritual exchanges. I think that it is through ritual that something like a shared Sidi identity is created which, at the same time, defines types of interactions with people of other status who follow different norms but are in need of ritual which services only Sidi can provide. Only Sidi - because they possess privileged access to the saint Bava Gor due to the "kinship relationship" between them and the saint.

The first requirement of ritual is a place. Arenas for ritual performances of the Sidi are provided by shrines which are distinguished by size and by the range of followers they attract. The *dargah* of Bava Gor in South Gujarat and the one in the Gir Forest in Saurashtra are the largest ones. The latter takes its name from the tomb of Nagarshi Pir who is said to have been the "younger brother" of Bava Gor.[69] Apart from these two comparatively large Sidi *dargahs* in terms of their followings, there are many more shrines dedicated to other brothers and sisters of Bava Gor. In each and every Sidi settlement – even if it sometimes consists of only three households – a common shrine dedicated to Sidi saints will be found. When the applicants compared their saints with a Hindu lineage deity they were implicitly referring to this fact: that a *kuldevta* is in its actual appearances as spatially represented as the lineage is genealogically segmented. In the case of the Sidi, however, it is less genealogical depth which is achieved but lateral extension. The lateral network of Sidi shrines interacting with each other spans a wide geographical region from Sindh to Bombay. Every settlement is marked by a shrine. These *dargahs* also serve as signs of the presence of African saints and thus of Sidi. A stranger, i.e. somebody who has no immediate Sidi relatives in a town, will turn to the *dargah* where he/she surely will find a place to eat and stay.

Most Sidi shrines are situated in an urban environment where many Sidi work as domestics. Although some *dar-gahs* are merely a room in a common courtyard, most of them consist of small shrines built around a tomb. In towns like Mandvi, Jamnagar, Ahmadabad, Surat and many more, the land on which the shrine is built was originally given by a local chief in exchange for domestic, body guard or military services rendered by slaves turned into ordinary domestics. The existence of these *dargahs* suggests that the Sidi, once purchased and added to the court of a local king, were then treated as any other category of court personnel. For their stay and subsistence they were given land to build their houses. Most Sidi settlements are therefore in towns, usually in the old craftsmen and servants quarters. Today, the shrines and the land assigned to it represent important assets in terms of securing Sidi access to urban spaces instead of relegating them to the slums of the destitute. Even though Sidi are generally poor, they are not destitute. The space marked by the shrines is thus both important for ritual and for more profane matters such as having a place to build one's house.

The second dimension manifested by the shrines refers to ritual constructions of kinship. Physical spaces are turned into representations of kinship through which potentially every Sidi shrine is connected with all the others. Any locally named saint can be ultimately related to Bava Gor as a brother or sister. Although siblings are distinguished according to age, there still remains a noticeable one-generation emphasis which seems to result in the erasure of time and the history of slavery. The Sidi seem to recognise three levels of genealogical existence. Usually genealogical knowledge of the Sidi encompasses no more than three generations.[70] The second level is occupied by saints, who are brothers and sisters for each other, but ancestors (*dada* = FF) to living Sidi. The final and most distant level, the level of Sidi "roots", is represented by Hazrat Bilal, an "Abyssinian" and the famous caller for prayer and companion of the Prophet. Everybody knows, however, that this is a symbolic kinship relationship since Hazrat Bilal reputedly had no offspring. Similarly, the local saints, considered brothers and sisters of Bava Gor, are called *dada* and *dadi-ma*, but few people assume "real descent". Sometimes the kinship ties to Bava Gor are re-inforced by reference to his army. Bava Gor, the legend tells, was a military man who led a Sidi army from distant Africa to India. Along with them came the sisters. They were on a moral mission, destined to destroy evil embodied by a "demoness". The battle took place where the *dargah* of Bava Gor is situated. On the way, some of his Sidi soldiers and their women stayed back and they are the one's who are venerated today at different local shrines.

Each shrine follows its own ritual routine of '*urs* celebrations. The shrines represent nodal points of networks that include related kin of different degrees. For example, an '*urs* held at the shrine of Bava Gor in Surat would attract members from all households living in Surat itself as well as their kin resident in more distant places. These are, for example, married daughters of a household with their husbands and children, sons residing temporarily in another place, a sister of the wife etc. A wider network of kin is mobilised at the '*urs* of Bava Gor which is attended by Sidi who permanently live some three- to four hundred kilometres away, mostly on the peninsula of Saurashtra. Not all of them are directly related to Sidi in Ratanpur.

Shrine rituals are performed by different actors. The Sidi have evolved a system of ritual roles related to the worship of their shrines some of which form the basis of permanent positions – for example the head of a shrine (*gaddivaras*), shrinekeepers (*mujavar*), *kotwal* (ritual guard) and some more. All are ultimately related to the organisation of a shrine in terms of ritual. Other roles are not permanently attached to specific families and persons, but may be assumed by different people at different '*urs* celebrations. Finally, there are musicians, dancers and those who regularly get possessed by Sidi saints during '*urs* performances. The roles people permanently or temporarily assume in the context of the cult of Bava Gor are related to a prestige system specific to the Sidi and the members of their caste. Moreover, the rituals performed at Sidi shrines are gendered in the sense that there is always a men's side and a women's side of the rituals performed. Few rituals exclude the participation of either men or women. Rather, the difference between male and female ritual roles is emphasised and their complementarity is enacted.

While, on the one hand, Sidi rituals structure gender relationships, on the other, they foster temporary identification between living Sidi and the ancestor-saints. Usually, a Sidi *'urs*-celebration includes several nightly drumming sessions in the course of which many Sidi, men and women, get possessed by one of the saints. This type is clearly distinguished as an auspicious form from evil spirit possession. Usually, women embody "sisters", men "brothers". At the climax, when large numbers of people are simultaneously possessed, the presence of Sidi saints among the living is experienced through the bodies chosen by the saints as vehicle. This happens during dancing sessions called *damal* or *goma*.[71]

Taken as a whole, the cult of Bava Gor links the Sidi as a collectivity to the wider society in Gujarat. People who suffer from various kinds of mental ailments conceptualised as evil spirit possession – in contrast to "auspicious saint possession" – visit local Sidi shrines and seek various cures and ritual services which Sidi ritual specialists provide. Moreover, the Sidi are part of a sectarian following of another Sufi saint in whose shrine rituals the Sidi act in a ritual role which is part of the larger universe of Sufi cults anchored amongst the prestigious Muslim category of religious *persona* of the Sayyid. Finally, the cult of Bava Gor also provides an arena for the inversion of secular relationships. Many of the permanent non-Sidi cult followers belong to the category of employers of the Sidi (*sheth*), they belong to higher Muslim service castes such as Bohra or Memmon, or even to Parsis. The same people who give secular employment as domestic servants to the Sidi are also the ones who seek their ritual services in terms of personal crisis.[72] It is then that the roles are reversed and the Sidi assume ritual authority over their superiors.

What should have become apparent from the above is the agency of the Sidi in creating a social universe of action within the host society of Gujarat. The idiom and the workings of the cult show many local variations but on the whole, a common idiom has been evolved in which the Sidi communicate in terms of "one's own people" as Africans. At the same time, the ritual connection established between the Sidi and Bava Gor and other saints provides for the roles they assume in relation to a wider field of popular Sufism and Muslim regional culture. Thus, the Sidi subculture seems to have evolved in response to the prevailing conditions in Gujarat which circumscribed and channelled Sidi agency in terms of caste.

Concluding Remarks

As demonstrated in this paper, the Sidi in Gujarat are neither completely isolated from the host society, nor have they completely merged with the local population. In interaction with the host society they created a social universe based upon their own cultic constructions of their past. As should have become apparent, the Sidi do not have a single, unified history. They look back to different strands of history, some have disappeared from the historical scene because the society they represented has ceased to exist. Many an Africans' forefathers might never have had any connection with those noble Sidi appearing in prominent battlegrounds. At different times, then, the Sidi were assigned and assumed different roles, such as slaves, soldiers, traders and finally, the dominant role in the present, *faqirs*. Since there is no historical continuity, one cannot speak of a "degradation" the Sidi allegedly underwent.

Notes

1. For Karnataka cf. Palakshappa *The Siddhis of North Canara* (Delhi 1976).
2. I carried out fieldwork supported by the German Academic Exchange Service (DAAD) from 1987 to 1989 in Gujarat. In 1994/1995 I spent several months in Sindh. This research was generously supported by Free University of Berlin.
3. cf. Joseph E Harris, 'African History from Indian Sources', *African Quarterly*(1969: 4). Omar Khalidi 'African Diaspora in India: The Case of the Habashis of the Dakan', *Hamdard Islamicus* Vol. XI, 4 (1993: 16).

4. The case of the Sidi would probably present a striking case for a process of invention of caste as a social fact, with a force independent of the will and agency of the people, caste "from below". For Muslim castes, see I. Ahmad *Caste and Social Stratification among Muslims in India* (Delhi 1978) and P. Werbner *The Migration Process. Capital, Gifts and Offerings among British Pakistanis* (Oxford 1990).

5. Helene Basu *Habshi-Sklaven, Sidi Fakire. Muslimische Heiligenverehrung im westlichen Indien.* Berlin, (1995).

6. Steingass *English-Persian Dictionary* (1904).

7. Abdulaziz Lodhi 'African Settlements in India', *Nordic Journal of African Studies* Vol. 1/1: 83-87 (1991: 83).

8. For example the succession of Muslim ruling dynasties of the Delhi sultanate included Turks and Afghan; the Mughal empire was founded by Mongol invaders. In Sindh, a period of Sayyid rule (Kalhora) was a regional exception, cf. Suhail Zaheer Lari *A History of Sindh* (Karachi 1994: 144.).

9. cf. R.W. Beachey *The Slave Trade of Eastern Africa* (London 1976).

10. R. Pankhurst *An Introduction to the Economic History of Ethiopia* (London 1961: 409.).

11. Richard F. Burton-Page 'Habshi', *Encyclopedia of Islam* 2nd edition (Leiden 1971: 14).

12. Mordechai Abir 'The Ethiopian Slave Trade and its relation to the Islamic World', in: J. R. Willis (ed.) *Slaves and Slavery in Muslim Africa.* (London 1985: 128.)

13. For an early detailed discussion of the slave-trade from the Horn of Africa, see Pankhurst, R. *An Introduction to the Economic History of Ethiopia.* (London 1961 372ff). And R. W. Beachey *The Slave Trade of Eastern Africa* (London 1976).

14. Trade between ports along the western coast of India and East Africa was already mentioned in the *Periplus.*

15. Ashin Das Gupta *Indian Merchants and the Decline of Surat, c. 1700-1750* (Wiesbaden 1979:408)

16. In Sindh and at the Malabar coast in South India.

17. Beachey op. cit.: 7.

18. op.cit.: 6.

19. Pearson op.cit.: 12.

20. Pearson op.cit.: 25

21. The Italian traveller Careri mentioned African slaves kept by the Portuguese in Goa in the 16th century, cf. Sen, S. (ed.) *Indian Travels of Thevenot and Careri,* (New Delhi 1949).

22. Beachey op. cit.: 7

23. Beachey op. cit.:48

24. Beachey op. cit. 38

25. India Office Pamphlet, quoted in Beachey (op. cit: 50).

26. Beachey op. cit.: 59.

27. Beachey op. cit.: 74.

28. Beachey op. cit.: 85f.

29. For the details of Islamic slavery, see R. Brunschvig, 'Abd', *Encyclopedia of Islam* (N. Ed. 1971). Slaves were distinguished in domestic and military slaves.

30. Daniel, Pipes, *Slave Soldiers and Islam. The Genesis of a Military*

System. (New Haven 1981 35).

31. Willis, John Ralph 'The Ideology of Enslavement in Islam', in: J. R. Willis (ed.), *Slaves and Slavery in Muslim Africa*. Vol. I (London 1985: 2).

32. The Quran, *sura* xxiv, 33, makes the liberation of slaves a major merit.

33. cf. Brunschvig op. cit.

34. Levtzion, Nehemia 'Slavery and Islamization in Africa', in: R. Willis (ed.) *Slaves and Slavery. Islam and the ideology of Enslavement*. Vol. I (London 1985: 194)

35. Sanders, Edith R. 'The Hamitic Hypothesis; its Origin and Functions in Time Perspectives', *Journal of African History* (1969, X, 4: 521-532); Ranke-Graves, Robert von und Raphael Patai *Hebräische Mythologie. Über die Schöpfungsgeschichte und andere Mythen aus dem Alten Testament* (Frankfurt 1986: 150).

36. Willis op. cit.: 8

37. Pipes, Daniel *Slave Soldiers and Islam. The Genesis of a Military System* (New Haven 1981).

38. Kulke, Hermann and Dietmar Rothermund *A History of India*. (Calcutta 1990: 162)

39. cf. Burton-Page op. cit.: 15

40. The most famous evidence of the early presence of Habshi slaves in India refers to the horsemaster of the Khilji Queen Radiyya, cf. Richard F.Burton-Page 'Habshi', *Encyclopedia of Islam* 2nd edition (1971: 14).

41. cf. Pankhurst op. cit.: 409.; Burton-Page op. cit.; Harris 1969 op. cit.; Khalidi op.cit.

42. Pearson, Michael N. *Merchants and Rulers in Gujarat: the response to the Portuguese in the 16th century*. (Berkeley 1976).

43. op. cit.: 67.

44. op. cit.: 151.

45. Burton-Page op.cit.: 16.

46. Muslim sultans were not so much interested in power at sea than in power over land and people, cf. Michael N. Pearson op. cit.

47. Das Gupta op. cit: 168.

48. Das Gupta op.cit.: 260

49. For the creation of Princely States in Gujarat by the British , see Robin Jeffrey, ed., *People, Princes and Paramount Power. Society and Politics in the Indian Princely States* (Delhi 1978).

50. Burton, Richard F. *Sind and the Races that inhabit the Valley of the Indus*. (Karachi 1973, Repr. of 1851)

51. Freeman-Grenville, G. S. P. 'The Sidi and Swahili', *Bulletin of the British Association of Orientalists* (1971)6: 3-18

52. Francis, Peter *Indian Agate Beads* (Lapis 1982: 4).

53. op. cit.: 4.

54. The names carry obvious associations to regions in Africa, Habash to Ethiopoia, 'Mishra' to 'Mishr' in Egypt. For the mnemonic role of these names, see Helene Basu "Theatre of Memory: Ritual Kinship Performances of the African Diaspora in Pakistan", in: Aparna Rao and Monika Boeck (eds), *Kinship and Precreation in Southasia* (in print).

55. Trivedi, R.K., ed., *Agate Industry of Cambay*, Census of India, V, Part

VII A (e) (Bombay 1961: 24)

56. op. cit.: 55.
57. J. Copland 'An Account of the Cornelian Mines in the Neighbourhood of Broach', *Transactions of the Literary Society of Bombay*, (1819) Vol. I: 294-295.
58. Lieut. George Fulljames, 'A Visit, in December 1832, to the Carnelian Mines, situated in the Rajpeepla Hills, to the Eastward of Broach', *Transactions of the Geographical Society Bombay* (1838).
59. Helene Basu 'The Sidi and the Cult of Bava Gor in Gujarat', *Journal of the Indian Anthropological Society* (1993: 28: 289-300).
60. 'Magar' means crocodiles which are kept at this shrine.
61. Burton op. cit.: 255-56
62. *Gazetteer of the Bombay Presidency* (Bombay 1899: 11).
63. After 1951 all religious institutions in Gujarat were administered by the Charity Commissioner's Office which also has to decide cases of succession disputes.
64. In Sufism *dhikr* refers to devotional singing.
65. 'Urs are termed the annual celebrations at Muslim shrines which vary with different traditions. Cf. Pnina Werbner 'Langar: Pilgrimage, Sacred Exchange and Perpetual Sacrifice in a Sufi saint's Lodge', in: Pnina Werbner and Helene Basu (eds), *Embodying Charisma. Modernity, Locality and the Performance of Emotion in Sufi Cults* (London 1998).
66. Khalidi op.cit.: 16.
67. D. K. Bhattacharya 'Indians of African origin', *Cahiers d'Études Africaines* (Vol. 77, No. 5/6: 1969, 579).
68. cf. Louis Dumont Homo Hierarchicus (London 1980).
69. see also J. Chakraborty and S. B. Nandi 'The Siddis of Junagadh: Some Aspects of Their Religious Life', *Human Science* (Vol. 33, 2: 1984, 130-137); R.K. Trivedi *Siddi. A Negroid Tribe of Gujarat*, Census of India, Volume V, Part IV-B, No. 1, Ethnographic Series (Bombay 1961); T.B. Naik and G.P. Pandya *The Sidis of Gujarat. A Socio-Economic Study and a Development Plan* (Ahmadabad 1981).
70. Often even less because an immediate forefather had been a slave from Africa.
71. Goma seems derived from Swahili '*ngoma*' for 'dance'.
72. Helene Basu 'Hierarchy and Emotion: Love, Joy, and Sorrow in a Cult of Black Saints in Gujarat, India', in: Pnina Werbner and Helene Basu (eds) *Embodying Charisma. Modernity, Locality and the Performance of Emotion in Sufi Cults* (London 1998).

THE AFRICAN DIASPORA IN SRI LANKA

Shihan de Silva Jayasuriya

Introduction

This paper explores the extent to which the Ceylon Kaffirs (referred to as Kaffirs hereafter) exhibit African cultural traits. In Sri Lanka (formerly Ceylon) people of African descent are called Kaffirs (from Cafre Portuguese). The Africans concerned in this paper are those of the negro race that occupy the African continent, South of the Sahara. It does not include the Africans who live north of the Sahara and belong to a Caucasic 'Mediterranean' race. The African diaspora (hereafter referred to as the diaspora) is usually associated with the slave trade. Although the slave trade was largely responsible for the movement of Africans out of Africa, it was not the only mechanism; there was also free migration in order to pursue a job or a trade. Africans began entering India in sizeable numbers from the 13th century onwards. They came as soldiers, sailors, policemen, traders, bureaucrats, clerics, bodyguards, concubines and servants[1]. Sri Lanka had trade contacts with Ethiopia from the beginning of the 5th century when the island was an emporium in the Indian Ocean. Trading activity centred around Matota (near Mannar) on the North West of the island [See map for geographic locations]. Cosmos Indicopleustes, the Greek traveller, who wrote about Sri Lanka at the beginning of the 6th century states that 'As its position is central, the Island is a great resort for ships from India, and from Ethiopia, and in like manner it despatches many of its own to foreign ports'[2].

Gerbeau[3] poses a post-modernist question: "Is it possible to write the history of silence?", and urges scholars not to reduce the study of the slave trade "to a paragraph in commercial history but to place it at the level of a history of civilizations". An analysis of the diaspora recognizes that the origins of the Kaffirs lie outside Sri Lanka. In order to examine cultural maintenance, cultural transformation and cultural transmission, it is necessary to define culture and cultural dynamics. Anthropologists define culture as a total lifeway of a society which includes kinship, political structure, language, literature, art, music, dance and religion[4]. All these elements, however, are not static to the same extent; some are more dynamic than others.

The story of the diaspora has been constructed by weaving together fragmentary evidence. The diaspora in Sri Lanka is analyzed in this paper by considering cultural factors, oral traditions, historical and demographic factors. The elements in the culture set which differentiate the Kaffirs from the indigenous population are Language, Religion, Music and Dance.

The Sirambiadiya (a village three miles from Puttalam in the North-Western Province) Kaffirs are living evidence of an African presence. It is important to study them before they also blend into multi-ethnic Sri Lanka.

The Indian Ocean is complex and there is a need for regional specialization and multiple language skills[5]. In the analysis of the diaspora, I have used my expertise on Sri Lankan history and culture (which includes language). Historians are only addressing a part of the diaspora. It will no longer suffice to date the cargoes and count the men and the piastres. The historian will also have to be an archaeologist, an ethnologist, a specialist in oral tradition, a biologist, a linguist and perhaps a psychiatrist, in order to analyze the diaspora[6]. This paper takes a multidisciplinary approach and draws attention to a forgotten minority in Sri Lanka, the Kaffirs.

The Ceylon Kaffirs

The history of the diaspora in Sri Lanka is complicated and multi-layered. Africans were brought to Sri Lanka by the Portuguese (1505-1658), the Dutch (1658-1796) and the

British (1796-1948) (the three successive European colonial powers). The geographical limits of the Portuguese seaborne empire in Asia were reached in the Chinese Port of Macau and Nagasaki in Japan[7]. Portuguese ships that sailed from Mozambique to India were accompanied by galeotas ('galliots') or patachos ('two masted vessels with square sails') manned by African slaves[8]. These Africans settled down in the Portuguese Asian colonies including Sri Lanka. Out of the 20,000 soldiers that garrisoned the Portuguese forts in Sri Lanka, only 1,000 were from Portugual[9]. The remainder were recruited from the Portuguese African and Asian colonies[10]. The Sinhalese victory over the Portuguese army led by Captain-General Constantine da Sa da Noronha, in 1630, at Randeni Wala, boosted the Sinhalese army's confidence, which then advanced to attack Colombo. A Sinhalese victory in Colombo was prevented only with the help of a Company of Kaffirs which arrived from Goa[11]. The Kustantinu Hatana, a war ballad about this episode was composed in the 17th century by Dom Jeronimo Alagiyavanna, the last classical Sinhalese poet, who had converted to Roman Catholicism. Verse 19 of the Kustantinu Hatana refers to the Kavisika ('Kaffir') and Abisi ('Abyssinian') mercenaries in the Portuguese army[12]. A distinction between Kaffirs and Abyssinians is also made in the Portuguese Roteiro do Mar ('Ship's Log Book') of Dom João Castro[13]. It states that the land of the Abyssinians was separated from the land of the Kaffirs who lived in the bush, which extended from Melinde to Mozambique. By 1634, there were only 284 Kaffirs in the Portuguese army in Sri Lanka. It is interesting to note that the Kaffirs introduced the assagai, a short wooden spear with a metal point, to Sri Lanka[14]. They were allowed a rice ration of two measures per day, a payment of 18 Xerafims (old currency in Portuguese India and the Orient) per annum, and a certain amount of cloth for their use[15]. In 1640, one hundred Kaffir archers had fought for the Portuguese against the Dutch in Galle[16]. On 13th March 1640, Galle had been seized by the Dutch and some Kaffirs had been retained to repair the ramparts. When the Portuguese Era ended, some Kaffirs had served under the Dutch; others had settled down in the

Kandyan kingdom which had remained under Sinhalese rule. King Raja Sinha II (1635-87), ruler of the Kandyan kingdom, had a "guard of Cofferies or Negroes in whom he imposeth more confidence then in his own People. These are to watch at his chamber door, and next his person"[17]. The Dutch Governor Van Goens Junior, (who served in Sri Lanka from 1675-80), stated that there were 4,000 Kaffirs working for the Dutch in Sri Lanka. At the beginning of the 18th century, the Dutch administration in Sri Lanka had begun to buy slaves from Madagascar[18,19]. The Dutch had employed Africans for demanding tasks. Malagasy slaves were grof van leedenen ('strong, robust and sturdily built') and were deployed for heavy work[20]. They were employed to build forts and battlements in the major cities of the Dutch empire such as Colombo and Batavia[21]. The Dutch colonizers had formed the Kaffirs into a labour pool when they set out to build their Castle fortress in Colombo. In the early 18th century, the Kaffirs had become aware of their increased numbers and had staged an insurrection within the ramparted citadel. They had sparked off many acts of violence in the streets, had caused damage to properties, and had conspired and murdered the Fiscal, Barent van der Swann, and his wife. The insurrection had been suppressed but the Dutch had contained the Kaffirs within the citadel, in case they staged another insurrection. They had been housed on an open stretch of land after their day's work in a domestic house or in an institution, where they answered a roll-call and were then ferried across the Beira Lake to Slave Island (adjacent to Colombo Fort), which got its name due to the old and sick slaves that were housed there. According to Roberts et al[22] in the late 18th century, the Dutch gentlefolk of Colombo went to Wolvendaal Church on Sundays in trikel carriages or in palanquins pushed or drawn by Kaffirs of both sexes. The Dutch had kept up the strength of the Kaffirs by immigration (implying that it was free movement) from the Cape, and the British had maintained the numbers by buying slaves from the Portuguese in Goa[23].

Bertolacci[24] remarked that he could not observe the descendants of the 9,000 Kaffirs recruited to Sri Lanka by the

Dutch Government at various times, and who were formed into regiments. They were not distinguishable among the then present inhabitants of the island. They had intermarried with the Portuguese Burghers. There are three documents in the Colonial Office papers relating to Kaffirs being recruited into the corps by Frederick North (1798-1805), the first British Governor in Sri Lanka (C.O. 54, 14. North to Hobart, 25 September 1804. Encl: Kaffir slaves (79 men, 2 women and 19 boys). Some Kaffirs had been purchased in Bombay and transported to Sri Lanka, while other Kaffirs (70 men and 8 women) had been purchased in Goa. Governor North had also contracted with one Monsieur Fortin to get down 500 able-bodied Kaffirs from Mozambique to be delivered at Galle or Colombo) [25].

A body of 700 Kaffirs had been added to the British garrison in Colombo and formed into a regiment[26]. Many of them had been slaves in the Portuguese settlement of Goa and had been purchased by the British Government. They had rejoiced in the change of status and had promised to become brave and hardy soldiers. They were nominally Roman Catholics and had no knowledge of any other religion. On Sundays they had marched to the Portuguese church which was situated two miles from the Colombo fort. Many had been accompanied by women and children which implies that this community would have been a few thousand strong. The Sinhalese monarch also included Kaffirs in the army. Eighty Kaffirs fought in the Sinhalese army during the British campaign against the Kandyan kingdom in 1803[27]. The Third Ceylon Regiment, in 1811, had 800 Africans in its ranks; they had been purchased in Goa and then inducted into the regiment[28]. During the British Era, the Kaffirs formed a large portion of the Ceylon Regiment, especially the Third and Fourth Regiments which included 874 Kaffirs[29]. They had made good soldiers and were remarkably long-lived. The British Government also had retained a body of Kaffirs to construct mountain roads. They had been brought to Sri Lanka by the Portuguese from Mozambique.

According to Selkirk[30], the Kaffirs had spoken Portuguese, were mostly Roman Catholics, had thick lips, high cheek bones, curly hair and were natives of Kaffraria in South Africa. They had seldom married outside their tribes. They had been part of the Ceylon Rifle Regiment which included Malays and English. Kaffirs had been brought from the Cape of Good Hope in South Africa (during the Dutch Era), and more Kaffirs had been brought when Sri Lanka fell into British hands[31].

In the 19th century, the Kaffirs had become extinct: "within recent years, a few were located on the sides of the principle roads of the interior, whence they were frequently milemen"[32]. Hardy[33] stated that 6,000 Kaffirs, 2,300 Portuguese and half-castes were killed by the Kandyans. He had not given details of the episode but it serves to illustrate the significant Kaffir presence in the island.

In recent Census Statistics Reports, the Kaffirs have been included in the 'Others' group, which does not give a breakdown of the ethnic composition, but the following figures are available for the late 19th (the first regular Census was in 1871) [34–36] and early 20th centuries[37–38]. The figures confirm that the number of Kaffirs had declined by the end of the 19th century. Kaffir men and women had ensured the continuance of Kaffir physiognomic features. The numbers fluctuated over the decades: 349 Kaffirs (195 males, 154 females) in 1871, 408 (204 males, 204 females) in 1881, 214 in 1891, 318 (166 males, 152 females) in 1901 and 253 (132 males, 121 females) in 1911. An exact figure is not available for the Kaffirs in the island today. The ethnic composition of contemporary Sri Lanka is: Sinhalese 73.95%, Sri Lankan Tamils 12.70%, Sri Lankan Moors 7.05%, Indian Tamils 5.52%, Malays 0.32%, Burghers & Eurasians 0.26% and Others 0.20%[39].

Language is generally accepted as the most important element in the culture set. Sri Lanka Portuguese Creole (SLPC), the lingua franca (language for trade and external purposes) from the mid-16th to the 19th century, became the mother-tongue of the Kaffirs. The Portuguese-based creole evolved when the Portuguese came into contact with the Sri Lankans in the 16th century. It is the successful solution to the intercommunication problems that arose when the Portuguese and Sri Lankans came into contact. It was also spoken by the Dutch and British colonizers who followed the Portuguese. Pidgins and Creoles are contact languages; they evolve when people who do not speak each other's mother-tongue come into contact. A Pidgin is usually short-lived but a creole is assured of a longer life span as it is the mother-tongue of a speech community. In Linguistics, the word 'Creole' has a specific meaning; Contact Linguistics is a specialized field of study which includes the analysis of Pidgins and Creoles. Unlike Afrikaans, a Dutch-based creole, which became an official language in South Africa, Sri Lanka Portuguese Creole did not become an official language due to sociopolitical and economic factors. If Sri Lanka Portuguese Creole had been given a new label, it would have established its individuality. Sri Lanka was known as Ceilão to the Portuguese; the creole could have been labelled Ceiles[40]. Ceiles is a new language with a unique grammar. It is not an inferior version of the Portuguese spoken in Portugal. It is not the result of imperfect learning. Edward Sapir[41], Linguist-Anthropologist states that, "Both simple and complex types of language of an indefinite number of varieties may be found spoken at any desired level of cultural advance. When it comes to linguistic form, Plato walks with the Macedonian swineherd, Confucius with the head-hunting savage of Assam".

Some Kaffirs had built a school in Kornegalle (modern Kurunegala) [42]. The British missionary, Robert Newstead, had given them elementary books and arranged to instruct them in Portuguese (which most probably was Sri Lanka Portuguese Creole, as it was the language used for communication). Newstead's translation of the New Testament into the creole printed as five editions is testimony to the usage of the Creole[43]. Today the creole is mainly spoken in the Eastern Province (Batticaloa and Trincomalee) and North-Western Province (Puttalam). The Kaffirs often belonged to the Burgher (descendants of Portuguese and Dutch) communities in towns. This is not surprising as both groups are Creole speakers par excellence. As the diaspora in Sri Lanka had diverse African origins, they would have spoken different African languages, but the Creole would have eliminated intercommunication problems. The languages in Sri Lanka today are Sinhala, Tamil, English, Sri Lanka Portuguese Creole, Sri Lankan Malay Creole, Veddha, Pali, Sanskrit and Arabic. While the Indo-Portuguese Creoles of India have become extinct, Sri Lanka Portuguese Creole (previously known as the Indo-Portuguese of Ceylon) has been able to withstand linguistic pressures from the other languages. Further research should reveal the rationale behind this interesting sociolinguistic phenomenon.

Religion is generally accepted as the second most important element in the culture set. The Kaffirs were predominantly Christians (Roman Catholics or Calvinists). Verse 33 of the Kaffir Song (see page 269) from the 19th century Sri Lanka Portuguese Creole manuscript in the Hugh Nevill Collection in the British Library, London, testifies to the Muslim presence on the island. African soldiers (both Christians and Muslims) were brought to the island during the Second World War, but they had not settled down on the island. However, they had had children from their relationships with Sri Lankan women. The majority of Sri Lankans are Buddhists, the religion that was introduced to the island in 600 BC. The 1981 Census of Sri Lanka records 69.30% Buddhists, 15.48% Hindus, 7.61% Christians, 7.55% Muslims, and 0.06% Others[44].

When the Kaffirs, Portuguese and Sinhalese came into contact in Sri Lanka, a new form of music, Kaffrinha, evolved. Kaffrinha (diminutive of Kaffir) is a fusion of three cultures: African, European and Asian. The music has two rhythms: 6/8 (fast and boisterous called Kaffrinha) and 3/8 (slow and majestic called chikoti - chicota 'whip' Portuguese)[45]. Kaffrinha later evolved into a dance. The appellation Kaffrinha suggests that the music has an African origin but the Sinhalese and the Portuguese Burghers contributed to the evolution of this music[46]. Today this music is also called Kaffrinha Baila perhaps in recognition of the Portuguese input[47]. Kaffrinha is popular music in Sri Lanka and illustrates cultural transmission.

The Goan dance, Mando, was once known as Cafrinho. The Sri Lankan Kaffrinha is a frenzied dance which has little in common with the plaintive tone and masochist lyrics of the Goan Mando[48]. Perhaps the Sinhalese input to the Sri

Lankan Kaffrinha differentiates the two dances. These two dances, however, have a common element, as the men use a brightly coloured handkerchief. In fact, this is also a characteristic feature in the Mandôas performed by the upper class Northern Mozambicans today. The percussion instruments used in Goa, Sri Lanka and Mozambique are somewhat similar. They all use a drum (ghumat in Goa), made of fired clay with one end open and the other covered with the skins of reptiles (alligator and iguana in Sri Lanka; alligator, iguana, cow and buffalo in Goa; crocodile, goat and antelope in Mozambique). Mozambique was once a province of Goa and there had been racial and economic interaction between the two territories.

The music of creole cultures has rarely been recorded on scores as creole communities lacked a knowledge of western music. Fernando (a Cambridge educated Sinhalese lawyer and a pianist), the pioneer researcher of Portuguese music in Sri Lanka, provides the scores for several creole songs. The songs, Cafferina, Caffri, Viltao de Mazambicu (which refers to Mozambique Island) and Zulu Baba (which refers to the Zulu tribe in South Africa) are of particular interest in this context. The musical instruments used by the Ceylon Portuguese (i.e. Burghers) are the violin, the tenor violin (viaule - a guitar-shaped instrument with thirteen strings), the mandoline (which the Portuguese refer to as the banderinha), the guitar and a small kind of tom-tom known as the rabana[49]. Fernando[50] adds that the mandoline and the guitar were fast becoming obsolete. The Ceylon Portuguese orchestra that he assembled to play Sri Lanka Portuguese Creole songs to the Royal Asiatic Society in Colombo, in 1894, consisted of two violins, two guitars, a tambourine, a triangle and a banderinha. The only viaule player in the island at the time was too aged and unable to perform on that occasion.

Sri Lanka Portuguese Creole music is fortunate on another account. The Hugh Nevill Collection in the British Library[51] includes a manuscript of Sri Lanka Portuguese Creole verse. It is the largest collection of Asian Portuguese Creole folk verse. The manuscript is divided into three groups. The second group "Cantiga De Purtigese - Kaffrein

- Neger Song Portiguese" ('Songs of the Portuguese - Kaffrinha - Portuguese Negro Songs') is relevant in the context of the diaspora. The manuscript is in Dutch orthography in places (See Figure). De Silva Jayasuriya[52-54] has translated the entire manuscript into Standard Portuguese and English. It is not possible to present a perfect translation for several reasons: the dynamic nature of a creole, the time that has elapsed since the recording of these verses, and the lack of creole dictionaries. I have used my knowledge of Standard Portuguese and my mother-tongue Sinhala in translating the verses. Wherever there was ambiguity, I interpreted the meaning based on my knowledge of Sri Lankan and Portuguese cultures. The song given below refers to negrinha ('little negress')(Verses 2, 5), a 12 year-old girl named Mariana. The chorus (Verse 9) refers to manga ('mango' Portuguese and Malagasy), a fruit abundant in Sri Lanka. It is used metaphorically for Mariana (Verses 9 & 10). The rose (a European flower) (Verses 15, 23, 31) and the jasmine (a Sri Lankan flower) (Verse 14) are also used metaphorically for Mariana. Fugitive meetings (Verses 25, 26), unrequitted love (Verses 41, 42), parental consent to marriage (Verse 34), the washerwoman who plays a purifying role in marriage ceremonies (Verse 27), precious stones in Sri Lanka which were an attractive commodity to the Portuguese (Verse 42), fishermen (Verses 7, 41), the sea (Verse 41), cockfights (Verse 4), Sri Lankan currencies - cents (Verse 8) and rupees (Verse 37) illustrate the interplay between Sri Lankan and Portuguese customs and values.

"Cantiga De Purtigese - Kaffrein Neger Song Portiguese"
'Songs of the Portuguese - Kaffrinha Portuguese Negro Songs'

Sri Lanka Portuguese Creole	Standard Portuguese	English
(1)		
Marianha basoo de mangara	Mariana debaixo da mangueira	Mariana underneath the mango tree
Kee tha faiya	Que fazes?	What are you doing?
Tha ganya	Ganhas	You are gaining
Pa Kadoo	Pecado	Sin
(2)		
Negareya portha saradoo	Negrinha detrás da porta fechada	Little Negress behind the closed door
Kee tha fieya	Que fazes?	What are you doing?
Tha ganya	Ganhas	You are gaining
Pakadoo	Pecado	Sin
(3)		
Toodoo pai pai	Todos os pais	All the fathers
Jaoffoi pera gara	Foram para a guerra	Went to the war

Kee ja ganya	O que ganharam	What did they gain
Bandaraa tha satha	A bandeira de seda?	The flag of silk?
(4)		
Toodoo pai pai	Todos os pais	All the fathers
Jaoffoi juga galloo	Foram ao jogo do galo	Went to the cock fight
Sim karnalies	Sim carnales	Yes carnals
Ja faeya aballoo	Abalaram	They have gone
(5)		
Negarenya barreya boodedoo	Negrinha barriga bojadora	Little Negress belly
		jutting out
Kee ja kumma	O que é que comeu?	What have you eaten?
Battalha	Batata doce	Sweet potato
Kuseedoo	Cozida	Boiled
(6)		
Toodoo pai pai	Todos os pais	All the fathers
Jaaffoi brink bolla	Foram jogar à bola	Went to play ball
Meu sosu	O meu sócio	My partner
Parme botha farra	Bota farra para mim	Throws fun for me
(7)		
Toodoo pai pai	Todos os pais	All the fathers
Jaffoi per praya	Foram para a praia	Went to the seashore
Kee ja kumma	O que comeram?	What did they eat?
Kee ja peska raaya	A raia que pescaram	The stingray that they
		fished

(8)

Ken kee ja da parvos	Quem lhe deu	Who gave you
Senko sattale	Cinco cêntimos?	Five cents?
Istie senko sattale pera	Estes cinco cêntimos	These five cents
Kompara panoo da brattale	Compram pano barato	To buy cheap cloth

| Chorres | Coro | Chorus |

(9)

Manya manga manya manga	Minha manga, minha manga	My mango my mango
Kambele ja perroda	Tão bonita, eu perdi-me	How beautiful, I lost myself
Partoo manusudoo manga	Pela tua mansidão manga	For your meekness mango
Kambele lo parrusa	Tão bonita vai parecer	How beautiful it will seem

(10)

Regallador na kama sonya	Regalado na cama sonho	I dream in bed blissfully
Au kune menya ben	Eu e os meus bens	I and my riches
Au ja ergu sobersetoo fica	Eu ergui-me sobressaltado	I got up startled
Sou sen ta manga	Estava sem ti manga	I was without you mango

(11)

Pasturoos kee santa	Pássaros que sentem	Birds that feel
Kee bunitos fia kanta	Que bem cantam	That sing beautifully
Fogo da amories ager	O fogo de amores hoje	The fire of love today
Bokes da kessa	Faz cessar suas bocas	Stops their mouths

(12)

Pasturoos kee kreeya	Pássaros que são criados	Birds that are brought up
Kee bunitoos pawpeya	Que bem cantam	That sing beautifully
Fogo tha su patie ager	Os fogos dos seus peitos hoje	The fires of their breast today
Bokes tha kessa	Faz cessar suas bocas	Stops their mouths

(13)

Bonetoo bailla meu nonna	Como baila bem minha senhora	How beautifully you dance my lady
Basa basa bailla	Você baila	You dance
Basa jatoi taem pera	Porque você tem jeito	Because you have style
Juntoe per kassa	Se casarmos podemos ficar juntos	If we marry we can be together

(14)

Fulla mugarim	Flor de jasmim	Jasmine flower
Charoda premarus	Cheiro primoroso	Excellent scent
Istee fulla kuwruker ja dora	O meu desejo por esta flor	My desire for this flower
Anno dora mea	Durou um ano e meio	Lasted for a year and a half

(15)

Orres margavadoo	Nas horas magoado	In aggrieved hours
Jaffoi au por passeya	Fui passear	I went for a walk
Aen kontraa oen rossa	Encontrei uma rosa	I found a rose
Passomadoo ja fica	Pasmado fiquei	I was amazed

(16)

Jaffoi passeya na manya	Fui passear na manhã	In the morning I went for a walk
Na kampos tha floris	Nos campos de flores	In the fields of flowers
Auw buska amor na manya	Eu busquei um amor na manhã	In the morning I sought a love
Kaen granthe amoris	Com grande amor	With great love

(17)

Veitha tha amaro amo	Por causa de amor profundo	Because of deep love
Ja kai na affasan	Caí na afeiçao	I fell in affection
Ja pertha menya igraiya	Perdi a minha igreja	I lost my church
Au ja pertha thavasaan	Eu perdi a devoção	I lost devotion

(18)

Amor ja falla	O meu amor falou	My love said
Va manya juntoo lo murra	Ela vem morar comigo	She will come to live with me
Ja oya pourassa perme	Ela viu pobreza em mim	She saw poverty in me
Larga ja kurra	Largou mim e correu	She forsook me and ran away

(19)

Vos ja thaa pallavra perme	Você deu a sua palavra para mim	You gave your word to me
Nunkoo thaa serthassa	Nada era certo	Nothing was certain
Vos pertha perme agora	Você perdeu-me agora	Now you lost me
Kee pervos grandasa	Por causa do vosso orgulho	Because of your pride

(20)
Jaffoi toodoo partee
Arowpaguna Jappan
Nunkoo treya natha farda

Kurca da bottan

(21)
Kadora kadora amor
Kee serves na porta
Kavasa kabardo amor
Sange kotha kotha

(22)
Rowsa tha bathanu
Mega charoo da geiyava
Bos brumain rowsa nona

Au kee desseyava

(23)
Pancha albery rowsa

Attardiya kai na chan
Manya rowsa anganasoo amor

Kerca da bottan

Fui a toda a parte
Um roupão do Japão
Não trouxe na farda

Casas de botões

A todas horas amor
Quem espera à porta?
Cabeça quebrada amor
Sangue caindo gota a gota

Botão de rosa
Meigo choro de jóia
Vos, rosa indefinida, senhora
Que eu desejo

Apanhei uma rosa do arbusto
Mais tarde caiu no chão
A minha rosa enganou o seu amor
Por causa dos botões

I went everywhere
A robe from Japan
I did not wear on the uniform
Button-holes

At all hours love
Who waits upon the door?
Head broken love
Blood dripping drop by drop

Rosebud
Tender cry of jewel
You, undefined rose, lady
That I desire

I picked a rose from the bush
Later it fell on the ground
My rose cheated her love
Because of the buttons

(24)

Amor valla mais de kee	O amor vale mais do que	Love is worth more than
Toodoo rikassa	Toda a riqueza	All the riches
Nantha larga man parme	Não me deixes	Do not leave me
Goila tha presasa	Jóia preciosa	Precious jewel

(25)

Iste orres tardu amor	A esta hora tardia amor	At this late hour love
Kee serves akee	Quem espera aqui?	Whoever waits here?
Kee nuntha nath amor	Quem não ama ninguém amor	The one who loves nobody
Prastha bos partee	Oferece-se à ti	Offers himself to you

(26)

Papa kee falla fiya	Papá que chama sua filha	Papa who calls his daughter
Bos kanda ovu	Quando você ouvir	When you hear
Astandoo per longer pervos	Por estar longe de você	Through being far from you
Natha nathiya vea	Não vê nada	Does not see anything

(27)

Veda tha amoru toodoo passoo	Vida de amor em cada passo	Life of love
Ja passa	Que passei	In each step that I stepped
Tarayo da mainathu	A lavadeira trabalhou	The washerwoman worked
Atha rappas ja lavaa	Até as roupas estarem lavadas	Until the clothes had been washed

(28)
Kee potha faiya jathero
Sorthe nosa mall
Na matoo sarradoo na
Boka tha animal

(29)
Pasturoos na rossara kee
Tamboos ja kantha
Masmoo istu rossa minya
Amor kee plantaa

(30)
Auw ten bossa sukre amor
Bos ten menya mal
Premur kee tanya ben arger
Killain ja ficca mal

(31)
Dansa menya orro amor
Rossa tha valler
Dosse framasara
Na korsan tarancha amor

---

(28)
Que será que eu fiz?
Para a nossa má sorte
No mato cerrada
Na boca do animal

(29)
Pássaros na roseira
Que em tempos cantaram
Como esta minha rosa
Que plantou amor

(30)
Eu tenho o vosso doce amor
Você tem o meu mal
Premeia quem tinha bem argui
Como ficou má?

(31)
Dança meu querido amor
Rosa de valor
Doce formosura
No coração escreve amor

What could I have done?
For our bad luck
In the thick wood
In the mouth of the animal

Birds on the rosebush
That sang in former times
Like this my rose
Who planted love

I have your sweet love
You have my bad
Whoever has good
rewards argues
How was that bad?

Dance my dear love
Rose of value
Sweet beauty
Writes love in the heart

(32)
Reppa riva gattoo amor
Ausker botha thaga na

Gattoo slatu bassoo amor
Perra paga rattoo na

(33)
Sera wiera tu amor
Logo ne momentoe na
Sober mohamet amor
Hoge joeremuntoe

(34)
Au tuwee ake amor
De paie suva mandadorna
Nossa paie maie amor
Manda koe racadae

(35)
Tode suva ranou amor
Eu lo dispawa va na
Per vasa ree amor
Tambem te mathavana

Amor o gato sobre a ripa
Ameaça atirar-se daí

O gato salta para baixo amor
Para pegar o rato

Teu amor virá
Logo num momento
Sobre Mohamet amor
Hoje juro

Eu vim aqui amor
Mandado pelo vosso pai
Os nosso pais amor
Mandam este recado

Todo o vosso amor rainha
Eu não decido
Porque o vosso amor rainha
Também mata

Love, the cat on the lath
Threatens to throw
himself from there
The cat jumps down love
To catch the rat

Your love will come
Soon in a moment
Upon Mohammed love
I swear today

I come here love
On your father's command
Our parents love
Send this message

All your love queen
I will not decide
Because your love queen
Also is killing

(36)

Amor iste tampoo nu keu	Este tempo amor	Love this time
Sava lava tun va na	Eu sei não levei	I know I have not brought
Eu ker tanda amor	Eu quero tanto amor	I want so much love
Paupeya nunthava na	Não estava a falar	I was not speaking

(37)

Amor istee tampoo nukoo	Este tempo amor	Love this time
Saba lava ben va na	Eu sei não levei	I know I have not
	bem	brought good
Kee valla soo rastoo kanda	O que é que vale o teu rosto	What has value is your face rupees
Ruppiya nunthava na	Quando não havia rupias	When there are no rupees

(38)

Eun deya artade amor	Um dia à tarde amor	One day in the afternoon love
Jaffoi passeyava na	Fui passear	I went for a walk
Eukontra un rosa amor	Encontrei uma rosa amor	I met a rose love
Passomadoo ja fee cavana	Pasmado ela confiou	Amazingly she trusted me
	em mim e conversou	and talked to me

(39)

Bossa rastoo tantoo luster	Tanto desejo no vosso rosto	So much desire on your face
Eu keyar kie joiyavana	Eu quero aquela jóia	I want that gem

Eu lo anda terra longee	Eu irei para uma terra longe	I will go to a far away land
Pervos lembra lo churravana	Pensando de você chorarei	Thinking of you I will cry
(40)		
Barkoo te kurava na	Porque estás a corar?	Why are you blushing?
Parkei ballansa vana	Porque estás a hesitar?	Why are you hesitating?
Eu koem munya amoroo	Eu com o meu amor	I with my love
Eunde lo diskan savana	Não descansarei ainda	Will not rest yet
(41)		
Marra kieriya passou	O mar queria levar	The sea wanted to carry
Passu keereya pascador va na	Queria levar o pescador	It wanted to carry the fisherman
Dossa anoo sou menena sava	Sei que sou uma menina com doze anos	I know that I am a twelve year old girl
Busca sou amarao na	Não procuro vosso amor	I seek not your love
(42)		
Korava da sol amor mau	Corado do sol meu amor	Blushing with the sun my love
Re koo padareya	A rica pedraria	The magnificent precious stone
Bos munya amor veda mau	Você meu amor minha vida	You my love my life
Eu kee disseya va	Que eu desejo	That I desire

The Sirambiadiya Kaffir Community

Although the Sirambiadiya Kaffirs may not be represen-
tative of all the Kaffirs that once lived in Sri Lanka, it provides the last opportunity to study a Kaffir community.
There are 60 families in this community but they do not
have a Chief as in an African tribe.

There are several theories about their origins. One
theory asserts that the Kaffirs arrived via Goa, the administrative headquarters of the Portuguese Oriental Empire
(Estado da India), and that they originate from a region
named Kaffa in Ethiopia, and that therefore they are called
Kaffirs.

Edirisinghe[55] states that a group of Kaffirs came to Galle
(a coastal town in the Southern Province) and later dispersed
to Trincomalee (a coastal town in the Eastern Province) and
to Mannar and Kala Oya (towns in the North-Western
Province). She states that another group of Kaffirs had
been brought by the British, in 1814, in order to capture the
Kandyan Kingdom (which they gained in 1815) and thereby
were able to colonize the entire island, a feat not achieved
by the two previous colonizers (the Portuguese and the
Dutch). After this episode the Kaffirs had been moved to
defend the Puttalam fort.

In the early decades of the 19th century, a detachment
which consisted of the Third Ceylon Regiment which
included mostly Africans, most of whom were Kaffirs, in garrison service at Puttalam[56]. Brohier adds that the Kaffirs in
Puttalam were descendants of the soldiery who kept the
British flag flying over the Puttalam fortress. In 1865, the
Government had disbanded the Regiment and levelled the
stockade to the ground. Then many soldiers and camp-fol-
lowers had settled down in Puttalam with their families.
Some had found employment in the salt pans as watchers
while others had taken to cultivation on land which was relatively sterile due to low rainfall in the region. Eventually the
Government had offered them land and facilities for irrigation and had encouraged them to form a colony. Thereby
the Kaffirs became small landholders in Sri Lanka; a Pareto
Gain for the Kaffirs. The Kaffir settlement in Sirambiadiya

originated together with others such as Tabbova in the Puttalam District. Then Kaffirs living in other parts of the island had begun to migrate towards Puttalam, perhaps viewing it as a cultural homeland.

A comprehensive history of African immigration (whether free or forced) to Sri Lanka does not exist. Stories about an African past have been handed down from Kaffir generation to generation through an oral tradition. Some of the recollections and views of the Sirambiadiya Kaffirs have been documented in what follows.

According to M J Elias, a 62 year old retired Kaffir Gramasevaka ('village headman') in Sirambiadiya, their ancestors came from an island off South Africa called Kaffa and therefore they are called Kaffirs. He is not aware that they had come via India. He also claims that the Kaffirs were brought in chains and eventually weaned out of their tribal customs and beliefs by the missionaries. He adds that some of his ancestors had constructed the railway line in Puttalam, worked in the kachcheriya ('government office') and in foreign homes.

Ana Miseliya (Elias's Mother), the 85 year-old grand matriach of this Kaffir community, is of the view that their ancestors (whom she states were North Africans) were first brought by the British to Trincomalee Fort to assist in a war. She adds that a Kaffir had captured the Trincomalee Fort and had placed the British flag on it. The British had planned to send the Kaffirs back to their homeland after the war was over; some had refused to leave and had been given land, and jobs in the kachcheriya and salt pans. She believes that the Kaffirs in Sri Lanka today are their descendants. These Kaffirs had been accompanied by Kaffir women and therefore had not contracted marriages with Sinhalese women. She is saddened by the loss of the younger generation's ability to speak the creole; they speak Sinhala. Sinhala is spoken by 73.95% of Sri Lankans as the mother-tongue; it is also the language of inter-ethnic communication as the Sinhalese do not speak the minority languages such as Tamil and Sri Lankan Malay Creole. The younger Kaffirs are marrying Sinhalese. When she was interviewed in 1998, she mentioned that she knew of only one in-marriage that was due to take place in 1999. She states that the children of the out-marriages will inherit the Kaffir's affinity for music. She considers music and dance to be the only forces that bind the community. Vincent Solomon, another member of this community, regrets that their characteristic curly hair is disappearing due to out-marriage. He agrees that music and dance will be the only distinguishing features of the Kaffir descendants.

B M Raphael, another elderly Kaffir, however, believes that his ancestors were brought from Madagascar, during the Boer War (1899-1902). They had been brought for their own safety and had arrived at Vellakaran Kuda and had been handed over to a Sinhalese aristocrat, Ratnayake Mudiyanse. The men had not been accompanied by their families and had been given jobs in the salterns, kachcheriya and in foreign homes.

Daniel Bruno, another Kaffir, was of the view that their ancestors had come as a regiment from Madagascar during the Boer War[57]. They had arrived at Galle; some had been stationed there but others had been sent to Trincomalee, Mannar and Colombo. According to Martin Marcus, another Kaffir, their ancestors had come to Sri Lanka as a battalion of Portuguese-speaking East African soldiers who had served in 'Queen Victoria's Regiment' and had come to Sri Lanka after their victory in the Boer War[58].

Oral traditions have mixed up the facts as information has been handed down through several generations. The non-homogeneity with respect to their African origin could perhaps be attributed to intermarriage, in Sri Lanka, among Kaffirs of different African origins.

Today only the elderly members of the Sirambiadiya Kaffir community speak Sri Lanka Portuguese Creole but everyone joins in the Creole sing-song sessions. The community speaks and writes Sinhala. The Kaffirs study in Sinhala medium schools. In 1994, Sri Lanka had a literacy level of 90.1%[59]. Education is subsidized by the Government at primary, secondary and tertiary levels and is therefore available to all Sri Lankans, regardless of their socioeconomic status.

The grammatical structure of the creole spoken by the

Sirambiadiya Kaffirs has been outlined in what follows. The Standard Portuguese (SP) word order is SVO (Subject Verb Object) while that of Sinhala is SOV (Subject Object Verb). The word order of the creole shows grammatical variation. The word order is SOV in (i) and similar to that of Sinhala but in (ii) it is SVO and akin to that of Portuguese. Grammatical variation is a linguistic phenomenon found among bi/multi-lingual speakers. Sinhala is the substratum language of the creole[60]. When languages come into contact and a new language evolves, the language of the more powerful group is called the superstratum language (Portuguese in this context) and the language/s of the other group/s are called the substratum language/s. In a contact language, most of the vocabulary is from the superstratum language. Accordingly most of the words in Sri Lanka Portuguese Creole have Portuguese etyma. There are two non-Portuguese words in examples (iv) and (vi): markat (market from English) and rupia (rupiyal 'rupees' from Sinhala).

(i) Mo (eo) casa tanda (SLPC): Eu vou a casa (SP): 'I go home/I am going home'

(ii) Nos te cume aros (SLPC): Nos comemos arroz (SP): 'We eat rice/We are eating rice'

Preverbal markers to denote Tense, Mood and Aspect are a typical feature of creole languages[61] and Sri Lanka Portuguese Creole is no exception. It employs an aspect particle to mark the present - 'te/ta' (tem/esta 'have/'is' Standard Portuguese - as in ii), a tense particle to mark the past - 'ja/ya' (from ja 'already' Standard Portuguese - as in iii), and a modality particle to mark the future - 'lo' (lo(go) 'soon' Standard Portuguese - as in iv) [62]. This is in contrast to Standard Portuguese which employs verbal inflections to denote Tense, Mood and Aspect. Some interesting linguistic features of the creole are the absence of verbal inflections, omission of prepositions, infinitive marker (pa), zero copula and the absence of plural marking in nouns. The creole genitive is distinct from that of the Portuguese; it could be based on an English model as illustrated in (viii). However, several other models, such as the Prakrits, Dutch and Malay have also been proposed.

(iii)   Yo (eo) casa ya/ja foy (SLPC): Eu fui a casa (SP) 'I went
        to the house'
(iv)   Yo (eo) markat anda fatu pa toma lovi (SLPC): Eu
        virarei ao mercado e levarei os fatos (SP): 'I will go to
        the market and I will bring clothes'
(v)   Yo (eo) aros ta cume (SLPC): Eu como arroz (SP): 'I eat
        rice'
(vi)   Unha midda aroskuruva dos rupia (SLPC): Uma media
        de arroz custa dois rupias (SP): 'A measure of rice costs
        two rupees'
(vii)   Minha idadi sesante ses (SLPC): Minha idade são
        sesante seis/Tenho sesante seis anos (SP): 'I am 66
        years old'
(viii) Minha nome Miseliya. Minha Pappas nome Peter
        Manuel, Mammas nome Dominica (SLPC): O meu
        nome é Miselia. O nome do meu pai é Manuel e o
        nome da minha mãe é Dominica. (SP): 'My name is
        Miseliya. My Father's name is Peter Manuel and my
        Mother's name is Dominica'.

The Sirambiadiya community represents one of the last
strongholds of a language which is becoming moribund. A
comparison with the creole spoken by the Burghers in the
Eastern Province (Batticaloa and Trincomalee) should
demonstrate if there is any influence from African languages in the Sirambiadiya variety.

The Sirambiadiya Kaffirs have not retained or revived
African religious beliefs or practices. There is no evidence to
suggest that they are trying to reconstruct African religions
or to revive African languages. The Sirambiadiya Kaffirs are
Roman Catholics. The following Sri Lanka Portuguese Creole
song, identified as a victory song by the Kaffir community,
was apparently sung by the soldiers en route to Sri Lanka.
Saint Antony is 'the finder of lost articles'. In this context,
these soldiers who had lost a home found another in Sri
Lanka by lighting candles to Saint Antony. Evidently, the
incoming Africans would have sung the song in another language.

[SLPC]

Male solo	Sinhor Santantoni suva vela namao o
Female chorus	Sinhor Santantoni suva vela namao ya oya
The whole group	Vela namao ya oya//, Canseru namao ya oya//
The whole group	Ya ganha ya ganha
	Ya ganha bandera//
	Ya oya ya oya - vela namao ya oya//

Lord St Antony's candle in the hand   [My translation]
We saw Lord St Antony's candle in the hand
We saw the candle in the hand, We saw the lantern in the hand
We have captured, we have captured
We have captured the flag
We saw we saw
We saw the candle in the hand

All these words have Portuguese etyma. While the lines are repeated some members back up the singers with hoi-hoi, aria-aria or konju po. The diverse African origins of the Kaffirs indicate that they could have spoken several African languages: Swahili, Macua, Amharic, Malagasy and Zulu. I have considered the etyma of these words in the above mentioned African languages, Portuguese and Sinhala. Amharic is the most widely spoken language in Ethiopia. Macua is spoken in the provinces of Nampula, Zambézia, Cabo Delgado and Niassa in Mozambique. It is the language of the Macua tribe. Swahili is also spoken in the Cabo Delgado province. However, there is no Bantu lingua franca in Mozambique. These words do not have Sinhala etyma; hoi hoi is an ideophone in Sinhala. In Swahili, hoi hoi 'noise, shouting' (from Persian 'mirth at a festival') [63]. Konjo can sometimes be heard as konzo ('a long pole which has been pointed and hardened by fire and used to kill serpents') [64]. Po is a particle of locality meaning where, when or while. Po is also an exclamation accompanied by spitting[65]. Aria 'part, section, party, following' is rarely heard, and is probably a corruption of raia 'subject of a kingdom' (Arabic, uraia 'citizenship', the condition or state of being a subject). Haria could be a variant of heria 'to strike a sail' and in Kimvita (dialect of Swahili around Mombasa) it is 'a cry of joy at seeing a sail on the horizon'[66]. Hoi hoi is a 'joyful cry of women' but in the dialects of Southern Africa, of Gasi in Mozambique, hoe hoe is 'a way of invocation in the chants'[67]. Heria is a cry raised on first seeing a dhow arriving. Heria is also a nautical expression 'let go the sheet' and it is used by winch and crane workers for 'lower' (Portuguese arrier). Areia 'sand' has a Portuguese etymon. Two words have Amharic etyma: hoy 'oh!', konjo 'beautiful'[68]. Konjo 'cunning/crafty/deceitful/skilful' and ary 'there/yonder signifying a distant place'[69] have Malagasy etyma. There are no Macua etyma for these words. In Zulu, konje is a conjunction 'so then', po is an ideophone of hooting, sounding a horn[70]. Swahili (Kiswahili) is probably the most widely spoken language in Africa and some have suggested that it should be adopted as a lingua franca in Africa. It is therefore not surprising that all the words have Swahili etyma. Perhaps these words are an expression of the Kaffirs' nostalgia for the countries that they left behind in Africa.

Although Sri Lanka Portuguese Creole is now a dying language and there are only about 500 speakers of the language in the island, the creole community is about 5,000 strong. The Sirambiadiya Kaffirs sing Manhas (from Marchinas 'little marches' Portuguese) at wedding ceremonies. The Manhas emanate from Portuguese Marchas 'marches'. In Portugal marchas are performed, during the feast of Santos Populares ('Popular Saints') which celebrates three saints (Saint Anthony, Saint John and Saint Peter). In Sirambiadiya, the bride and groom cut the wedding cake, drink wine and sing Manhas together with relatives and friends who hold hands and dance in circles. Manhas are short compositions.

Fifteen years ago, the musical instruments of the Sirambiadiya Kaffirs included a pink three-stringed long-necked wooden lute with a trapeziform resonator, a drum, and home-made instruments such as a glass bottle with a metal spoon, two coconut halves and a wooden chair/stool or a metal vessel with two wooden sticks. Today the musical instruments are limited only to those made at home. Their music starts slowly and gathers momentum and force, ending in a mele. This is in contrast to the regular 6/8 or 3/8 beat of the Kaffrinha and Chikothi. Striking features of the Sirambiadiya Kaffirs' dance are, the waggling or shaking of hips, bending forwards, arm and elbow movements, all of which signal an African origin.

Discussion

In addition to the Konstantinu Hatana which has been mentioned earlier in this paper, there are other Sinhala literary works that testify to an African presence on the island. The Kappiri Hatana, a Sinhala victory poem refers to the Kaffir regiments in the British army that came to Sri Lanka at the end of the 18th century and the beginning of the 19th century[71].

In the Kapiri Nadagama, the hero is a Kapiri (Kaffir) [72]. The Nadagama (folk opera) is the first fully-fledged theatrical performance of the Sinhalese Theatre, and was composed in the 19th century. Therefore the Kapiri Nadagama is one of the earliest theatrical performances of the Sinhalese theatre. These literary works await to be explored further in the context of the diaspora.

The specific ethnic identity and the place of origin of African slaves in Asia were unimportant to the slave dealers and slave masters[73]. It contributes to the difficulty in ascertaining the ancestry of the Kaffirs. The evidence from historical sources and oral traditions suggests that the Kaffirs originate from several African countries: Ethiopia, Mozambique, Madagascar and South Africa. Some Kaffirs have come through India (Goa and Bombay). Pankhurst[74] and Basu[75] analyze the diaspora in India. The slaves of the Portuguese in early 17th Century Goa originated from three places: Bengal, Far East and East Africa[76].

The Kaffirs recruited in Mozambique Island could have been Mozambican or from other neighbouring African states. Because of its excellent harbour and the protection which it provided against storms, Mozambique Island was the regular stopping place for the India fleets. It became the focal point of Portuguese trade on the East African coast due to its central position. A factory was set up on the island in 1507-8 and a fortress was erected to protect it. According to Schurhammer[77] the negroes who lived in Mozambique Island had gleaming black skin, dazzling white teeth, flat noses and curly hair. In the 18th century, Mozambique Island supplied India with ivory but in the 19th century the ivory trade shifted north beyond Portuguese control. Then Mozambique turned increasingly to slave trading[78].

Through the 1820s and 1830s more than 15000 slaves were exported annually from Mozambique Island alone[79]. Medeiros[80] deals with the contribution of the Mozambican diaspora in the development of cultural identities in the Indian Ocean Islands. The Sirambiadiya community sing about Macua[81]. The Portuguese had contacts with the Macua on the mainland opposite Mozambique Island and occasionally with groups encountered in the coastal estuaries[82]. Mozambicans were also brought to Sri Lanka during the Dutch and British Eras. The Macua tribe in north-west Madagascar is purely African. There is also a Macua tribe in northern Mozambique. But since Macua and Mosambiki were synonymous with 'slaves' until the end of the 19th Century, it is not possible to be certain if there has been free migration from Africa to Madagascar or not.

Newitt[83] analyses the diaspora in Madagascar. Slave exports from the south of Madagascar began with the arrival of the Portuguese in the 16th Century[84]. The Arabs probably first introduced East African slaves to Madagascar. Portuguese travellers in the 16th Century mention boats from Mombasa and Malindi that came to buy slaves from Madagascar. Maintirano (in mid-west Madagascar) was the focal point of the two-way slave traffic[85]. It retained its pre-eminence as slave entrepôt for the entire west coast. Malagasy women and children captured in the interior of the country awaited distribution to the Mascareines, the Comoros Islands, Arabia and Western India from Maintirano. Slave movement was both eastwards and westwards from Madagascar. Malagasy slaves were taken by Arabs, Portuguese, Dutch and the British, especially in the 18th Century, and sold to Ile de France (Mauritius), Ile de

Bourbon (Réunion), Cape Colony (in South Africa), Caribbean and North America. Hintjens[86] deals with the African diaspora in Réunion and Houbert[87] deals with that of Mauritius. Some Malagasies of African origin relocated to Sri Lanka during the Dutch Era.

The development of Ethiopic into a semi-syllabic script could have been due to the exposure of Ethiopian traders from the 5th Century onwards to the already well-established semi-syllabic scripts in Sri Lanka and the Indian ports which were influenced by the Prakrits[88]. However, there has been no record of Ethiopian settlers from that time. When Ibn Batuta (a Moroccan) visited Sri Lanka in 1345, Colombo was in the hands of a Muslim (wazir and ruler of the sea), Jalasti, who had a garrison of 500 Abyssinians[89,90]. This explains the distinction made between the Abyssinians and Kaffirs in 17th century Sri Lanka as is evident from Sinhala literary works, but today all people of African descent are given the appellation Kaffir. According to Goonatilleke[91] the Sirambiadiya Kaffir community represents a group of "late settlers" who are Ethiopian in origin and who have come from Lisbon. He adds that there is a document about them in the Lisbon Archives. Their music and dance, substantiate this assertion. The manhas, differentiate them from the other Kaffirs and link them to Portugal.

Kaffirs have also migrated from Cape Town and Kaffraria in South Africa. The Oxford Dictionary of the World[92] defines a Kaffir as a member of the Xhosa-speaking people of South Africa, many of whom were settled in a Cape Colony reserve known as British Kaffraria, which was established by the British in 1847 on land lying between the Keiskamma and Kei rivers. Kaffraria extended from the Kei River on the East, to the boundary of Natal on the North East[93]. The song 'Zulu Baba' ('Zulu Father' or 'Zulu Boy'), sung by the Kaffirs is a link with the Zulu tribe in South Africa. The etymon of baba could be Swahili ('father') [94] or Sri Lanka Portuguese Creole 'boy'[95]. The Zulus are Bantus and some migrated from Portuguese East Africa to South Africa[96].

The number of Kaffirs reached a maximum during the Dutch Era. In 1809, Sir Alexander Johnstone, the British

Chief Justice in Sri Lanka at that time, was sent to England to present to the government, a proposed plan to end slavery and enforced labour. On 12th August 1816, as an expression of gratitude to the government for having granted to the people of the maritime provinces a charter and the privilege of trial by jury, all the proprietors of domestic slaves came to a resolution that all children born of their slaves after that date should be freed. Measures were taken, in subsequent years, for the cessation of slavery throughout the island. When the British abolished slavery in the Indian Ocean region, the movement of human capital from Africa decreased. However, free African migration continued in the Indian Ocean region. Alpers[97] compares this phenomenon with that of the Atlantic Ocean.

The Kaffirs contributed to many aspects of Sri Lankan society. They were mercenaries, archers, naval officers, singers and musicians (in regimental bands), body guards, domestic workers, labourers, mile-men, cultivators, watchers (in salt depots), nurses and government servants. The Sirambiadiya Kaffirs are mainly chena cultivators who cultivate on a small plot of land allocated to them by the Government. A few work as nurses in the Puttalam General Hospital and as white collar workers, peons or labourers in government offices. Most women opt to stay at home and manage the domestic affairs. Some women migrate to the Middle East in search of well-paid employment, a phenomenon common to other ethnic groups in the island. Recently, 38 year-old Marie Jacintha has formed a band which consists of ten musicians from the Sirambiadiya Kaffir community. They intend to earn a living by playing their music in Colombo, the capital of Sri Lanka. Given the socioeconomic conditions prevailing in modern Sri Lanka and the small number of Kaffirs, their achievements are not atypical to the other ethnic groups. In Sri Lanka, however, there has been no person of African origin rising to a prominent position as in India, where Malik Ambar (Ethiopian born and sold to slavery) became the regent-minister in the kingdom of Ahmadnagar in 1602 until his death in 1626, when his son, Fettah Khan, succeeded him. Islam provided a common denominator for cultural identification and facilitated the political and military success of Malik Ambar.

There are no restrictions placed upon intermarriages in Sri Lanka and the Kaffirs intermarried with the Portuguese Burghers during the Dutch Era. This, however, is not surprising as they shared a common language and religion, the two most important elements in the culture set. Thananjayarajasingham & Goonatilleka[98] state that some of the Portuguese Burghers in Batticaloa display African facial features.

When a Kaffir woman marries outside her community, the offspring take the ethnicity of their father. In Sri Lanka, statutorily, the Father's race determines the racial identity of the children, particularly for statistics and census purposes. Out-marriages dilute the gene pool and the Kaffir physiognomy is gradually disappearing.

The Sirambiadiya Kaffirs, however, display Negroid physiognomic features. B M Raphael comments that he came across another Kaffir community in Kandy during the second world war, when he was serving in the army. They had accused Raphael of pretending to be of their race as he was lighter skinned, a fact that Raphael attributes to out-marriages in his community. With inbreeding heredity is all-powerful; determination is absolute: the group, the population, the caste or race are invariable. With outbreeding, heredity disintegrates; gene recombination produces unpredictable variability, endless innovation. Organised uncertainty, dominates the population, not merely the organism; determination in controlling evolution is transferred to the selective power of the environment[99]. In-marriage between Kaffirs would lead to the entire progeny being phenotypically Kaffir. In a Kaffir-Sinhalese marriage, the physiognomy of quarter of the progeny will be Kaffir, quarter will be Sinhalese and half will combine characteristics from both the ethnic groups.

It is surprising that a few hundred Kaffirs in Sirambiadiya have been able to maintain their distinctiveness. It appears that the non-absorptive and compassionate nature of the Sinhalese Buddhists (who form the majority in Sri Lanka and to which category I also belong) enabled the Kaffirs to maintain their separate identity.

Concluding Remarks

The only African cultural elements prevailing among the Kaffirs are music and dance through which the African presence is evident in contemporary Sri Lanka. Language and religion also have differentiated the Kaffirs from the indigenous population. The Kaffirs have neither attempted to reconstruct African religions nor to revive African languages. The two most important elements in the culture set (firstly language - Sri Lanka Portuguese Creole, and secondly religion - Roman Catholicism) are identified with the Portuguese colonizers of Sri Lanka who would have been bilingual in Portuguese (their mother-tongue) and Sri Lanka Portuguese Creole (which was needed to communicate with the Sri Lankans). The Kaffirs have been marginalized due to the sociopolitical changes that occurred in the island, particularly as the Portuguese Creole ceased to be the lingua franca (which was replaced by English) and also due to the introduction of other Christian denominations by the Dutch and the British colonizers[100].

Notes

1. Irwin, G W (1977). Africans Abroad: A Documentary History of the Black Diaspora in Asia, Latin America and the Caribbean During the Age of Slavery. Columbia University Press, New York, p.138.
2. Nicholas, C W & Paranavitana, S (1961). A Concise History of Ceylon. Colombo: Ceylon University Press, p.163.
3,5,6. Gerbeau, H (1979). The Slave Trade in the Indian Ocean: Problems Facing the Historian and Research to be Undertaken. In: The African Slave Trade from the Fifteenth to the Nineteenth Century. Reports and Papers of the Meeting Organised by UNESCO in Haiti. 31 January - 4 February 1978. pp. 184-207.
4. Thornton, J (1992). Africa and Africans in the making of the Atlantic World, 1400-1680. Cambridge, p. 206.
7. Chaudhuri, K N (1985). Trade and Civilisation in the Indian Ocean: An Economic History from the Rise of Islam to 1750. Cambridge University Press, Cambridge, p.75.
8. Trinidade, P da. 1961 (ed). Conquista Espiritual do Oriente. Introdução e Notas de F Felix Poles. Lisboa.
9. Coelho, F A (1880-86). Os dialectos románicos ou neolatinos na África, Ásia e América. Boletim da Sociedade de Geografia de Lisboa. Republished in J Morais-Barbosa (ed). 1967. Estudos linguisticos crioulos. Lisboa: Academia Internacional de Cultura Portuguesa, p.45.

10. Bartens, A (1995). Die Iberoromanisch-Basierten Kreolsprachen. Peter Lang, Germany, p.159.
11. Tennent, J E (1860). Ceylon: An Account of the Island - Physical, Historical and Topographical. London: Longman, p.41.
12. Fernando, M E (1933). Alagiyawanna's Kustantinu Hatana. Catholic Press, Colombo.
13. De Castro, J (1541). Roteiro do Mar Roxo, p.63.
14,15. De Silva, C R (1972). The Portuguese in Ceylon 1617-1638. H W Cave & Company, Colombo, p.188-189.
16. Anthonisz, R G (1929). The Dutch in Ceylon. Vol. I. Early Visits and Settlement in the Island. CAC Press, Colombo, p.51.
17. Knox, R (1681). An Historical Relation of the Island Ceylon. Tisara Prakasakayo Ltd, Sri Lanka.
18. Pieters, S (ed & trans) (1911). Memoir of Hendrik Zwaardecroon. Colombo, p.21.
19. VOC 215, Resolution Gentlemen XVII 11 August 1692.
20. Barendse, R J (1995). Slaving on the Malagasy Coast 1640-1700. International Institute for Asian Studies, University of Leiden, The Netherlands. Working Paper Series 2, 137-155, p.142.
21. Arasaratnam, S (1995). Slave Trade in the Indian Ocean in the Seventeenth Century. In: Merchants, Mariners and Oceans: Studies in Maritime History. Ed: K S Mathew. Manohar Publishers, New Delhi, India, p.200.
22. Roberts, M, Raheem, I & P Colin-Thome (1989). People Inbetween. Vol. 1. Sarvodaya Book Publishing Services, Ratmalana, Sri Lanka, p.22.
23. Tennent, J E (1860). Ceylon: An Account of the Island - Physical, Historical and Topographical. London: Longman, p.259.
24. Bertolacci, A (1817). A View of the Agricultural, Commmercial and Financial Interests of Ceylon. Black, Parbury & Allen, London.
25. De Silva, C R (1953). Ceylon under the British Occupation 1795-1833. Colombo Apothecaries Company, Sri Lanka, p.274.
26,27. Cordiner, J (1807). A Description of Ceylon, Containing an Account of the Country, Inhabitants and Natural Productions. Longman, Hurst, Rees & Orme, London, p.65,213.
28. Beachey, R W (1976). The Slave Trade of Eastern Africa. Rex Collings, London, p.28.
29. Hardy, S (1864). Jubilee Memorials of the Wesleyan Mission, South Ceylon 1814-1864. Colombo: Wesleyan Mission Press, p.17.
30,31. Selkirk, J (1844). Recollections of Ceylon after a Residence of nearly thirteen years; with an account of the Church Missionary Society's operations in the island and extracts from a journal. Hatchards: London.
32,33. Hardy, S (1864). Jubilee Memorials of the Wesleyan Mission, South Ceylon 1814-1864. Colombo: Wesleyan Mission Press, p.17-22.
34. Census of the Island of Ceylon 1871: A General Report. W H Herbert, Government Printer, Colombo (1873).
35. Lee, L. Census of Ceylon 1881: General Report and Statements.
36. Lee, L. Census of Ceylon 1891: A General Report. G J A Skeen, Government Printer, Colombo, Ceylon (1892).
37. Arunachalam, P (1902). Census of Ceylon 1901. H C Cottle, Acting Government Printers, Colombo, Ceylon.

38. Denham, E B. Ceylon at the Census of 1911 Being the Review of the Results of the Census of 1911. H C Cottle, Government Printers, Colombo, Ceylon (1912).
39. Statistical Pocket Book of the Democratic Socialist Republic of Sri Lanka (1998). Department of Census & Statistics, Ministry of Finance & Planning, Colombo.
40. De Silva Jayasuriya, S (1997). Hugh Nevill Collection of Indo-Portuguese Verses: Portuguese and English Translations of Oersaan and Falentine. Journal of the Royal Asiatic Society Sri Lanka, Vol. XLII, pp. 107-211.
41. Sapir, E (1921). Language. New York. Harvest Books, No. HB-7.
42. Hardy, S (1864). Jubilee Memorials of the Wesleyan Mission, South Ceylon 1814-1864. Colombo: Wesleyan Mission Press, p.17.
43. De Silva Jayasuriya, S (1999). 'On the Indo-Portuguese of Ceylon': A Translation of a Hugo Schuchardt Manuscript. Portuguese Studies, Vol. 15, pp. 52-69. King's College, University of London.
44. Statistical Pocket Book of the Democratic Socialist Republic of Sri Lanka (1998). Department of Census & Statistics, Ministry of Finance & Planning, Colombo.
45. Fernando, C M (1894). The Music of Ceylon. Journal of the Royal Asiatic Society Ceylon Branch, xiii, p.183-189.
46. Ariyaratne, S (1985). Baila Saha Kapirinna. Dayawansa Jayakody Publishers: Sri Lanka.
47. De Silva Jayasuriya, S (1999). Echoes of the Tagus: Music of Sri Lanka. The Indian Ocean Review Vol. 12, No. 1, p.18, Curtin University, Perth, Australia.
48. Cabral e Sá, M (1997). Wind of Fire. The Music and Musicians of Goa. Promilla & Company Publishers, New Delhi, p.88.
49,50. Fernando, C M (1894). The Music of Ceylon. Journal of the Royal Asiatic Society Ceylon Branch, xiii, p.183-189, p.188.
51. Nevill, H (1904). Portuguese Songs, From the Collection of Manuscripts, Chiefly Sinhalese Purchased from the Executors of Hugh Nevill. London: British Library.
52. De Silva Jayasuriya, S (1995). Portuguese and English Translations of Some Indo-Portuguese Songs in the Hugh Nevill Collection. Journal of the Royal Asiatic Society Sri Lanka, Vol. XL, pp. 1-102.
53. De Silva Jayasuriya, S (1996). Indo-Portuguese Songs of Sri Lanka. The Nevill Manuscript. Bulletin of the School of Oriental & African Studies, University of London, Vol. LIX, Part 2, pp. 253-267.
54. De Silva Jayasuriya, S (1997). Hugh Nevill Collection of Indo-Portuguese Verses: Portuguese and English Translations of Oersaan and Falentine. Journal of the Royal Asiatic Society Sri Lanka, Vol. XLII, pp. 107-211.
55. Edirisinghe, P (1996). Melting Pot of Multi-races - Puttalam. The Sunday Observer. Sri Lanka. January 1st.
56. Brohier, R L (1973). Discovering Ceylon. Lake House Investments Ltd, Colombo, p.24.
57. Hettiaratchi, D E (1969). Linguistics in Ceylon I. Current Trends in Linguistics. Vol. 5. Linguistics in South Asia. Ed. T A Sebeok. Mouton, p.747.
58. Goonatilleke, M H (1983). Report of an Interview with the Portuguese Speaking Community in Puttalam. Department of

National Archives, Colombo, Sri Lanka, p.4.

59. Statistical Pocket Book of the Democratic Socialist Republic of Sri Lanka (1998). Department of Census & Statistics, Ministry of Finance & Planning, Colombo.

60. De Silva Jayasuriya, S (1999). Portuguese in Sri Lanka: Effects of Substratum Languages. Journal of the Royal Asiatic Society of Great Britain and Ireland Series 3, Volume 9, Part 2 pp. 251-270.

61. Bickerton, D (1981). Roots of Language. Ann Arbor, Karoma, USA.

62. De Silva Jayasuriya, S (1999). Tense Mood Aspect in Asian Portuguese Creoles: A Comparison. The Third Biennial Conference of the Association for Linguistic Typology, held at the University of Amsterdam, Netherlands.

63. Rechenbach, C W (1967). Swahili-English Dictionary. The Catholic University of America Press, Washington DC 20017, USA, p.135.

64. Krapf, L (1882). A Dictionary of the Suahili Language. Trubner & Company: London, p.170.

65-67. Sacleux, C (1939). Dictionnaire Swahili-Français. Institut d'Ethnologie, Paris. p.754, p.279, p.285.

68. Leslau, W (1976). Concise Amharic Dictionary. Harrassowitz, Wiesbaden. p.422 & p.277.

69. Richardson, J (1885). A New Malagasy-English Dictionary. The London Missionary Society, Antananarivo, p.65 & 354.

70. Doke, C M & Vilakazi, B W (1953). Zulu-English Dictionary. Witwaterstrand University Press, p.437 & p.682.

71. Nevill, H (1904). Kappiri Hatana; Kaberi Puvata (Kavi); Kappili Hatana. From the Collection of Manuscripts, Chiefly Sinhalese Purchased from the Executors of Hugh Nevill. London: British Library.

72. Sarachchandra, E (1966). Folk Drama of Ceylon. 2nd edition. Department of Cultural Affairs, Sri Lanka.

73. Harris, J E (1971). The African Presence in Asia. Evanston, Illinois, USA, p.50.

74. Pankhurst, R (2002). The Ethiopian Diaspora to India: The Role of Habshis and Sidis from Medieval Times to the End of the 18th Century. In: The African Diaspora in Asia. Eds. S de S Jayasuriya & R Pankhurst. Red Sea Press, USA.

75. Basu, H (2002). Slave, Soldier, Sailor, Faqir: Fragments of African Histories in Western India (Gujarat). In: The African Diaspora in Asia. Eds. S de S Jayasuriya & R Pankhurst. Red Sea Press, USA.

76. Subrahmanyam, S (1993). The Portuguese Empire in Asia 1500-1700: A Political and Economic History, Longman, p.229.

77. Schurhammer, G (1977) (Trans). Francis Xavier: His Life, His Times. Vol. II. India 1541-1545. Trans. M J Costelloe. The Jesuit Historical Institute, Rome, Italy, p.78.

78,79. Curtin, P, Frierman, S, Thompson, L & Vansina, J (1978). African History. Longman Group Ltd, London, p.394, p.395.

80. Medeiros, E (2002). Contribution of the The Mozambican Diaspora in the Development of Cultural Identities in the Indian Ocean Islands. In: The African Diaspora in Asia. Eds. S de S Jayasuriya & R Pankhurst. Red Sea Press, USA.

81. Jackson, K D (1990). Sing Without Shame: Oral Traditions in Indo-Portuguese Creole Verse. John Benjamins, Netherlands, p.84.

82. Newitt, M (1995). A History of Mozambique. Christopher Hurst, London, p.63.
83. Newitt, M (2002). Contribution of the African Diaspora in Madagascar. In: The African Diaspora in Asia. Eds. S de S Jayasuriya & R Pankhurst. Red Sea Press, USA.
84,85. Campbell, G (1981). Madagascar and the Slave Trade, 1810-1895. Journal of African History, Vol. 22, pp.203-227. p.220, p.224.
86. Hintjens, H (2002). From French Slaves to French Citizens: The African Diaspora in Réunion Island. In: The African Diaspora in the Indian Ocean. Eds. S de S   Jayasuriya & R Pankhurst. Red Sea Press, USA.
87. Houbert, J (2002). Creolisation and Decolonisation in the Changing Geopolitics of the Indian Ocean. In: The African Diaspora in the Indian Ocean Eds. S de S Jayasuriya & R Pankhurst. Red Sea Press, USA.
88. Baker, P (1996). The potential for the development of Arabic-based and other contact languages along the maritime trade routes between the Middle East and China, from the start of the Christian era. In: Atlas of Languages of Intercultural Communication in the Pacific, Asia and the Americas. Eds S A Wurm, P Mühlhäusler & D T Tyron. 637-672, p.665.
89. Gibb, H A R (1929). Ibn Batuta. Travels in Asia and Africa 1325-1354. London: Routeledge, p.260.
90. Hulugalle, H A J (1969). Guide to Ceylon. Lake House Investments Ltd, Colombo, p.10.
91. Goonatilleka, M H (1998). Personal Communication.
92. Munro, D (Ed) (1995). Oxford Dictionary of the World. Oxford University Press, Oxford.
93. Silver, S W & Co (1875). Handbook of South Africa. S W Silver & Co., London, p.440.
94. Sacleux, C (1939). Dictionnaire Swahili-Français. Institut d'Ethnologie, Paris. p.82.
95. De Melo, T (1910-20). O Oriente Portuguez. Revista da Commissao Archaeologia da India Portugueza. Nova Goa: Imprensa Nacional.
96. Bryant, A T (1949). The Zulu People: As they were before the White Man Came. Shuter & Shooter, Pietermaritzburg, p.11.
97. Alpers, E (2002). The African Diaspora in the Indian Ocean: A Comparative Perspective. In: The African Diaspora in the Indian Ocean. Eds. S de S Jayasuriya & R Pankhurst.Red Sea Press, USA.
98. Thananjayarajasingham, S & Goonatilleka, M H (1976). A Portuguese Creole of the Burgher Community in Sri Lanka. Journal of the Indian Anthropological Society 11, 225-236, p.228.
99. Darlington, C D (1969). The Evolution of Man and Society. George Allen & Unwin, London, p.674.
100.De Silva Jayasuriya, S (2000). Portuguese Cultural Imprint on Sri Lanka. Lusotopie, pp. 253-259, Paris, France.

Index